SOCIAL-SKILLS TRAINING

Jeffrey A. Kelly is Associate Professor of Psychiatry (Psychology) at the University of Mississippi Medical Center. He received his B.A. from Case Western Reserve University and his Ph.D. in clinical psychology from the University of Kentucky in 1975. Dr. Kelly is the author of many professional journal articles on behavior therapy, is a consulting editor for the *Journal of Consulting and Clinical Psychology,* and received the President's New Research Award from the Association for the Advancement of Behavior Therapy in 1980 for his work in social-skills training. His responsibilities at the University of Mississippi Medical Center include the clinical and research supervision of psychology residents, direction of psychological and psychiatric outpatient services, and supervision of the child and adolescent behavioral psychology clinic.

SOCIAL-SKILLS TRAINING

A PRACTICAL GUIDE FOR INTERVENTIONS

Jeffrey A. Kelly, Ph.D.

Foreword by Cyril Franks, Ph.D.

Springer Publishing Company
New York

No part of this publication may be reproduced, stored in a retrieval system, or transmitted in any form or by any means, electronic, mechanical, photocopying, recording, or otherwise, without the prior permission of Springer Publishing Company, Inc.

Springer Publishing Company, Inc.
200 Park Avenue South
New York, New York 10003

82 83 84 85 / 10 9 8 7 6 5 4 3 2 1

Library of Congress Cataloging in Publication Data

Kelly, Jeffrey A.
  Social-skills training.

  Bibliography: p.
  Includes index.
  1. Social skills. 2. Behavior therapy. I. Title.
HM251.K447   302   81-13555
ISBN 0-8261-3580-3   AACR2
ISBN 0-8261-3581-1 (pbk.)

Printed in the United States of America

This book is dedicated to my family, whose lifelong support has made this project possible.

CONTENTS

CONTENTS

FOREWORD

Because virtually all our waking hours are spent in some form of social interaction—either on a one-to-one basis or across a diversity of groups—the conduct of our lives is determined at least partly by the range of our social skills. In bygone eras life was simpler, if not easier; systems were fewer, social mobility was less, and relationships were relatively straightforward, with clearly defined roles for each of us to follow. In contemporary Western society, the pace of life is faster and more complex, and rules change according to the system within which we are operating at the time. All too often we are compelled to function in two or more systems simultaneously, and this requires considerable social dexterity. The need for social skills and the wherewithal to acquire these skills is no longer a simple matter.

The twentieth century has witnessed remarkable achievements with respect to the mastery of technical skills. Sophisticated but elegantly simple training procedures are now routine in technologies ranging from house painting and the factory assembly line to nuclear engineering. Even in the helping professions, the emphasis is still on the acquisition of technical competence rather than on social and interpersonal skills. Highly competent physicians, teachers, and top management executives who know their subject matter well but who do not interact constructively with patients, students, or employees are commonplace. Recognition of the need for social-skills training is a comparatively recent development.

In the mental health field the situation is complicated further by the fact that most practitioners are psychodynamic in orientation. They tend to view their patients as psychiatrically disturbed and in need of therapy or even hospitalization. More often than not, therapy focuses on the underlying bases to the maladaptive behavior rather than the teaching of effective coping skills. The attempts to correct deficits in interpersonal functioning have been predicted upon the psychodynamic assumption that social-skills training is secondary to the remodeling of the underlying personality structure. Such enduring personality traits as neuroticism or dependency are presumed to be characteristic of that individual and poor behavior is attributed to deviant traits. With slight variations, this position seems common to most dynamic theorists, ranging from Freud, Jung, and Adler through Horney, Sullivan, Hartmann, and the ego psychologists to a slew of contemporary psychodynamically-oriented writers. Thus, a person who finds difficulty in relating in social situations is presumed to be an introvert and altering personality structure, rather than specific social-skills training, becomes the primary aim of therapeutic intervention. Traditional therapists put more stress on the early life course of interpersonal deficits as the determinants of social relationships in the present than do behavior therapists—this despite the numerous clients who graphically describe their social-skills deficits that have incapacitating consequences for their present lives. Some therapists go as far as to suggest that the teaching of social competencies is potentially destructive to the subtleties of the patient-therapist relationship and hence to the values embodied in nonintrusive therapy. If social skills are considered at all, the problem is viewed in terms of motivational rather than skills deficits.

The behavior therapist, especially the social learning theorist, enjoys a quite different perspective. To a large extent we are as we function, think, feel, and behave, and our repertoire of social skills is very much a part of this totality. Although originally acquired through previous experiences, our responses to social situations are being modified continually by ongoing social consequences. This is not, or course, a passive process in which the individual is influenced exclusively by the behavior of others; rather, the interaction is reciprocal, whereby each individual in a group of two or more can modify the social behavior of the other(s). This, in turn, serves to modify our own behavior. We are neither the slaves of our inner thoughts, nor are we controlled by our external environments. It is this program of mutual, reciprocal interaction—the core of contemporary social learning theory—which forms the basis of social-skills training as practiced by the sophisticated behavior therapist.

Social-skills training aims to extend the repertoire of behavioral competencies across a variety of situations as part of an interactional process in which individuals feel comfortable both with themselves and their relationships with others. In so doing, as Kelly notes, the emphasis is as much upon cognitive well-being and systematic strengthening of desirable characteristics as it is upon the elimination of unacceptable behaviors.

The learning theory principles employed in social-skills training and the philosophy that underlies them are no different from those which accompany any behavioral intervention. Good social-skills training must be considered within the total behavior therapy context. Successful social-skills training in one sphere is likely to generate progress in others. Social-skills training should not be viewed as the mechanistic application of a series of isolated techniques.

Sometimes social-skills training is inappropriate, sometimes it becomes low in the hierarchy of therapeutic priorities, and sometimes clinical strategy demands that it be made the initial focus of attention despite the presence of more profound problems.

If, when, and how to apply social-skills training is a decision for the skilled clinician. One does not jump into such training as one does into a bathtub at night. As with all behavioral interventions, an essential first step is the comprehensive behavioral assessment, followed closely by the development of a provisional therapeutic plan, which may or may not include social-skills training. If social-skills training is to be used as part of the therapeutic program, it too becomes subject to reevaluation as therapy progresses. Thus, social-skills training is only as good as the sophistication and experience of the coordinating clinician. In this respect we are fortunate indeed.

Jeffrey Kelly is a seasoned clinician, and he provides the necessary conceptual framework without which social-skills training becomes little more than a patchwork of isolated techniques. A conceptual framework alone, however, is not sufficient; for implementation the practitioner must have a strong command of procedure. It is here that this book excels. Procedural details and case material are provided in a manner that avoids the cookbook flavor common to many texts of this nature. Information is presented in a practical, technically correct but not overly technical fashion. Although a working background in behavior therapy or some close liaison with a practicing behavior therapist would be an obvious asset, it is not necessary to be an expert in the field to appreciate the significance of this book. What Kelly does with great success is to bridge the gap between research and application. The progression from theoretical principles to direct service follows smoothly and effortlessly, with successive chapters addressing themselves to a variety of settings and populations. But the main thrust is directed toward those who work with clients in such outpatient settings as residential programs, mental health clinics, counseling centers, and schools. This is a clearly written, much needed book that makes a timely contribution to the armamentaria of practicing clinicians and their associates.

Cyril M. Franks
Graduate School of Applied and Professional Psychology
Rutgers University

PREFACE

Clinicians, therapists, and counselors frequently observe the extreme difficulty that many of their clients encounter in handling interpersonal relationships. By client report or by therapist observation, it is evident that a large number of clients lack the skills to deal effectively with others during everyday interactions. In childhood, these may be the children who appear unable to establish cooperative play relationships with peers and fail to exhibit the prosocial interaction skills necessary to develop and maintain friendships. By adolescence, an individual is faced with new situations requiring more complex social skills, including the initiation of heterosocial or dating behavior and the use of other conversational skills to meet people and establish friendships. Assertive expression, the ability to effectively handle nonroutine interactions such as job interviews, and conversational abilities are still other skills that many adult clients find difficult to acquire; situations in which they are needed create anxiety for them.

Traditional theories of personality development and behavior change have long recognized that successful interpersonal functioning is both an antecedent and a consequence of psychological adjustment. However, while traditional theories attach substantial importance to the social behavior of clients, most attempt to describe the early-life causes of interpersonal deficits rather than to provide practical therapeutic techniques for actually equipping clients with more adaptive social competencies.

During the past ten years, behavior therapists have investigated and developed procedures to directly increase the social-skill repertoire of clients. The general description of "social-skills training" actually refers to the treatment approach for a number of specific interpersonal deficits, including lack of refusal and commendatory assertiveness, heterosocial or date-initiation skills, general conversational skills, job-interview effectiveness, and prosocial skills in children. Social-skills training has been reported in the research literature as being successful with a wide range of client populations, including: chronic psychiatric patients and mentally retarded individuals who exhibit severe and pervasive skill impairment; isolated, withdrawn, or unassertive children;

socially anxious individuals; nondating adolescents and college students; and high-functioning outpatient clients who lack the ability to effectively handle very specific types of situations, such as job interviews or interactions requiring assertiveness. Regardless of the exact type of skill being taught and the nature of the client population, all social-skills training approaches rely on the social learning theory principles of modeling, instruction, behavior-rehearsal, reinforcement, and feedback to shape more appropriate skill performance. These principles are first applied during structured practice in the treatment setting and then in the natural environment.

However, while social-skills training procedures have been widely reported in the research literature, and while many therapists in applied settings recognize the importance of increasing their clients' interpersonal competency, there have been few empirically based comprehensive guides to assist the practicing therapist who wishes to implement these techniques in his or her applied setting. The purpose of this book is to bridge the gap between the research literature on skills-training and its applications in direct-service settings.

Initial chapters of *Social-Skills Training: A Practical Guide for Interventions* summarize the conceptual foundations and learning theory principles that form the basis for training, as well as behavioral procedures for assessing client social-skills competency. Techniques for determining the format and conduct of training interventions are discussed. These include specific training techniques, individual versus group treatment, identification of the specific skill-components that will be taught to clients, behavioral evaluation of the intervention's success, and procedures to facilitate the generalization of improved skill performance from training sessions to troublesome situations in the natural environment.

Later chapters address specific types of social-skills training. Each of these chapters summarizes the behaviors that comprise overall competence in that type of skill, behaviors that can be taught to the socially deficient client. Self-report inventories for client assessment are reviewed. Then, potential applications of that form of skills-training are discussed, including the types of clients or settings for which it is most relevant, specific issues involving the procedural handling of treatment sessions, and assessment of client behavior-change. Representative clinical research on each form of skills-training is presented, especially as it relates to applied interventions.

This book is directed toward the empirically oriented therapist or practitioner treating clients in an applied setting, including outpatient and residential programs, mental health clinics, student counseling centers, schools, and similar treatment environments. While all skills-training principles and evaluation techniques are based upon empirical behavior research, the orientation of this book is toward applied and clinical applications of social-skills training in the direct-service setting.

ACKNOWLEDGMENTS

Many persons have contributed to the development and refinement of this book in both direct and indirect ways. My deepest thanks go to Ellen Berler and Andrew S. Bradlyn, who provided skilled research assistance and shared their ideas, suggestions, and comments at all stages of the manuscript's development. My discussions with Janne Patterson, C. Gerald O'Brien, and Jim Hollandsworth provided valuable ideas for the book. My friend Allan Hauth provided support and encouragement throughout the book's time-consuming preparation. Mary Winford, Jeri Cox, and Susan Peeler each provided valuable secretarial assistance; Barbara Watkins, editor at Springer, was most helpful in bringing the book into production in a manner far smoother than I thought could be possible. My faculty colleagues and psychology residents at the University of Mississippi Medical Center and Jackson VA Medical Center have always provided an environment of research and clinical stimulation, which makes a writing task such as this not only possible but enjoyable. Finally, a special thanks to the Krystal Number Four, where much of this book was written.

Chapter 1

Social Skills and Psychological Adjustment: Conceptual Foundations

Almost everyone knows people who can be described as interpersonally skillful or socially competent. These are individuals who seem to exhibit the ability to handle other people effectively and who are highly reinforcing to those with whom they interact. At a social gathering, these are the people who can easily meet others, converse effectively with them, convey and elicit information freely during conversations, and leave others with the feeling of enjoyment following the interaction. At a business meeting, this might be the person who can clearly state personal viewpoints or opinions, lead others to believe that he or she understands and appreciates their opinions, and offer disagreeing views without causing others to feel they have been attacked. During a job interview, this is the applicant who is able to convince an employer, within just minutes of time, that he or she is vocationally competent, well-rounded, diligent, responsible, and the ideal person to hire.

Some people appear to have developed and refined a social style that permits them to achieve rewarding interpersonal outcomes, while at the same time leaving others with favorable opinions of them; terms such as "extroverted," "socially ascendent," "assertive," and "socially skilled" are all used to describe persons with these response capabilities. However, these are not the terms typically used to describe the behavior of our clients. Ranging from the pervasive social impairment observed among institutionalized persons, such as chronic psychiatric patients or the mentally retarded, to the much more well-defined and situationally specific social deficits of higher-functioning persons, it is evident that interpersonal behavior represents a problematic area for many individuals. The modification of client social skills is often an important aim of therapy.

Interpersonal impairment is a defining characteristic of many emotional and behavioral disorders. Bellack and Hersen (1978), for example, have noted that there are literally hundreds of theories concerning the development of schizophrenia. These often discrepant explanations range from biochemical to

1

dynamic to behavioral to genetic theories. Yet, regardless of the clinician's theoretical position on the development of schizophrenia, almost any clinician would use an extremely uniform and consistent set of descriptors to describe the behavior or appearance of a "chronic schizophrenic." The "chronic psychiatric patient" is almost invariably described in terms of massive social deficiency: extreme nonresponsiveness to other people, withdrawal, lack of appropriate emotional reactivity to others, and the presence of various interpersonal appearance "cues" that others find idiosyncratic, peculiar, or odd. It is, most prominently, the social behavior of chronic schizophrenic individuals that sets them apart from other people. As Bellack and Hersen note, it is unclear whether these social deficits are always a consequence of schizophrenia or whether they may be contributory to the diagnosis of that disorder. Similarly, there seems to be variation in whether such individuals had earlier acquired an effective social-skills repertoire, but then ceased to exhibit those skills following long-term hospitalization, or whether effective social skills had simply never been acquired during development. Those issues notwithstanding, it is apparent that persons labeled as "chronic schizophrenics" typically exhibit massive social deficits, which impair their ability to establish appropriate relationships and function normally in the community. Without intervention, it is unlikely that such individuals will develop friendships, find or hold jobs, or adapt successfully to noninstitutional environments.

Similarly, mentally retarded persons often exhibit relatively generalized social-skill impairment. Mental retardation has been conceptualized historically in terms of both intellectual subnormality and interpersonal deficiency (American Association on Mental Deficiency, 1977), and investigators have long noted that the social functioning of retarded individuals within the mild to moderate range of impairment is a substantial predictor of vocational, interpersonal, and independent-living adjustment (cf. Doll, 1953). Presumably, if skills-deficient retarded citizens could be taught more appropriate social skills, they too could be integrated more successfully into various community settings and would achieve better interpersonal acceptance among nonretarded persons. There is evidence suggesting that the greater the number of cues that an individual exhibits conveying that he or she is retarded, the more others will respond unfavorably to that person (Kelly & Drabman, 1977; Rosenberg, 1959). Thus, an aim of skills-training with this client population would be to reduce interpersonal cues or behaviors indicative of retardation and to increase more appropriate social skills, which would facilitate the client's development of relationships.

In the case of institutionalized or formerly institutionalized psychiatric patients as well as retarded persons, skills deficits may be quite pervasive, cross-situational, and strikingly apparent. Yet, among higher-functioning clients, interpersonal skill deficiencies can also be problematic. Clinicians, counselors, and therapists have long observed that interpersonal relationships are often directly identified by clients as reasons for seeking treatment. Examples include clients' complaints of their inability to form or initiate social relationships with others, social anxiety, loneliness and shyness, being rejected by others, or the inability to assert themselves when confronted with unreasonable behavior from other people. Often, very direct references to interpersonal skill difficulties are made by clients in their earliest interviews with the therapist or counselor. At other times, clients present in treatment with initial vague complaints of anxiety or depression, and it is not until somewhat later that the therapist discovers specifically that unsatisfactory interpersonal relationships are the basis for more generalized mood or anxiety-related difficulties. It is evident, then, that while some low-functioning client populations are characterized by massive social deficits that are immediately apparent upon even casual observation, difficulties in handling and establishing interpersonal relationships are reported by even high-functioning clients seen in almost any counseling or treatment setting.

What Are Social Skills?

We can define social skills as those identifiable, learned behaviors that individuals use in interpersonal situations to obtain or to maintain reinforcement from their environment. When conceptualized in this manner, social skills can essentially be viewed as behavioral pathways or avenues to an individual's goals. Let us direct our attention to three aspects of this definition of social skills: (1) viewing socially skilled behavior in terms of its ability to lead to reinforcing consequences, (2) the interpersonal situations in which social skills are exhibited, and (3) describing skilled behavior in an identifiable, objective manner.

Social Skills as Behaviors That Elicit
Reinforcement from the Environment

One approach to categorizing or defining interpersonal skills is based on their function or utility for an individual. Some interpersonal skills serve the purpose of facilitating the establishment of relationships with other people. Other skills, although used in an interpersonal context, serve to obtain goals or reinforcers that are not themselves social in nature. Still other social-skill behaviors function primarily to prevent others from removing or blocking reinforcement to which an individual is entitled.

Social Skills That Facilitate Relationship Development

The establishment of relationships with other people is, for most individuals, a desired goal or rewarding experience; consequently, social relationships can be considered to be reinforcing events for most people. These interactions might include such things as dating, having friends with whom one can comfortably converse, and meeting new people easily at parties or other informal gatherings. However, attaining each of these desirable social goals requires that the individual first engage in a set of relatively well-organized skill behaviors. For example, in order to date another person, the individual wishing to attain that goal: (1) must be in a setting where potential dates can be met; (2) must initiate an appropriate conversational interaction, which provides the potential date with a favorable impression; and (3) must make a specific request to continue or renew the interaction at a later time. The constellation of these and similar social behaviors that effectively lead to the establishment of dates has been termed "heterosocial or date-initiation skills."

A related but more general type of social competency is needed for the purpose of establishing conversations or friendships with others whom one does not yet know. Here, the goal is perhaps not to obtain a date, but to have an enjoyable conversational interaction. This short-range goal of conversation is also a prerequisite to the development of closer friendship relationships, and the behaviors that lead to those outcomes can be termed "conversational skills." In similar fashion, "commendatory skills," or "commendatory assertion," has been described as an important aspect in the establishment of positive relationships with other people (Wolpe & Lazarus, 1966). "Commendatory skill" refers to the ability to warmly and convincingly compliment the good actions of other people, which in turn may foster a reciprocation of their positive responses.

Date-initiation, conversational skills, and commendatory social skills seem primarily relevant to adolescents or adults. Prosocial-play skills in young children also serve to facilitate the development of their peer relationships. Certainly, many of the behaviors that constitute effective prosocial-play skills among children are different than those adults might use to establish friendships, but the purpose is the same: to exhibit peer-valued social skills, which promote the development of relationships and the reciprocation of positive actions from others.

All of the interpersonal skills that facilitate the building of relationships have in common with one another the fact that they increase the social attractiveness or reinforcement value of the person exhibiting them. Because others respond positively to individuals who are skillful in conversation, date-initiation, commendatory behavior or, in the case of children, prosocial-play skills, these competencies serve not only as avenues by which a person can initiate reinforcing relationships, but they also increase the likelihood that others will seek out further opportunities to interact with the individual.

Social Skills Used in an Interpersonal Context to Bring About Nonsocial Reinforcement

In some cases, socially skilled behavior serves to help an individual attain desired and reinforcing goals that are not themselves interpersonal in nature. For example, job-interview skills occur in the context of a social interaction—the interaction between the applicant and the interviewer—but the reinforcer sought by most applicants is being hired, rather than building a relationship for its own sake. Job-interview skills thus represent the constellation of social behaviors that are capable of leading to the nonsocial but nonetheless important reinforcer of being hired for employment. A number of investigators have examined the manner in which job-interview skills, or the social behavior exhibited by an applicant in the job-interview situation, can influence whether or not the applicant will be hired (cf. Furman, Geller, Simon, & Kelly, 1979; Hollandsworth, Glazeski, & Dressel, 1978; Kelly, Wildman, & Berler, 1980).

Social Skills That Prevent the Loss of Current Reinforcement

In contrast to those skills that principally enhance a client's own reinforcement value and facilitate approach responses from others, or those skills that permit a person to attain other kinds of desired nonsocial goals, different competencies may be needed to handle the unreasonable behavior of others. "Refusal assertion" serves such a purpose. When a person is engaged in some rewarding activity or wishes to express feelings, beliefs, or personal opinions, it is possible that others may attempt to block or inhibit that individual's own goal-directed behavior. In essence, some other person would then be unreasonably attempting to remove current activities that the individual finds reinforcing, or to keep the individual from doing things that are potentially rewarding. Refusal assertion refers to those competencies that a person can use to prevent others from blocking his or her own goal-directed behavior; they provide the client with appropriate social avenues for expressing feelings, disagreements, and requests for the antagonist to change his unreasonable behavior.

While each of these different types of social skills represents strategies for obtaining reinforcement of some kind or preventing its loss, the behaviors that constitute each type of skill differ. As we will discuss in more detail shortly, many of the skill behaviors one would use to initiate a date are quite different than those one would use in a job interview. Similarly, many of the actions that comprise an effective refusal-assertive response are not the same as the behaviors that make up the skill of assertively commending the positive conduct of another person.

It is apparent, then, that a wide range of qualitatively and functionally different behaviors are subsumed under the generic term of "social skill" or "social competency." Social-skills training derives its meaning only within the context of the teaching of a specific type of skill. Social-skills training denotes the general treatment approach of applying learning principles for the purpose of increasing the interpersonal competencies of clients; clinical interventions must be targeted toward a specific type of goal skill, such as refusal assertion, conversational skill, date-initiation behavior, or job-interview skill, based upon the exact nature of client deficits and needs.

Situational Specificity of Social Behavior

Traditional psychometric measurement of social behavior has often assumed that social competence can be represented as a single range, continuum, or dimension. For example, some measurement approaches have described a linear social-competence continuum, with high competence at one end of the range and low competence at the other (cf. Bernreuter, 1931; Cattell, Eber, & Tatsouka, 1967; Drake, 1946; Eysenck, 1947). Presumably, a given individual could then be "located" at some point along this dimension, usually based on responses to a self-report measure of general social competence. Similar formulations and measurement procedures have been used to create continuum models for generalized traits of introversion-extroversion, orientation toward others or away from them, social dominance versus submissiveness, and so on.

However, there appear to be several major limitations associated with the conceptualization of social competency in terms of generalized, continuum-like traits. As suggested in the previous section, what we term social skill or competence is a collection of different types of skills, which are used for different purposes. There may be little correspondence between the ability of a given individual to effectively exhibit one type of social skill and the ability of the same individual to effectively exhibit another type of social skill. Wolpe and Lazarus (1966), for example, have noted that some clients are able to effectively assert themselves when confronted with the unreasonable behavior of an antagonist (refusal assertion), but lack the commendatory skills repertoire to communicate positive or affectionate feelings to others. Other investigators have found that training skills-deficient clients in more effective commendatory social skills largely failed to improve their ability to handle situations requiring refusal assertion (Geller, Wildman, Kelly, & Laughlin, 1980; Kelly, Frederiksen, Fitts, & Phillips, 1978). A similar situation probably exists for some college students who handle many everyday interactions successfully but lack the skills repertoire needed to present themselves effectively during employment interviews. This may be due to infrequent exposure to the job-interview social situation and to the relatively specialized skills needed to effectively handle it. It appears unwarranted, then, to assume that individuals will be consistently skillful across different types of social competency, and it may be more useful to construe the various kinds of social skills as functionally discrete abilities.

The degree to which a particular type of skill will be important or functional for an individual depends upon how frequently the person is in situations where that skill is needed, as well as the importance or value of the goal that can be attained by using the skill. Effective date-initiation behavior is more salient for individuals who are single and seeking to establish date relationships than for persons who are already happily married. Conversational skills may be more important for individuals who must frequently meet others than for people with a small group of friends and more solitary pursuits. Effective job-interview behavior is more salient to the individual seeking employment than to the individual who has been working contentedly at the same company for years. We would expect that individuals are likely to most develop and exhibit social skills that permit goal-attainment in situations that they encounter frequently or, conversely, we may expect that individuals are likely to experience greater dissatisfaction if they do not have the social-skills repertoire that is needed to handle those interactions that could lead to personally salient goals.

There may be little necessary correspondence between an individual's ability to exhibit one type of social skill and the same person's ability to effectively handle situations calling for another kind of skill; in addition, even a single type of social skill, such as assertiveness or conversational skill, is not consistently exhibited across all situations. Mischel (1968) has argued that while clients and therapists may perceive a high degree of consistency in social behavior across different situations, objective assessment often indicates that the social behavior or skills of the same individual are determined by the situation the individual is in. Thus, a person may exhibit effective refusal-assertion skills in one situation but fail to exhibit the same skills in a different situational context. Eisler, Hersen, Miller, and Blanchard (1975) found that the quality of effective assertion among psychiatric patients varied depending upon such factors as whether the antagonist in a role-play situation was portrayed as familiar or unfamiliar to the client, whether the antagonist was a male or a female, and the circumstances surrounding the need to be assertive. Other investigators have found that clients who could generate appropriately assertive responses during role-plays of troublesome situations were considerably less effective in handling the same incident when it occurred in the natural environment (Bellack, Hersen, & Lamparski, 1979).

These findings make intuitive sense. If we were to observe a given individual across various interpersonal situations in which another person behaves unreasonably towards him, we would expect to find that the manner in which the person handles an antagonist would vary, depending upon many situational variables. These might include whether the antagonist was a family member, a close friend, an acquaintance, a stranger, a co-worker, or a supervisor at work. The sex and age of the antagonist may also determine a client's response; one might well behave differently toward a peer than toward a very elderly person, even if the two individuals acted identically. Cognitive factors, such as the perceived intent of the antagonist, can influence whether an assertive response will occur and, if so, the verbal or nonverbal nature of that response. For these reasons, construing assertiveness as a generalized, cross-situational trait appears both behaviorally inaccurate and simplistic (Mischel, 1968).

A similar pattern of situational specificity appears likely for other types of social skills. The quality, competence, or ease of conversational interactions exhibited by a client will depend upon situational factors, including the familiarity of the other person in the conversation, the sex of the client, the sex of the partner, and the purpose of the interaction (e.g., talking with a stranger to pass some time at a bus stop, conversing with one's boss, or conversing with the intention of asking the other person for a date).

Failure to Exhibit Socially Skilled Behavior

An individual's failure to exhibit socially skilled behavior in a given situation can be explained in a number of different ways, as we shall discuss below.

Lack of skill acquisition or learning.   It may be that a specific type of social skill was never acquired or was inadequately learned, and therefore is never exhibited in any situation. In this case, the client does not have the appropriate skill behaviors in his or her repertoire. Consequently, the skill never is exhibited, or rarely is exhibited, regardless of the situation in which the client finds himself or herself. This might account for the ineffective behavior of the chronically institutionalized patient who seems to exhibit relatively pervasive social impairment; of extremely withdrawn clients with little exposure to situations where they could perform the skill and be reinforced for its exhibition; or of higher-functioning clients with little or no experience history in specific situations requiring that skill, such as adolescents just learning to date or inexperienced job-seekers going on their first interviews.

Lack of skill use in certain situations.   In this case, a specific type of skill is learned and exhibited effectively in a certain situation but fails to appear in other situations. Here, various environmental, interpersonal, or setting cues (or "signs") may govern the exhibition of social-skill responses; when those cues are present in a situation, the skillful behavior will occur. In situations with cues dissimilar to those in the setting of original skill-learning, the individual will not engage in those behaviors, and may not even perceive them as response options. An example of this might be a child who will display appropriate peer social behavior in a highly structured game situation, but not in an unstructured free-play setting. Here, the structure of the setting is a cue affecting the social behavior of the child. Similarly, an individual might have no difficulty conversing with same-sex persons, but may experience anxiety and exhibit diminished skills in the same situations when interacting with opposite-sex persons. In this case, the sex of the other person appears to be a discriminative cue, such that same-sex partners elicit a skilled type of response, while opposite-sex partners elicit a much less effective social-skill response.

Situational variables may affect reinforcement. A specific type of social skill may result in different consequences, such that in some situations it is reinforced, while in other situations it is not reinforced. As we will elaborate more thoroughly in Chapter 2, it is likely that social skills of almost any kind are learned and refined naturalistically as a result of their ability to lead to reinforcement. If a skill is reinforced consistently in some situations but not in others, an individual should learn to identify or discriminate those situations in which a particular interpersonal strategy is most functional or capable of leading to reinforcement. Thus, for example, the assertive skills that one would use to effectively resolve a disagreement with his brother might be different than the skills the same person would exhibit when disagreeing with a hot-tempered supervisor at work. A college student's interactions with her roommate will be quite different than her conversation on a job interview or with her college advisor, because somewhat different behaviors are likely to be reinforced in each of these situations. Ideally, individuals learn what social skills will be reinforced in different settings, and adapt their behavior accordingly. However, problems can arise if a person either enters a situation and does not know what social skills will be reinforced or if the person's social style is so inflexible that a skill is rigidly used even when it is not adaptive. For example, people may handle many situations in a passive manner, even when assertion is appropriate, because they have not been previously reinforced for exhibiting assertive behavior.

Describing Socially Skilled Behavior in an Objective, Identifiable Manner

In order to teach clients new social skills, it is necessary to objectively define those behaviors that make a given type of interaction skillful. Let us assume that we are watching a number of people while each is confronted with the unreasonable behavior of another person toward him or her. We might observe and label as "assertive" the way one person handles an antagonist, and label as "unassertive" the way another handles the same situation. Labeling an interpersonal response as assertive or unassertive is a result of our observation of various behaviors included in the response; the behavioral components of refusal assertion might include the presence of such nonverbal characteristics as eye contact, firm affect, verbal fluency, appropriate loudness, gestures, and short latency or delay between the conclusion of the antagonist's comments and the individual's response. Verbal content components of an effectively assertive response could include a statement conveying recognition of the antagonist's viewpoint but verbal noncompliance or disagreement with the other person; a request for specific antagonist behavior change; or the proposal of an acceptable solution to the conflict (cf. Eisler, Miller, & Hersen, 1973; Linehan, Goldfried, & Goldfried, 1979; Mullinix & Galassi, 1978; Woolfolk & Dever, 1979). Thus, the social ability termed "refusal assertion" can be broken down behaviorally into a constellation of identifiable behavioral components. Since these component behaviors can be specified and described in a relatively clear-cut and objective fashion, the social-skills training therapist can assess the extent to which each component is present in a client's interactions and then train those components that are absent or deficient. If the identified components are the salient determinants of an effective response, one can teach the skill by teaching the components comprising it.

This behavioral mode of skill-analysis may be applied not only to refusal assertion, but to any form of social competency. One can observe how skillful individuals initiate or maintain conversations, handle job interviews, meet persons whom they wish to date, or commend the actions of others. In the case of children, it is possible to observe play and social-behavior differences between popular and unpopular children. In social-skills assessment and training, one seeks to determine those specific behavioral components that constitute the desired type of skill, and then to systematically teach the identified component behaviors to the skills-deficient client.

Social Skill Functioning and Psychological Adjustment

Traditional theories of personality and psychopathology have long recognized relationships between social functioning and emotional adjustment; these relationships have been most thoroughly elaborated in the personality development descriptions of Harry Stack Sullivan, Alfred Adler, Karen Horney, and other neo-Freudian interpersonal theorists. Sullivan, for example, rejected the notion of an internal personality construct, arguing instead that what we term "personality" exists and can be defined only in the context of interpersonal relationships. To the extent that an individual successfully interacts with others, that individual will receive accumulating positive social feedback and come to label his or her self in a positive fashion (Sullivan, 1953). On the other hand, when relationships with significant other people are characterized by anxiety, frustration of needs, or negative feedback, the individual's self-appraisals will be correspondingly negative, distorted, and regressive. Such constructs as self-esteem or self-concept are thereby determined by the interpersonal relations and feedback that an individual receives during the course of development.

Horney's theoretical approach to personality also stresses interpersonal functioning in relation to adjustment. According to her formulation, the social insecurity of a child early in life produces an enduring disturbance in that person's later social interactions, which takes the form of excessive and maladaptive "movement toward people," including "neurotic" and lifelong needs for affection; "movement away from people," characterized by social avoidance or independence to prevent being hurt; or "movement against others" (Horney, 1945). When an infant or child has experienced parental social inconsistency, overindulgence, hostility, or deprivation, later relationships then become recurrently maladaptive as the individual attempts to reduce the basic social anxiety that had been created earlier. In similar fashion, Adler's description of personality stresses the relationship between detrimental early life experiences (including parental pampering, neglect, physical or emotional inferiorities, and absence of sibling contact) and corresponding later disturbance in social functioning (see Adler, 1931).

These theories provide a descriptive linkage between early social relationships and personality. However, while Sullivan, Adler, and Horney eloquently describe maladaptive or deficient aspects of client social functioning, each theorist views current interpersonal behavior as symptomatic or secondary to a more basic developmental disturbance, usually rooted in faulty parent-child relationships. As a result, therapy based on these traditional interpersonally oriented theories is directed toward an analytic, interpretive reconstruction of early-life experiences and does not directly focus on teaching a client new social competencies. Additionally, client social functioning is characteristically described in an imprecise and traitlike fashion (such as Horney's descriptions of the interpersonal orientations of movement toward, away from, or against other people).

It is possible to conceptualize psychological adjustment in a different manner, with socially skillful functioning the prerequisite for adjustment, rather than its consequent. As we have noted, social skills are the strategies that people use to obtain reinforcing consequences from their environment. Reinforcers are not absolutes, and goals that one person considers highly desirable may be quite unimportant to someone else. However, achievement of most of the goals sought by clients (and anyone else) does require reasonably successful interaction with other people. The goal of establishing friendships requires that a client initiate and maintain certain types of informal conversational interactions; without those skills in his or her repertoire, it is unlikely that the client can develop satisfactory friendships. In order to establish dating relationships, a more specialized set of social-skill competencies are needed. To maintain feelings of self-worth and to feel that one can communicate beliefs or opinions to others, assertive capabilities must be present in the individual's skills repertoire. To achieve the goal of being offered a desirable job, a candidate must first convey socially to a potential employer that he or she will be a competent, achieving employee; in order to be promoted to a better job, requisite social skills include the ability to interact effectively with subordinates, peers, and supervisors across a variety of different work situations.

To the extent that a client's interpersonal repertoire permits the attainment of goals that the client deems reinforcing, that individual is likely to evaluate himself or herself in positive terms. Thus, favorable self-evaluation (including such global descriptors as "self-esteem" and "self-confidence") forms as a consequence of a social-skills repertoire that permits the attainment of personally meaningful goals. In addition, as social skills are practiced and become reinforced within specific goal-oriented situations, it is likely that they will continue to be exhibited and that the skills repertoire of the client will become further elaborated. For example, the individual who has the skills to initiate interactions with others will not only be reinforced for those initiations, but will also develop close relationships conducive to the practice, refinement, and learning of additional social competencies.

On the other hand, if a client has failed to acquire the social-skills repertoire necessary to attain personally significant goals in the environment, a much more detrimental pattern is probable. As a result of an intitial skills deficiency, a client may be persistently unable to achieve sought-after goals, and attempts at social initiation may actually be punished. In this way, the child who lacks peer-valued play and social skills could be such an unrewarding agent that other children seek to minimize their contact with the skills-deficient child. An adolescent who is severely deficient in date-initiation skills may have his or her attempts to initiate dates repeatedly rejected. The formerly institutionalized psychiatric patient with severe social-skills deficits will find it extremely difficult to establish appropriate social relationships in the community, especially if he or she "looks like" a former psychiatric patient to most people outside of the institution. An unemployed mother who has been on Welfare, but who in fact is employable and seeks work, may be consistently rejected for employment because she lacks the social skills to portray herself as vocationally competent under the stress and novelty of an interview.

Under such repeated failure conditions, it is likely that clients will develop negative self-evaluations and begin to cognitively label themselves as socially awkward, unsuccessful, undesirable, or unattractive. Thus, the initial skill deficits of clients are antecedents for the failure to attain personally reinforcing goals, which in turn gives rise to persistent negative self-evaluation. As a result of unsuccessful social interactions, a client is also likely to develop failure-oriented cognitions and anticipate anxiety when confronted with situations that he or she feels unprepared to handle effectively, based on past experience. Meichenbaum and his associates (Meichenbaum & Cameron, 1974) have described the manner in which such failure-oriented cognitions can foster social anxiety and, under the disruptive influence of this anxiety, result in even further impaired social-skill performance. A likely consequence of this pattern is that the client's attempts to handle the troublesome situations will extinguish as a result of nonreinforcement, punishment, or the uncomfortable anxiety associated with attempts to attain goals when the requisite skills for doing so are insufficient. Avoidance of the situations, social isolation, or abandonment of the desired but unattainable goals are predictable outcomes.

Unfortunately, this pattern of initial skill-deficiency may well perpetuate continued skills deficits in the future. By avoiding situations that require social competencies that he or she lacks, the individual is not likely to be in a position to learn more appropriate skills. The socially isolated child, by virtue of reduced opportunities for peer interaction, will be less likely to observe and interact with skillful peer models and less likely to be reinforced by others when skillful prosocial behaviors do occur. The formerly institutionalized adult who lacks everyday conversational skills may be so avoided by other people that there will be continued isolation and few opportunities to learn more effective social skills in the natural environment, thereby perpetuating continued skill-deficiency.

By intervening to teach clients more appropriate social skills, it is possible to interrupt this cycle. The aim of social-skills training is to directly increase the behavioral competency of individuals so that they can achieve successful outcomes in those types of social situations where their current skills are inadequate. Thus, the target for intervention is the individual's current social behavior itself, rather than postulated early-life contributors to the observed deficits. As a client learns and practices new social skills in the therapy or training environment, and then exhibits them in previously troublesome situations in the natural environment, more satisfactory outcomes in those situations should be achieved and the client's self-evaluation and self-perception of competence will correspondingly become more positive.

Skills-Training and Client Growth

Some observers have suggested that most traditional psychotherapies seem principally oriented toward the "removal" of sources of psychological discomfort (Hollandsworth, personal communication, 1979). Clinicians and counselors have directed a great deal of attention to techniques that reduce client anxiety, reduce client depression, and reduce client conflict. If troublesome behaviors and characteristics could only be eliminated from a client's functioning, that individual would then be able to cope and adapt more successfully. Thus, traditional treatment often appears more oriented to removing undesirable characteristics than to systematically strengthening desirable response capabilities. In contrast to this essentially pessimistic "discomfort reduction" model, social-skills training approaches seek to build new behavioral competencies in clients. In this manner, skills-training adds to the adaptive and social repertoire of the client, rather than simply reducing discomfort.

Behavioral treatment approaches have been criticized by some clinicians on the grounds that they are inherently mechanistic, controlling, coercive, or that they fail to recognize the potential for "personality growth" (Breger & McGaugh, 1965; Portes, 1971; Rogers & Skinner, 1956; Shoben, 1963). However, behavioral social-skills training explicitly recognizes and requires the ability of clients to change as a result of their learning experiences, perhaps more than in almost any other treatment approach. Social-skills training assumes that regardless of why a client has not learned how to handle certain interpersonal interactions successfully, that client can be taught more effective behavioral competencies if the desired competencies are identified clearly and if learning principles are systematically applied to increase them. Since training requires that the client actively practice and rehearse new responses to troublesome situations, the client becomes actively and directly involved in treatment, rather than being a passive recipient of the therapist's advice or interpretation. As we will see, the learning theory principles that are employed in social-skills training are the same as those learning theory principles that presumably operate to facilitate social-skills learning in the natural environment. Thus, skills-training intensifies or compresses naturally-occurring learning experiences within treatment sessions, and utilizes the potential of clients to benefit from the intensive learning exposure. There is also an explicit optimism that once clients have added new skills to their interpersonal repertoire in the training setting, they can then learn to generalize or extend the exhibition of these skills to previously troublesome social interactions in the natural environment. Equipped with new competencies, the individual should experience more successful outcomes in the situations targeted for treatment. Naturally-occurring reinforcement contingencies (including more positive reactions from others in interpersonal situations, the formation of relationships with others, feelings of personal satisfaction due to more effective expression of beliefs, and more satisfactory attainment of goals) can then maintain improved social skills beyond the initial training environment. Once more appropriate skills are exhibited and reinforced in the environment, the client's increased confidence will allow him to be exposed to still other social interactions, accompanied by enhanced opportunities for the natural learning of additional competencies.

Chapter 2

The Social-Learning Theory Model
of Skills-Acquisition

If we conceptualize social skills as learned strategies that serve purposeful or goal-directed functions, it becomes appropriate to determine how they are normally acquired during development. If the factors responsible for the naturalistic learning of social competencies can be specified, it should then be possible to incorporate similar principles in training interventions for clients who have not yet acquired those skills.

Social-learning theory has provided the foundation for viewing social competencies as learned behaviors. This theory postulates that the development of behavior, including the interpersonal style of an individual, can be accurately described, explained, and predicted based on learning theory principles. If one can determine the specific learning history of an individual, it will be possible to account for the manner in which that person handles situations, such as those situations requiring socially skilled responses. Social-learning theory, as applied to skills development, has the principles of instrumental or operant conditioning as its basis. The operant approach emphasizes the importance of environmental antecedents and consequences in the development and maintenance of behavior. However, such theoreticians as Bandura, Rotter, Mischel, and Meichenbaum have elaborated learning principles to include the effects of vicarious (modeled) sources of learning, cognitive expectancies and subjective reinforcement value, situational specificity of behavior, and the role of cognitive behaviors (such as self-statements and self-instructions).

Social-Learning Mechanisms and the Naturalistic Development
of Social Competencies

Social skills are acquired naturalistically as a consequence of several basic learning mechanisms. These mechanisms include: direct positive reinforcement of the skills; vicarious or observational learning experiences; receiving

15

interpersonal feedback; and the development of cognitive expectancies concerning interpersonal situations. Let us review each of these mechanisms.

Skills-Learning as a Result of Direct Reinforcement

Even during very early infancy, it is apparent that rudimentary social behaviors can be developed and maintained by their reinforcing consequences. Infants appear to learn very quickly those behaviors capable of eliciting positive consequences from the environment, including: crying to bring food, attention, or relief from discomfort; smiling and cooing to bring social attention and stimulation from others; and the exhibition of motor skills, which lead to physical and attentional responses from other people (Engen, Lipsett, & Kaye, 1963). Over time, the interpersonal repertoire of behaviors exhibited by the child becomes much more elaborated, diverse, and verbal, just as the variety of events that assume positively reinforcing properties becomes increasingly diverse, social, and removed from primary (body-need) functions. To the extent that various types of social interactions lead to positive consequences for a child and later for an adult, it is likely they will be reinforced and included in that person's interpersonal repertoire.

The manner in which direct personal reinforcement history operates to shape the naturalistic development of social skills appears to be governed by a number of factors. One of these is the subjective value of the events that can serve as reinforcers. Reinforcement is not an absolute property, and reinforcers are defined in terms of their functional ability to increase the likelihood of the behaviors that they follow. The extent to which such social outcomes as play with peers, conversations with others, dates, or positive comments from other people serve as functional reinforcers varies across individuals. If such events do not function as salient reinforcers for a given individual, it is likely that the social skills that lead to those outcomes will be less developed. Rotter, for example, notes that predicting the likelihood for a given behavior to occur must take into account the subjective reinforcement value of the consequating event to the individual (Rotter, 1954).

Interestingly, autistic and some severely retarded children appear highly unresponsive to the interpersonal attention that most children find reinforcing, and remain oriented toward primary (biological-need) rather than secondary (social) forms of reinforcement. This may partially account for the impaired social-skills development of these persons, since many interpersonal consequences of skill-exhibition do not seem to be salient reinforcers for them. Even in less extreme cases, the potency or subjective value of reinforcement available through use of various types of social skills affects the skills' development.

A second mechanism influencing the direct learning of skills involves the specificity of circumstances under which they are reinforced. Mischel (1973) has pointed out that very few social behaviors are reinforced consistently across all situations or settings, and we observed earlier that social skills differ both functionally and qualitatively depending upon the nature of an interpersonal setting. Similarly, whether or not a given type of skill will be exhibited across differing situations can be determined by the individual's reinforcement history for behavior in those situations. This becomes particularly important when people approach novel situations in which they have had no direct learning experience. If an individual approaches a novel interpersonal situation that is perceived and cognitively labeled as *similar* to other past situations in which a certain type of social response was effective (or which provides cues similar to those present in past learning), the individual is likely to behave in a manner consistent with behavior that worked in the past (Mischel, 1973). To the extent that the skill behavior will also be effective in the new situation, this form of response-generalization will prove adaptive. On the other hand, novel social situations can be problematic if different social skills are needed to handle them and if the person has little reinforcement history for engaging in those skills, as well as if the new situation was incorrectly perceived and different response contingencies are, in fact, operating.

Finally, basic research on reinforcement scheduling has demonstrated that new behaviors are most efficiently established under conditions in which they are reinforced on a consistent basis, with each instance of the desired, correct behavior being reinforced whenever it occurs (Reynolds, 1958). Unfortunately, most social skills are not reinforced on such a consistent basis when they are first being acquired. An individual's early attempts to express assertion, to ask someone for a date, to interview for a job, or to meet new people following discharge from an institution may not be reinforced with consistently positive responses from others. This is especially likely when the person has not yet fully mastered the skill and is relatively less able to engage in it effectively. If a social behavior is repeatedly attempted but does not lead to some positive consequence, especially during the earlier stages of learning, it may well extinguish and cease to be exhibited.

Skills-Learning as a Result of Observational Experiences

We learn how to handle interpersonal situations as a result of our direct experience in those situations and, more specifically, as a result of reinforcement histories for handling them in certain ways. Another potent source of skills-learning is observing how other people handle situations.

Bandura (1969) has described the influence of observational or vicarious learning (termed "modeling") on social behavior, and demonstrated its effect in a large number of studies. Exposure to a model can have any of three types of effects: (1) the modeling effect, in which the observer of the model acquires a new behavior that he or she did not exhibit previously as a consequence of the observation of the model; (2) the disinhibitory effect, in which exposure to the model causes the observer to more frequently exhibit a behavior that had been present earlier; and (3) the inhibitory effect, in which the observer exhibits a behavior less frequently after exposure to a model than before exposure to it (Bandura & Walters, 1963). With respect to social skills-development, the modeling and disinhibitory effects appear most important.

Children, adolescents, and adults develop new competencies to handle situations by observing how live models around them, including parents, siblings, friends, co-workers, and supervisors, handle those situations. Thus, social-skill knowledge can be acquired initially without personal learning experience in the relevant situations. For young children, parents and older siblings are among the most potent sources for imitative social learning; in time, other models in the environment become important sources of observational learning and supersede the influence of family models. This appears particularly true in adolescence, when peers become extremely influential sources for modeling social-skill behaviors (Lasseigne, 1975).

A number of studies have investigated the circumstances under which modeled learning is most likely to occur and when the observer is most likely to actually exhibit a new behavior seen in a model (cf. Bandura & Huston, 1961; Bandura & Kupers, 1964; Bandura, Ross, & Ross, 1963). Some of the factors that appear to facilitate observational learning include:

1. *Age of the model,*   particularly in childhood and adolescence. Children are most likely to imitate the behavior of a model similar in age to the observer or slightly older. Social behaviors exhibited by younger models are less likely to be imitated.

2. *Sex of the model,*   with models of the same sex as the observer exerting a stronger influence than opposite-sex models.

3. *Likeability of the model,*   with models high in warmth and affectionate characteristics more salient in influence than cold, unaffectionate-appearing models.

4. *Perceived similarity to the observer.*   If an observer perceives or is told that a model is similar to himself or herself, a greater degree of imitative learning will occur than if the model is seen as highly dissimilar.

5. *Observed consequence to the model when the model engages in the social behavior.*   If the observer watches a model engage in a social behavior and also sees that the model achieves a positive outcome as a result of it, there is increased likelihood that the observer will imitate that behavior. This is termed "vicarious reinforcement," since the observer sees the reinforcing consequence achieved by another person. On the other hand,

observed (vicarious) punishment of a model's social behavior decreases the likelihood of imitative behavior.

6.   *The observer's own direct learning history for engaging in the same or similar social behavior as seen in the model.*   In many cases, the observer has had some direct, personal experience handling situations similar to those in which the model is seen. The observer may have engaged in similar social responses as well. If the observer has a personal history of being rewarded for behaviors similar to those now exhibited by the model, it is more likely that the observer will actually exhibit the modeled social behavior than if the observer has been personally punished for behaviors now seen in the model. In this way, the observer's expectancies concerning what would happen if he or she actually engaged in the modeled behavior influence the likelihood of performing that skill.

While live models are a source of much observational learning, other forms of modeling also account for social-skill acquisition during development. These include portrayed realistic models, such as television or filmed portrayals of others; portrayed nonrealistic models, including cartoons, or animated nonhuman models; and symbolic models, such as idealized, elaborate verbal descriptions of the conduct of another person (a good Christian, the perfect Eagle Scout, or the ideal employee of a company).

A good deal of clinical and research attention has been directed toward studying the manner in which naturalistic modeling can exert a detrimental effect on behavior. This has been particularly emphasized with respect to the effects of portrayed, televised violence and sexual misconduct, as well as the effects of live peer-modeling of antisocial or delinquent behavior during early adolescence (Bandura, 1965; Bandura, Ross, & Ross, 1963; Rosekrans & Hartup, 1967). However, it seems likely that for most people, adaptive and prosocial skills are more often learned observationally than are antisocial behaviors.

In early childhood, the ways in which parents and older siblings handle social situations can be observed and copied, rather directly, by the young child. During school years, children appear to imitate the social behavior and play-skills exhibited by other children, particularly those classmates and friends who exhibit the characteristics that are associated with increased likelihood of imitative learning (e.g., same sex, same age or slightly older, warm, and successful when exhibiting the behaviors). Adolescents and adults also learn how to handle many social situations by imitating the behavior of others; initiating friendships and dates, learning how to handle job interviews or college-admission interviews, disagreeing with others, and expressing oneself assertively are skills acquired, in part, by directly watching other people in those situations or receiving detailed verbal modeling instructions from them.

Especially when approaching novel situations, people often visualize, recall, and imitate the social skills that have been seen in others and used successfully by them.

If modeled learning is an important mechanism for the naturalistic development of social competencies, one might specify some conditions under which it might fail to occur. If a child lacks appropriate live models due to isolation from parents, older siblings, or peers, there would be correspondingly less opportunity to observe how they handle interpersonal situations. Several studies provide indirect support for this pattern. Miller and Maruyama (1976) and Shrader and Leventhal (1968) have reported that "only" children or children who are the oldest in their families (and therefore lack older-sibling models) exhibit more frequent peer difficulties and behavior problems, at least through later childhood. This effect appears to dissipate over time, presumably as the role of family models becomes less crucial and the presence of peer models outside the family increases during school and later years (Birtchnell, 1972). At the same time, prolonged peer isolation in childhood has been associated with a variety of more frequent coping and social-interactive problems in adult life (Elkins, 1958; O'Neal & Robins, 1958; Stennett, 1966).

Individuals who have fewer opportunities to interact with socially skilled peers will also have less opportunity to watch and observationally learn from them. A child with few friends will be more isolated from peers during free play at school, during after-school activities, and at other times. In addition to diminishing the probability that the child will be directly reinforced for appropriate interaction skills, the simple physical isolation from others also decreases exposure to more skilled models. The same patterns can exist well beyond childhood. The shy adolescent or adult who has always shunned social activities in favor of solitary and nonsocial pursuits will have correspondingly less exposure to the conduct of skilled models; when this individual approaches new interpersonal situations, the strategies for handling them may not be based on the observed behavior of others, but only on a trial-and-error system from limited personal and direct social-learning experience.

The absence of appropriate skill models is extremely evident in the environment of institutionalized persons, such as retarded or emotionally disturbed children and adults. Within a confined institutional setting, there may be very few peer models who exhibit those social skills that are adaptive in the noninstitutional environment; in fact, social behaviors that are modeled in residential facilities for chronically low-functioning persons may be quite unadaptive outside that setting. Most therapists who work in long-term residential facilities such as retardation centers and psychiatric hospitals are well aware of the low level of social-interaction quality within them. From a social-learning perspective, the relative absence of skillful models significantly impairs opportunities for those clients to observationally learn more adaptive competencies and also reduces the likelihood that appropriate skills, if exhibited, will be actively reinforced by other clients in that setting.

The potential for modeling-induced social-skills learning to occur is also diminished in those kinds of interpersonal situations in which people rarely have the opportunity to observe others. The social skills needed to effectively convey to one's boss the "case" for a raise or promotion may be unclear if one has never observed this situation well-handled by someone else. Effective job-interview behavior can be especially troublesome to the inexperienced applicant, who has had little personal experience in that specialized situation and who has not observed successful models exhibit job-interview skills. Disharmonious couples, especially those who are isolated from very close couple friends, are unlikely to observe the effective conflict-resolution skills exhibited by others; this occurs primarily because a couple's adaptive conflict-resolution strategies rarely occur under circumstances in which others can observe them.

Thus, all people acquire social competencies not only as a result of personal learning experience and their direct-reinforcement history, but also by observing the modeled behavior of others. Under circumstances where opportunities for modeled learning are reduced, the development of those skill competencies may be correspondingly weaker.

Skills-Learning and Interpersonal Feedback

As individuals gain practice in handling a certain type of social situation and develop adaptive skills that bring about favorable outcomes, their behavior becomes more refined and well-honed. The initial attempts of a previously unassertive person to behave in an appropriately assertive fashion may be somewhat awkward, stilted, and uncomfortable, but will become progressively more refined under favorable, reinforcing conditions. The early date-initiation behavior of a young adolescent is usually less effective than that adolescent's dating skills two years later. Adults often feel less at ease and behave less skillfully when first meeting a new person in conversation, but more at ease during subsequent interactions. If social behavior in a given situation is reinforced through some positive outcome, it will not only tend to recur, but will change and become more effective over time.

An important mechanism contributing to the refinement and sharpening of skills is feedback. In social contexts, feedback is the information one receives from another person that communicates his or her response or reaction to one's behavior. If someone is conversing with an acquaintance about interests and hobbies, that person may notice that the conversational partner becomes much more attentive when certain topics are discussed, such as tennis and sports, and much less attentive when other topics are mentioned, such as family problems. Consequently, the person adapts his or her social behavior in response to the feedback provided by the other individual. Feedback can be positive in nature, strengthening certain aspects of social skills. Examples of such positive feedback might include another person's increase in eye contact, posture movement toward the individual who is speaking, or verbal comments conveying explicit interest in what is being said. Feedback may also be negative, thereby weakening aspects of the particular behavior. Negative feedback could include such responses as reduced eye contact, yawning, or movement away from the speaker. In a sense, what we term "feedback" can be actually viewed as social reinforcement (or the lack of it) administered contingently by the other person in the interaction. Some researchers have suggested that feedback, by definition, is only a molecular or "process" form of reinforcement over the course of social interactions (Madsen, Becker, & Thomas, 1968).

A number of studies have demonstrated that contingent feedback can alter the social behavior of clients, even without their awareness of it (see Greenspoon, 1955). Ideally, however, feedback should be direct and convey relatively specific information for the person to whom it is directed. To exert its maximum impact, feedback will be associated with a specific aspect of behavior and will be communicated clearly and verbally to the individual. With the information provided through feedback, the person receiving it will be better able to change and enhance his or her impact on others.

In some cases, clear feedback is provided during the course of an everyday interaction. Examples of this might include being told: "It made you look honest when you looked me right in the eye"; "I didn't believe that you were really being firm because you were smiling"; "You talk too much about your problems"; or "You make me feel comfortable because you get me to talk about myself." In these examples, the person receiving the comments is in a position to either maintain or eliminate certain social-skill behaviors, since the informational nature of the feedback is clear-cut.

In many routine interactions, social feedback is more ambiguous or essentially absent. If an adolescent attempts to initiate dating behavior and is repeatedly rejected, he usually does not receive very specific feedback as to why he is turned down by the prospective dates. What aspects of his style were deficient? Were there verbal or nonverbal elements of his date-initiation behavior that led to repeated rejection? If so, what were the deficient or inappropriate aspects? Without such information, the individual is not likely to know how he is being perceived and will not be in a position to change these behaviors.

Similarly, an individual may feel that he is making an appropriately assertive response to some troublesome behavior from another person. However, others may be quite perturbed by his behavior and consider it highly aggressive, rather than appropriately assertive. They are, perhaps, identifying certain aspects of the response (hostile tone, antagonistic comments, no verbally conveyed recognition of their position) that make the response noxious and ineffective. Unless the individual receives specific feedback from others on those aspects, they may be quite difficult to change. Unfortunately, with the exception of occasional feedback provided by close friends at the request of an individual, most everyday interactions provide little opportunity to receive this kind of clear-cut information. It must often be inferred, without great precision, from the more global and general reactions of others; as feedback becomes less precise and less tied to identifiable behavior, it also loses its ability to help people refine their own social skills.

Skills-Learning and Cognitive Expectancies

Julian Rotter introduced the notion that the subjective value of a given reinforcer must be taken into account in order to accurately predict whether an individual will engage in a behavior leading to that reinforcer (Rotter, 1954). Thus, as we noted earlier, social skills will assume greater importance and meaning if they lead to outcomes that a client values highly. Another predictor of social behavior, first noted by Rotter, is the individual's cognitive expectancy for success in a given situation.

Cognitive expectancies are beliefs or predictions concerning the preceived probability of successfully handling some situation. According to Rotter, expectancies develop as a result of experience in a situation or in other situations similar to it. If a person has learned through direct experience, modeling, or feedback that he or she is able to handle a social interaction effectively, a positive cognitive expectancy for future success will develop. Assuming that the interaction is also enjoyable, rewarding, or significant (and therefore has relatively high reinforcement value), the individual is likely to approach that situation. On the other hand, the probability is low that one will enter into situations requiring skills that one feels unequipped to exhibit satisfactorily, even if the potential outcome might be quite desirable; such skills carry a low cognitive expectancy for success. In short, Rotter's formulation can be interpreted to suggest that individuals will enter into situations requiring socially skilled behavior if both (1) the potential outcome from using those skills is sufficiently reinforcing and (2) the individual has developed, based on experience, the cognitive expectancy that he or she will be able to exhibit the skills needed to handle the situation effectively.

What are the mechanisms that comprise cognitive expectancies for success or failure in handling a given situation? In the previous chapter, we noted that the way in which clients label situations and what they actually tell themselves about their performance can influence skills-development and -exhibition. More specifically, if a person has a history of success in handling some type of interaction (such as those requiring general conversations with others, assertive expression, job-interview skills, date-initiation, or commendatory skills), the person is likely to label those situations as enjoyable, stimulating, or challenging, and to label his or her own behavior as competent, successful, or effective. Conversely, negative expectancies are probably acquired as a result of past difficulties in handling the troublesome situation and are maintained by cognitions of failure concerning performance in that situation. Two related approaches seem useful for reducing negative expectancies and the related anxiety that maintains them. One is to directly alter the detrimental manner in which clients label and covertly talk to themselves when they are anticipating the troublesome interaction (see Meichenbaum & Cameron, 1974). However, unless a skills-deficient client does actually acquire more adaptive ways to handle the social situation and achieve greater success in it, the success of cognitive modification alone appears unlikely. Thus, a second approach is to directly increase the behavioral skills-competency of the client to successfully handle those interactions that have proven troublesome.

Social-Learning Principles: The Active Ingredients of Skills-Training Interventions

The learning of social competencies in the natural environment is determined by such factors as history of direct reinforcement for skilled behavior, imitative or observational learning history, feedback and the shaping or refinement of skills, ample opportunities to practice newly acquired behaviors, and the development of increasingly positive cognitions or expectancies for performance. Regardless of why certain competencies were not acquired naturally in socially deficient clients, the same learning principles can be used to teach those skills in our treatment interventions. The treatment principles that appear crucial to any type of clinical social-skills training intervention are: instruction and rationale provided to the client, modeling exposure, opportunity for actual practice of the skill, reinforcement and feedback on the client's behavioral practice, and generalization of skill-improvement to the natural environment. Let us consider first how these general social-learning treatment principles can be applied to skills-training and then we will examine several interventions that have actually used them. In Chapter 4, implementation of the principles will be considered in more detail and applied to specific types of skills-training interventions.

Instruction and Rationale Provided to Client

At the beginning of any social-skills training session, it is important to clearly convey to the client the exact skill-behavior or component that will receive attention that day and to provide a rationale for its importance. For example, an assertive-training intervention may be intended to increase several verbal and several nonverbal components of assertion, such as eye contact, voice tone and loudness, affect, verbal noncompliance, and statement of position. If increasing client eye contact is the aim of a particular session, the therapist might begin that session by verbally telling the client how eye contact is defined, why it is important to exhibit eye contact during interactions, and so on. For complicated verbal behaviors, clear identification of the component skills for the client is even more important, and examples may be given to illustrate the verbal behavior that will receive training attention that day. The purpose of beginning each session with brief instruction and explanation of the component by the therapist is to ensure that clients understand that day's expectations for their performance.

Modeling Exposure

Client exposure to a model who correctly exhibits the skill-component being targeted for training in the session permits the observational learning of that component. While verbally presented instructions or examples of a skill-behavior given by the therapist may provide an initial purpose for that day's session, a client's own observation of how a model actually exhibits the skill-component often conveys more clearly the nature of the desired behavior.

Models during training sessions can be live or portrayed. An example of live modeling might be two therapists interacting during a role-play with one another. One of the therapists serves as a model for the client to observe, and the therapist model exhibits the skill being targeted in that day's session. In assertiveness-training, for example, one therapist might play an antagonist with whom a second (model) therapist interacts. If verbal noncompliance and the statement of one's own position are the behavioral components of assertion to be trained in a particular session, the model exhibits these components in his or her response to the antagonist. If the purpose of the intervention is to teach a client conversational skills, and if the skill-component selected for training that day is getting one's conversational partner to talk about himself or herself, the two models might engage in a brief conversation with one another. In this modeled conversation, verbal behaviors, such as asking appropriate questions to elicit information from one another, could be illustrated. The important function here is that the live models exhibit, correctly and clearly, the desired skill-component for the client to observe.

Modeling exposure can also be accomplished using portrayed models, such as videotapes, which show the models exhibiting socially skilled behavior. In assertion-training, a video film might demonstrate a model handling the unreasonable behavior of another person and exhibiting all components of assertion. Conversational-skills-modeling films could show two people engaged in effective conversation, again exhibiting the behavioral components that will eventually be trained to the client. In job-interview or date-initiation training interventions, the film could show a model successfully handling those respective situations. The advantage of exposing clients to a videotaped model exhibiting the relevant skill, rather than exposing them to a live therapist model, is that the filmed model's behavior can be controlled and predetermined to ensure that the skill components are correctly, consistently shown. It also permits the therapist to observe the filmed model along with the clients and to point out important aspects of the model's behavior to them as they occur. This could not be as easily done if the therapist were simultaneously modeling the skill.

Overt Practice or Behavior Rehearsal

After a client is instructed on what component behaviors comprise an effective skill and he or she observes them in a model, it is then important to have the client actually practice that skill. Overt practice or rehearsal in handling a troublesome interaction adds the skill-components into the client's behavioral repertoire, beyond the simple understanding of what he or she should do differently. In all cases, practice or rehearsal within sessions is intended to approximate, as closely as possible, the actual troublesome situation of the natural environment. Rehearsal assumes that when a client is able to handle an interaction more effectively in training, and when new skills have been added to the previously deficient repertoire, the client will then be in a position to exhibit those skills outside of treatment. Overt practice or behavior-rehearsal within training sessions is one of the factors that most dramatically sets social-skills training apart from traditional interpersonally oriented forms of psychotherapy.

Procedures for client behavior-rehearsal depend upon the type of skill being trained, the specific kinds of situations that a client reports as troublesome, and the nature of the intervention (such as whether training is being conducted with a single client or a group of clients). Four forms of rehearsal or practice that have been widely used in social-skills training are structured role-plays, semi-structured extended interactions, unstructured social interactions, and informal rehearsal verbalization of examples of the skill-component within training sessions.

Role-plays. Assertive-training role-plays consist of a narrated description of some situation the client has found difficult to handle in the past. Another person, perhaps a therapist, plays the part of an antagonist in that situation and behaves unreasonably toward the client. The client then practices making assertive responses to the antagonist, focusing on the correct use of the component behavior receiving attention in that training session. Several different troublesome situations are usually role-played in the same session, since the aim of training is to teach the client to handle a variety of situations more successfully.

Role-play forms of rehearsal during sessions are most suitable when the aim of training is to teach clients to handle the relatively specific comments or behavior of another person. Role-played rehearsal techniques have been used extensively to allow clients to practice refusal-assertion skills when confronted with the unreasonable behavior of others (Butler, 1976; Ochiltree, 1977), commendatory skills to reciprocate the positive behavior of another person (Sloat, Tharp, & Gallimore, 1977), and effective job-interview skills when presented with questions that are frequently asked by personnel managers during employment interviews (Hollandsworth, Dressel, & Stevens, 1977).

Semistructured practice. In other cases, the type of social interaction that is being targeted for training is of longer duration and is difficult to present in highly structured form with the behavior of the partner relatively fixed. An example of this is a conversation, which seems more difficult to structure into a role-play than to engage in naturally. Date initiation and heterosocial skills-training have also relied upon semistructured practice interactions. For example, in a date-training project, Melnick (1973) allowed a male client to interact for several minutes with a female confederate. During these interactions, the confederate always maintained certain general constraints on her behavior (such as not monopolizing the conversation, requiring the client to maintain the conversational initiative, remaining consistently warm, etc.), but she did not deliver predetermined role-play comments or statements to the client. Clients were instructed to use the date-initiation component behaviors that they had just been taught during the course of their practice interaction with the female. Thus, the practice or rehearsal was semistructured and approximated a date-initiation situation that might occur outside of training. In similar fashion, Kelly, Urey, and Patterson (1980) utilized semistructured conversations between psychiatric aftercare clients and confederates who served as interaction partners to teach components of conversational skill.

Unstructured practice interaction. A form of rehearsal further removed from highly structured role plays is the unstructured practice social interaction. Here the nature of the rehearsal interaction and the behavior of the practice partner are quite unstructured and natural. In a study on social-skills training with isolated children, O'Connor (1969) placed each child in a free-play setting with other children immediately after training sessions and instructed the treated child to be sure to use the prosocial-play skills that had just been taught. The free-play interactions themselves were unstructured and the other children in them were simply playing naturally, rather than role-playing. Similarly, a project intended to teach everyday conversational skills to a group of retarded adolescents utilized unstructured practice interaction for behavior rehearsal purposes (Kelly, Wildman, Urey, & Thurman, 1979). Here, two group members were placed in a room together following each training group, and were asked to get to know one another better for about 8 minutes; they were instructed to exhibit the conversational skill they had just discussed in the group-training session. Again, they were not role-playing a conversational interaction, but instead were actually having a conversation.

Informal rehearsal verbalization.   Finally, it is possible to utilize the principle of behavior-rehearsal somewhat more informally in training sessions by asking the client to practice verbalizing examples of the verbal social-skill component. For example, when clients in a job-interview skills-training group were being taught how to convey information about their past work experience, each client actually practiced saying aloud these statements about experience that he or she would later want to say to a real interviewer (Kelly, Wildman, & Berler, 1980).

Regardless of the practice procedure followed, overt rehearsal in handling difficult situations is a key element of social-skills training. It generates not only a sample of the client's actual ability to exhibit a type of social skill, but also provides the client with the opportunity to actually practice new competencies, rather than merely talk abstractly to a therapist about them, or think about them. In addition, when a client is asked to practice or rehearse using a social skill, the therapist is in a position to directly assess the behavioral adequacy of the client's practice and determine whether the client has behaviorally acquired new skill-components.

Reinforcement and Feedback to Shape Behavioral Practice

While behavior rehearsal of social skills is a necessary aspect of training, it alone is not sufficient to improve performance. Even with ample opportunity to practice new social competencies during training, it is possible for clients to repeatedly perform them incorrectly. Further, even if clients do exhibit improved performance during their rehearsal handling of troublesome situations, they may be unaware of how they improved unless they also receive specific feedback and reinforcement during training sessions.

There are a number of techniques for providing both feedback and reinforcement following client behavior rehearsal.

Therapist-administered verbal feedback   on the client's performance is one of the most basic techniques. If a client rehearses responses to an interviewer's questions during a job-interview training role-play, the therapist might offer feedback on the quality of the client's role-played responses. Feedback would be tailored to the specific component-behavior that received training attention in that session and not to aspects of the client's performance that had not yet received treatment attention. As we have noted, to be maximally effective, any form of feedback should be direct, clear, and "tied" to a specific aspect of the client's behavior. Comments such as "I think you could do a little better" do not represent effective feedback because the behavior to which they refer is unclear. Better examples might include: "You maintained a lot of eye contact, much more than last time. It made you more believable"; "You spoke much more about your previous work experience when the interviewer asked about it; that's terrific"; or "You spoke loud enough to be heard well, just as we'd been working on." These examples not only reflect clear, behaviorally referenced feedback, but they also constitute verbal reinforcement of the desired skill-component. The client is explicitly told that he or she performed well, and is also told why the performance improved.

Verbal praise and specific feedback serve to strengthen and maintain appropriate skill-exhibition in behavior-rehearsal; they also function to correct client misapplications of skill-components during practice. An example of this might be when a client is practicing increased eye contact, but is then observed to continually stare at the practice partner. In other cases, an unassertive client may overdo verbal noncompliance toward an antagonist and appear hostile rather than appropriately assertive. Instructional feedback provided by the therapist can suggest behavioral alternatives and shape or refine the client's rehearsal performance.

In some instances, clients may immediately learn new component-skills and exhibit them successfully during their first practice interactions. However, this is often not the case. The purpose of rehearsal is not to yield one tentative performance of the targeted skill-component, but instead to firmly establish a new behavior in the client's repertoire. Thus, if an initial rehearsal is unsuccessful or if feedback suggests the need for additional refinement of the component-behavior receiving attention, further opportunities for the client to practice the behavior are indicated

Client-administered verbal feedback.   In group skills-training interventions, feedback and reinforcement on behavior rehearsal can come from both the therapists and from other group members. Client-administered verbal feedback following another client's rehearsal serves the same function as therapist-administered feedback and may even have increased credibility for some individuals, since the feedback and reinforcement are from peers.

Self-observation   represents a third type of feedback technique that may be used, when equipment for videotaping and replaying client behavior rehearsal is available. Here, the client and therapist together observe a film of the behavior rehearsal that just occurred. Feedback and verbal praise for correct instances of the skill component-behavior targeted for training in that session can be pointed out by both the therapist and the client when they are watching the film.

In summary, the learning-theory principles of instruction, modeling, overt practice, feedback, and reinforcement can be incorporated within social-skills training sessions. Implied in this training approach is the notion that these principles can be used to successively shape the various component behaviors that comprise a socially skilled response. While the verbal and nonverbal component behaviors receiving attention at a given time change over the course of the intervention, the actual conduct of any single training session remains relatively constant and incorporates each of these learning principles.

By the conclusion of a skills-training intervention, clients should have mastered each of the social-skill component-behaviors that had been targeted for training. If the components taught to clients are, in fact, those behaviors that comprise an effective overall social skill, the client will then be exhibiting socially skilled responses during rehearsal or practice periods within the session. Once clients have learned more effective ways of handling troublesome situations and demonstrate those newly acquired skills within the treatment setting, it is then necessary that they exhibit the same new skills when actually confronted with the troublesome situations in the natural environment.

Generalization of Skill-Improvement to the Natural Environment

In spite of the emphasis on rehearsal and practice, the ultimate purpose of social-skills training is not to assist clients in more effectively handling the behavior of another person during practice interactions within training sessions. Instead, the skills-training therapist seeks to establish change during these controlled practice approximations of the troublesome situation and then, most importantly, to facilitate generalization of the client's enhanced skills back to the problematic situations that occur in the natural environment. If clients exhibit appropriate social skills during rehearsal in the training setting, but then fail to do so in the natural environment, the intervention has served no clinical function.

"Generalization of training effects" refers to the presence of a newly learned response or skill under conditions different than those surrounding the initial learning of the skill. There are several types of generalization relevant to the skills-training therapist. These include generalization across time, across physical setting or environment, and across interpersonal situations.

Generalization across time refers to the maintenance of a skill in the individual's repertoire for a period of time after it has been originally learned. If a job-interview skill-training intervention effectively improves a client's ability to handle interviewer questions during role-play practice sessions, that improvement must then be maintained throughout the period that the client is job-hunting. If the improvement was only transitory and diminishes immediately after the intervention is concluded, little client benefit can be derived from training.

Generalization across physical setting or environment refers to the presence of the skill under different "surrounding" conditions than those of training. If training physically takes place within an office at a clinic, hospital, or school, but if the real troublesome situations occur in a client's home, workplace, or with friends and neighbors, the client must exhibit his or her new ways of handling the natural environment situation when it actually occurs.

Generalization across interpersonal situations. It is not possible for clients in social-skills training to rehearse handling every possible troublesome situation they will encounter. In assertive-training, one can construct a series of role-play approximations of the situations that a client reports difficulty in handling effectively. However, that individual will inevitably encounter other different situations in the natural environment that also call for assertive responses but that never were specifically rehearsed. In these cases, clients must generalize their use of newly acquired social skills to interpersonal situations slightly different than those that had originally been the subject of training or rehearsal. This argues against teaching clients simply to "memorize" specific things to say or to do in specific situations, which might have limited generalization potential; instead they should learn a more general way to approach and behave in a given type of situation.

Specific training techniques for incorporating the principles of instructions, modeling, rehearsal, and feedback or reinforcement will be discussed more fully in Chapter 4; procedures for enhancing generalization will also be presented in detail later. However, the major approaches for fostering generalization of social skills from the training setting to the natural environment include: (1) selecting situations for rehearsal or practice which approximate, as closely as possible, the actual troublesome situations experienced by a given client; (2) presenting a variety of role-play or practice rehearsal situations during training to increase the likelihood that a client will exhibit the skill under stimulus-differing conditions; (3) focusing training so that clients learn and understand the general principles of their training, rather than simply memorizing what to say in a situation; (4) making clients aware of situations in their daily environment that they can use to try out newly acquired skills; (5) directly reinforcing clients when they report using, or are observed to be using, the newly acquired skill behaviors in the natural environment; and (6) directly modifying clients' cognitive self-statements so that cognitions facilitate socially skilled behavior, rather than inhibit it. These generalization procedures can enhance the initial performance of new social skills in the intended natural environment; once more adaptive, functional skills become well established in the client's repertoire, naturally occurring reinforcement can then take over to maintain their use.

One Skills-Training Intervention That Illustrates Social-Learning Treatment Principles

Let us briefly examine one social-skills training study to more concretely illustrate the general application of instruction, modeling, rehearsal, feedback, and reinforcement within treatment sessions.

Hollandsworth, Glazeski, and Dressel (1978) reported their treatment of a 30-year-old college graduate who experienced extreme anxiety during placement-service job interviews on campus. Although the client had good academic credentials, he had been unable to obtain a job offer after more than 60 unsuccessful interviews. Before treatment was initiated, role-play assessment or "diagnostic" job-interviews were conducted; in these role-plays, a therapist acted as the interviewer and directed a series of standard interview questions to the client. Evaluation of this role-play performance indicated the client's need to make direct, unambiguous, or focused responses to the interviewer's questions; to direct relevant questions to the interviewer; to maintain eye contact and verbal composure; and so on. With these behaviors isolated as components of job interview effectiveness in which the client was deficient, training sessions were then initiated.

Each session began with a brief discussion between the therapist and the client regarding the component or aspect of effective interview behavior that was to receive training that day. Instruction, examples, and the rationale for the component were presented by the therapist. A modeling videotape was then shown; the film demonstrated a socially skilled individual being interviewed for a job and exhibiting all components or aspects of skill in that situation. The client was asked to focus his attention on how the model exhibited the skill component that was to receive attention in that day's training session. Immediately after the modeling exposure, the client himself engaged in the role-play interview, with the therapist playing the part of the interviewer. This "in-session" role-play provided the client with an opportunity for actual practice or behavior rehearsal of the skill. The client's practice interview was videotaped and then replayed with both the client and the therapist watching it. Feedback, corrective instruction, and reinforcement were provided by the therapist as each observed the videotape of the client's just-completed practice role-play interview. Training sessions continued until all previously deficient aspects of the client's job interview behavior were successively improved during practice interviews, and the client was encouraged to use his newly acquired skills during genuine interviews outside of the treatment environment. Happily, Hollandsworth et al. (1978) reported that the client obtained job offers on each of his first three genuine interviews following the completion of training.

This example illustrates quite clearly how the social learning principles of instruction, modeling, rehearsal, reinforcement, and feedback can be incorporated to increase the skills of an interpersonally deficient client. Whether conducted with an individual client or with a group of clients, social skills training applies to behavior in the training session those learning principles that account for skills acquisition in the natural environment. As we have noted, social-skills learning in the natural setting often occurs under incomplete or unfavorable circumstances, including few opportunities to practice a given skill, inadequate observation of appropriately skilled models, inconsistent reinforcement or feedback from others, and so on. However, within the treatment setting, it is possible to create an environment conducive to the development of skilled behavior by applying the same learning principles in a more consistent, potent, and directed manner. We will consider the implementation of these techniques in more detail in Chapter 4. Let us now turn our attention toward identifying the exact behaviors that can be taught to skills-deficient clients and the procedures that can be used to assess client social behavior.

Chapter 3

Assessing Client Social Competency and Identifying Skills for Training

Before any skills-training can take place, it is essential to consider the issue of client assessment. In this chapter, we will review four aspects of the social-skills assessment that precedes a treatment intervention itself. First, a therapist must determine the kind of skills-training that is needed for a given client and obtain rather specific examples of real-life situations that require that skill and in which the client currently experiences difficulty. Next, the therapist constructs approximations of those specific interpersonal problem situations within the training or clinic setting so that the client's method of handling them can be scrutinized. In order to evaluate the adequacy of the client's behavior in these sample interactions, it is necessary for the therapist to know what behaviors or components make up a skilled interaction; for this reason, we will review those components that appear to comprise various forms of social competency. The final aspect of assessment is to then compare how the client behaves in the sample interaction with those behaviors that comprise skill in that kind of interaction. This is accomplished by objectively rating various elements of the client's social behavior; when the client fails to exhibit behaviors or components known to contribute to social skill, they can then be identified or targeted for training attention in the treatment intervention itself.

Determining the Purpose or Goal Skill for a Training Intervention

In the preceding chapters it was noted that "social-skills training" is the general description of a behavior change approach, but one that can be applied to many different varieties or types of interpersonal skills. It is therefore necessary to identify exactly what kind of social skill a given intervention is intended to increase. We can term this final, desired end product of training the "goal social skill" of the intervention.

Social-skills training is intended to teach clients to more effectively interact with others in certain kinds of situations. For example, refusal-assertion training increases the competence of persons to handle situations in which others may take advantage of them or attempt to stifle their right to expression. Cooperative-play-skills training is intended to increase the ability of children to make friends in situations that provide the opportunity to interact with peers. Similar goal skills, such as effective date-initiation, conversational abilities, job-interview skills, or commendatory assertion, are each competencies that are needed in a particular kind of interpersonal situation (meeting a person one would like to date, meeting an unfamiliar person, being interviewed for a job, etc.). When clients consistently report having difficulty in handling a certain kind of interpersonal situation, or when they are observed by others to have difficulty in those situations, skills-training tailored to the problematic interactions is indicated.

Let us consider several case examples illustrating how the need for skills training might be discovered during an early interview or therapy session with a client.

Kathy is a 19-year-old who is attending a local junior college while living at home with her parental family. Her initial presenting and identified problems include loneliness, an absence of friends, and discomfort when meeting others for the first time. This discomfort is sufficiently great that she actively avoids situations where she will need to talk with others at any length. She also reports becoming depressed over the past few months. The therapist is aware, and indeed Kathy is aware, that her feelings of loneliness are a result of her failure to meet others, engage them in conversations, and develop friendships. Kathy says that she would very much like to have friends, but simply does not. When questioned about why she cannot more actively meet others and establish social relationships with them, Kathy reports that she has always been shy, it has been difficult for her to talk with people for as long as she can remember, and she often doubts whether she has anything interesting to talk about with others. Kathy spends most of her time studying, reading, and engaged in other solitary pursuits. During the interview, it is apparent that Kathy *does* appear very shy, speaking in a soft and tentative voice, and rarely looking directly at the therapist.

Even with this relatively limited information, one can form some preliminary observations concerning the client's area of social skill deficit. We can hypothesize that this client appears to lack the skills needed to initiate and maintain everyday conversations with others; because of this deficit, she has developed few close relationships and is reporting the emotional feelings of isolation, loneliness, and depression. While there seem to be opportunities for establishing friendships, such as during interactions with other students on campus, she feels ill-equipped and anxious about taking advantage of those situations. An aim of social-skills training in this case might well be teaching Kathy the skills needed to initiate and maintain informal conversations with others. From this perspective, by directly enhancing the client's conversational repertoire, it will be possible to equip her with the skills needed to meet others, make friends, and consequently, improve her self-evaluation and confidence.

Robert is a 35-year-old middle-management employee in a large company. He has come to a mental health clinic complaining of job dissatisfaction, a short temper, and feelings of frustration in his work and, more generally, his life. He has become irritated with his family, especially after "bad days" at work; occasionally, this takes the form of anger, while at other times Robert becomes sullen and uncommunicative. The focus of the clinic interview has been narrowed to Robert's work environment, since it appears that many of his difficulties arise there. Upon specific questioning, the client discusses several problem areas at work. One involves his interactions with subordinates who are accountable to him in the department he supervises. Robert reports difficulty confronting them about lax performance and their failure to adopt procedures he feels must be followed. It appears that Robert rarely asserts himself with subordinates on matters involving inadequacies in their job performance and fails to clearly communicate his opinions and positions. Consequently, his department's overall performance is poor and Robert is himself beginning to get pressure from his own bosses to "shape things up." This is frustrating for Robert because he wishes to be liked by his subordinates and certainly doesn't want to be thought of as an aggressive, hostile supervisor. Robert adds that he also has trouble speaking up in company meetings with other managers and does not feel he can offer opinions to them, either. At the end of the interview, both Robert and the therapist agree that many of the problems stem from his unsatisfactory handling of interpersonal situations at work.

This interview summary illustrates a case in which an individual seems unable to assert himself satisfactorily with others in the work environment. Thus, assertion training is the type of skill intervention that would appear most useful. Since the troublesome situations are reportedly confined to interactions with others at work (involving subordinates, professional peers, and supervisors), assertion training might be even more specifically targeted toward those situations. Once again, determining the type of skills-training needed for this client requires that the therapist identify those situations that were reported to be problematic. Whereas for Kathy, conversational and social initiation competencies were deficient, the type of skill that Robert appears to lack involves the expression of refusal assertion in work-related interactions.

Some clients may be able to identify, quite quickly and accurately, the nature of their interpersonal difficulties and the exact situations they find troublesome. Some persons may even be able to identify the kinds of skills-training they will need (they may say: "I need to learn to behave more assertively with people who try to take advantage of me"; or "I get very nervous in job interviews and just do not come across effectively"). However, many clients are unable to easily identify problem areas. It is frequently necessary for the therapist to evaluate or infer whether or not a client's difficulties are a result of the inability to handle interpersonal situations and, if so, the exact nature of those situations that consistently prove troublesome. Once this can be assessed, it is possible to then determine the type of skills-training that will be most useful.

Client reports of how they behave with others, or their descriptions of social situations they find difficult, provide one source of information on the type of social-skills training that is needed. Another source of similar information is through the direct observation of a client's social interactions.

The staff of a state hospital residential program for emotionally disturbed adults has long observed the very low quality of informal social interactions among patients in the program. In the day activities lounge of the facility, most patients sit by themselves, often staring aimlessly and almost unaware of the other individuals around them. The principal free-time activities were predominantly solitary in nature and usually consisted of watching television, reading, or smoking cigarettes. Most clients in the hospital had been diagnosed as schizophrenic, but very few were actively psychotic or acutely disturbed at present; instead, the general atmosphere was one of withdrawal, lack of social responsiveness (other than during structured activities such as recreational therapy), and isolation. Because of an increased emphasis on deinstitutionalization and community-based services, many of these patients would soon be leaving the residential facility to live, or perhaps to work, in the community. However, the program staff was well aware that these patients would have great difficulty establishing relationships, finding and obtaining employment, and adjusting to the social demands of community living. Could they be taught, quite simply, to look and act less like "former mental patients" before they left the hospital?

As we noted earlier, clients in residential facilities often exhibit social-skill deficits in a number of areas. These deficits are often sufficiently severe and long-standing that it is necessary to rely on staff observations rather than client reports to suggest the need for skills-training. For example, the patient who has been socially withdrawn for a considerable period of time may not have the appropriate skills to initiate interactions and may not even find interactions to be reinforcing any longer. Here, treatment might be based more upon staff observations of the need for social-skills training than the patient's own descriptions of troublesome interpersonal situations. The type of skills-training intervention is determined by the deficits observed in individual patients or groups of patients, as well as the interpersonal situations they will need to handle effectively in the future. Patients who hope to work following hospital discharge might benefit from training in the effective handling of job interviews. Patients who are passive and susceptible to being exploited by others could benefit from assertiveness training; still others may require general conversational-skills training.

Children represent another population group whose appropriateness for social-skills training must often be based on external observation. Because many children have difficulty accurately verbalizing interpersonal problems, information on the types of situations the child cannot handle effectively may principally come from therapist observations, as well as observational reports from teachers and parents.

Tammy, a 5-year-old girl, was brought to the clinic by her parents, who were concerned about the child's peer difficulties at school. Tammy's teacher also had recommended that the child receive assistance. The parents reported that Tammy was an only child who was doing well academically in her first-grade class. However, she appeared to have trouble making friends and preferred activities in which she did not have to interact with other children. The parents reported that their daughter rarely had friends over to the house, although the parents would welcome friends if they were to visit. On those occasions when Tammy's parents had observed her playing with others, she seemed aloof, shy, and sought out the company of adults nearby rather than other children. The parents reported no family difficulties nor other recent problems. Contacted over the telephone by the therapist, Tammy's teacher confirmed this pattern of social isolation. When the therapist inquired about specific examples of Tammy's behavior, the teacher indicated that during recess, the child would invariably play by herself rather than with others. Also, during unstructured classroom activities, such as art projects, Tammy would always work alone. The teacher felt that Tammy had no friends and appeared unhappy. Other children had become disinterested in Tammy because she made no efforts to reciprocate any of their approaches toward her; occasionally, classmates would pick on her by calling her names. During the clinic interview, Tammy was generally quiet and provided little information. She said that she got along well with her parents and had fun with them. However, when she was asked who were her best friends at school, she shook her head and said that she didn't have any.

In this case example, relatively few details of the problem could be presented by the child client herself. The teacher had greater opportunity to observe and detail those situations that were troublesome for the child. The formulation at which we might arrive based on the information presented here is that Tammy lacks social skills needed to interact with peers. This seems particularly true in the case of free play or unstructured classroom activities. Because Tammy does not exhibit social skills in her relationships with classmates, they find her an unrewarding play partner and largely ignore her presence. The aim of treatment might most logically be to increase the child's skills for initiating verbal interactions with peers, joining others in play, and then playing cooperatively with them. If such peer-valued social behaviors could be increased, it is likely that Tammy would gain greater acceptance by others, be included in their activities, and eventually come to value social play more than solitary activities.

To summarize, the type of skills training needed for a given client is determined by the nature of those social situations in which difficulty is experienced. Initial information can be obtained by carefully interviewing the client to determine the nature of troublesome situations, or by direct observation of a client's interpersonal deficits if he or she is in a residential setting, school, or some other observationally accessible environment.

Gathering Specific Information on Troublesome Social Interactions

If it were possible for a therapist to follow a client about all day every day, eventually the therapist would see the individual encounter some of the situations that are reported to be troublesome. The therapist could then observe just how the client behaved in those situations and would be in a position to closely pinpoint deficiencies in the client's handling of troublesome interactions. Unfortunately, this kind of direct, exhaustive observation is almost never possible and the therapist must devise some alternative, time-efficient strategy to assess a client's social skill behavior. This can be accomplished by devising sample interaction tasks to approximate the situation that a client does not seem to handle well at present.

Let us take the case example of Robert, as it was described earlier. We recall that the clinical formulation in this example was that Robert seemed unable to assert himself in the work environment, most particularly during interactions requiring firmness and making opinion statements to his subordinate employees and his fellow managers. According to our initial formulation, Robert's general feelings of frustration and irritability could be attributed to his ineffectual handling of such problematic work situations. Thus, assertiveness training appeared a reasonable treatment approach.

However, we still have not learned much about the exact situations that this client appears to have difficulty handling, and we know very little about his precise current behavior in those situations. A more thorough interview is needed to generate specific examples of situations that Robert finds difficult. Whom, exactly, does he have trouble with? Can we pick several situations that have actually occurred over the past week and determine what circumstances led up to them, the basis for the conflict, what the other person said to him, how he responded, and so on? The aim of this detailed inquiry is to learn and note, as precisely as possible, the exact situations that present difficulty.

In some cases, a client simply does not engage in difficult social interactions. One example of this was Kathy, the shy 19-year-old student who felt awkward during conversational interactions and could establish few friendships. Here, it was not readily possible to learn more about difficulties she had while engaging in interactions, because she routinely avoided them. In this case, the therapist might discover examples of those situations where Kathy could meet others. Upon detailed questioning, the therapist might discover that Kathy has the opportunity to converse with others before classes, at the campus cafeteria, during informal "mixers" at school, and during the course of church volunteer work. Again, the interview is directed toward identifying, in precise fashion, specific occasions when more adaptive social skills could be exhibited.

There are several reasons why the therapist must pinpoint the exact interpersonal-environmental situations where a client experiences difficulties or where more adaptive social skills will need to be exhibited. The first is that training cannot be conducted in an abstract fashion. For example, if one teaches assertiveness, the aim is not to teach assertive responses to abstract, hypothetical situations. Instead, we seek to teach more adaptive skills for use in those situations that the individual client *personally* finds difficult. Since assertion is situational in nature, it is likely that the situations in which one client needs to be assertive are not the same situations in which another client needs to be assertive. Thus, to appropriately individualize training, it becomes important to determine the precise situations that a given client finds troublesome. In similar fashion, assessment preceding other forms of social-skills training should be tailored to those specific situations that a client wishes to handle better.

Apart from ensuring that the training intervention is targeted towards those situations that an individual client personally finds difficult, the therapist also needs specific situational information to construct relevant behavior assessment situations. To continue with our assertion example, when we learn the exact interpersonal situations that the client reports as troublesome, we will then be able to construct assessment role-plays that duplicate those same situations. This will permit behavioral assessment sample interactions that closely approximate the situations that the client will need to handle more effectively.

While some clients are able to provide specific examples of past difficult interpersonal situations or are able to pinpoint those situations they would like to handle better in the future, many clients are unable to provide this detailed information in a single interview. In those cases, it may be useful to ask the client to self-monitor interpersonal problems that he encounters between interview sessions with the therapist. This might take the form of a daily diary recording procedure. Depending upon the type of skills-training intervention anticipated, clients might be asked to record each day those social situations in which they felt frustrated, wished they had asserted their opinions, had the opportunity to meet new friends, wanted to initiate a date, and so on. When clients record this information between initial interview sessions to bring their recordings to the therapist, they should record the events briefly but with sufficient specificity that the therapist can make an assessment of the interpersonal situations that closely approximate the actual troublesome interactions experienced by the client. In the case of children with social-skills deficits or lower-functioning adults with very limited skills repertoires, it may prove more desirable to have someone make such recordings who is in a position to closely observe the client. Thus, a teacher might keep a record detailing the interpersonal situations in which a child was observed to have peer difficulty at school, or the staff of a residential facility might record those situations in which an institutionalized client seems to exhibit the most severe social-skills deficits.

This information-gathering phase of assessment continues until the therapist has a clear understanding of those specific interactions in the natural environment in which the client seems to exhibit social-skills deficits. When we can describe the exact interpersonal situations that have caused problems in the past, or can identify quite precisely the interpersonal situations that we wish the client to handle well in the future, it is possible to devise approximations of those interactions for behavioral assessment purposes.

Constructing Role-Plays, Semistructured and Unstructured Interactions within the Treatment Setting

There are several ways for the therapist to create behavioral assessment interactions in the clinic or treatment setting to sample the client's initial or pretreatment social competence. These are role-plays, semistructured extended interactions, and unstructured extended interactions. Each requires that the client interact with some other person, with the therapist observing the client's skill during the simulated interaction. Let us consider how each of these techniques can be used.

Structured Role-Play Assessment Procedures

Role-play techniques for assessing social skills appear most useful when the client must learn how to respond to the relatively structured or discrete comments and behavior of another person. Types of skills interventions that often rely on role-play assessment include those targeting refusal and commendatory assertion capabilities, as well as job-interview skills. In each of these cases, it is possible to structure the behavior of a role-play partner by having that partner make planned comments to the client. For example, in a refusal assertion role-play, a partner can make unreasonable comments to the client and the therapist can observe the adequacy of the client's assertive response. In commendatory assertion role-plays, the partner might make warm or complimentary comments directed to the client; in job-interview skills assessment role-plays, the partner could play the part of an interviewer and direct standard interview questions to the client. In these forms of role-play assessment, the partner's behavior is structured, scripted, or planned; the situation that is being role-played duplicates a situation that the client wishes to handle more adequately; and the therapist observes the adequacy of the client's role-played response.

Most role-plays used in social-skills assessment consist of three parts: (1) a narrated background description of the particular situation in which the client finds himself or herself; (2) some comment made by a role-play partner and directed to the client; and (3) the client's response to the partner. Material presented in the narrated description of a role-play scene is derived from information provided by the client on actual troublesome situations. Robert, the unassertive manager used as an earlier example, may have told the therapist that one of the problems he encountered at work was dealing effectively with an employee who always came in late. The therapist could learn details of this situation, including the time that the employee usually came in, what the employee said to Robert, the sex of the employee, and so on. From this information, a role-play might be constructed as follows:

Narrated Description: "Imagine that you are at work one morning and it is now 9:30. One of your employees, Bill Smith, has just come in the door. He was due in at 9:00 and has just missed an important sales appointment. This has happened several times in a week and you are not happy with his continued failure to come in on time."

Role-Play Partner's Comment *(to the Client):* "Good morning, Robert. Traffic was really bad today."

Client's Response *(to Role-Play Partner):* _____.

In this role-play example, the focus of the therapist's attention is evaluating the client's response to the partner's comment. However, here there is only one structured comment made by the partner and only one response made by the client. It is often desirable to extend the role-play interaction by adding an additional partner comment (and an additional opportunity for the client to respond) within the same scene. For example, following Robert's first response, the role-play partner might then say, "I'm only thirty minutes late." Robert is then given a second opportunity to respond in the same role-play scene.

A similar role-play approach has been used in job-interview skills assessment. Here, the scene description "sets the stage" for a simulated job interview. The partner, playing an interviewer, delivers questions, while the client plays the part of the applicant:

Narrated Description: "Imagine that you have applied for a job as a salesman at the Evergreen Shoe Company. You are in the office of Mr. Wills, the sales manager, and you are being interviewed by him. After setting down your application form, he says:

Role-Play Partner's Comment *(to the Client):* "I don't like to read application forms. Can you tell me about your experience?"

Client's Response *(to Role-Play Partner):* _____.

In this example, the role-played interview would not be confined to a single question and answer. Instead, the partner delivers a second question following the conclusion of the client's first response, and continues doing so until a reasonable number of interview questions have been asked. The client's responses to all of the questions can then be evaluated.

Logistics of the Role-Play Assessment Procedure

Conducting assessment role-plays ideally requires the presence of three persons: the therapist; a second treatment staff-person, who functions as the role-play partner; and the client. The therapist can serve as the scene narrator and as observer of the client's responses while the role-play interaction is taking place. Physical setting requirements for role-plays are minimal; role-plays can easily take place in an ordinary office, with the partner and the client seated in chairs facing one another. Since the therapist is not ordinarily involved in the interaction itself, he or she should be positioned to observe the role-play unobtrusively, such as from a corner of the room and out of the client's line of sight.

It is important that the client understand the nature and purpose of any role-play assessment. Specifically, clients should be instructed to imagine that they are actually in the situation described to them and that the partner is actually the other person in that imagined situation. The client is to interact directly with the partner, avoiding parenthetical comments to the observing therapist during the role-play. Clients should be instructed to behave in the role-play just as they normally would act if the situation were genuine.

When role-play-assessment precedes a skills-training intervention, it is also important that the evaluation be quite comprehensive and sample the client's behavior across a number of situations requiring the use of a certain type of social skill. Thus, if a client appears unassertive and if earlier interview or self-monitoring data generated nine different examples of problematic situations where that client could have been more assertive, it would be desirable to construct separate role-play scenes for each of those situations. In the case of job-interview training, there is only one situation that will receive treatment attention (the interview itself), but within an interview are a number of different questions that will be asked of an applicant. Therefore, an assessment role-play job interview should include a variety of different questions that applicants must know how to answer.

Another practical issue when constructing role-plays of social situations involves planning the behavior of the partner. In most cases, the role-play partner's behavior should be planned and structured before the assessment session takes place. For example, the partner may follow a written script of the role-played interaction that specifies what comments the partner will direct to the client for each role-play situation.

Validity Issues in Role-Play Client Assessment

A central assumption of role-play assessment procedures is that clients' behavior in structured role-plays approximates the manner in which they really behave during similar interpersonal situations in the natural environment. Several recent studies have provided evidence that this assumption may not always be warranted, and that clients' responses during role-plays do not always predict the way they will handle similar situations outside of the clinic assessment setting (cf. Bellack, Hersen, & Lamparski, 1979). It appears plausible that this may be due to clients' perception of the setting in which assessment takes place. Most clients are likely to perceive role-plays as relatively safe and nonthreatening; if one behaves assertively toward a role-play antagonist, it is not likely that any real negative consequence to the client will occur. In the natural environment, clients may be less certain of the consequences of their assertion toward an antagonist and may inhibit behaviors they can emit in the assessment role-play. In spite of this potential limitation, it does appear likely that role-play assessment offers more detailed, accurate, and training-relevant information on client social-skill behavior than do more traditional assessment techniques. For example, a number of client self-report inventories on assertion and other social skills have been developed (cf. Gay, Hollandsworth, & Galassi, 1975; Twentyman & McFall, 1975; Watson & Friend, 1969; Wolpe & Lazarus, 1966). While these can be useful as general self-report screening devices, they provide little information on the exact situations that clients find difficult or on the client's actual behavior in those situations.

Several steps can be taken to maximize the validity of role-play client-assessment procedures. First, and as noted earlier, it is important that all role-play situations or scenes be individualized to a client's own needs. Some investigators have developed standadized sets of role-play scenes to assess client assertiveness across a number of situations, such as having someone cut in front of the client in a lunch line, being served an overcooked steak in a restaurant, being overcharged for car repairs, and so on (cf. Eisler, Miller, & Hersen, 1973; Eisler, Hersen, Miller, & Blanchard, 1975). While the use of standardized role-play scene batteries to measure client assertiveness is useful in social skills research, it is preferable to "tailor" or individualize role-play scenes in clinical applications of social-skills training. Similarly, job-interview skills assessment using role-played interviews will be valid only if the role-play interviewer asks the same kinds of questions that a client will be asked in a genuine interview.

A related strategy to increase the validity of role-play assessment is to ensure that role-play scenes are presented as realistically as possible and that cues from the troublesome situations in the natural environment are included accurately in the role-plays of those situations. For example, if a client has particular difficulty interacting with opposite-sex persons, the role-play partner should also be an opposite-sex individual. If a client reports trouble in self-assertion primarily when an antagonist acts hostile or angry, the role-play person should direct comments to the client in a hostile tone. A role-play assessment scene will be most valid when it closely approximates the stimulus characteristics of the intended situation in the natural environment.

A final validity issue involves the reactivity of role-plays. Some clients appear able to adjust quickly to the idea of a role-play by interacting directly with the partner, actually imagining themselves in the situation being role-played, and disregarding the presence of the therapist observing the interaction. Other clients may have greater difficulty role-playing situations and feel self-conscious, uncomfortable, and nongenuine. Certainly, one would not expect skills-deficient clients to handle role-plays of troublesome situations effectively and without discomfort, since they presumably do not handle these situations well in the natural environment. Thus, feeling embarrassed or not knowing what to say in a role-play may accurately reflect the client's deficient behavior during similar in-vivo situations and provide important information on later training needs. However, it is desirable to repeat the same role-plays on several different occasions before training is initiated. This permits the client to grow accustomed to the role-play procedure and permits the therapist to obtain a more stable, consistent initial baseline of the client's social competency in the assessment situations.

Semistructured Extended-Interaction Assessment Procedures

While role-plays are useful when the therapist is seeking to learn how clients handle the relatively specific comments or behavior of other people, some forms of social interaction cannot easily be duplicated with a role-play partner who makes standard or predetermined comments to the client. This seems particularly the case in more extended interactions such as conversations or date-initiation. Here, it would be difficult to "script" the comments of a partner during simulations of these situations, and semistructured, extended-assessment interactions may prove more useful. In the assessment of clients' conversational skills, several studies have used paradigms in which the client is asked to interact with another person for a set period of time (see Kelly, Urey, & Patterson, 1980). The partner in this contrived interaction is a confederate of the therapist, in the same manner that a role-play assessment partner was a therapist confederate. However, rather than requiring the client to respond to fixed comments delivered by the partner, in the extended-assessment interaction the client and partner interact in a less structured fashion.

As an example of this technique, we might consider again the case of Kathy, the shy 19-year-old who reported difficulty meeting other people. Based on interview or self-monitoring data, the therapist may have learned that Kathy has the opportunity to meet other people at her campus snack bar, where students congregate informally between classes. However, she rarely initiates interactions with others there and the therapist would like to assess her current conversation-initiation skills. A semistructured procedure for doing this might involve first presenting Kathy with a hypothetical situation description, as follows:

Narrated description: "Imagine, Kathy, that you have just walked into the snack bar on campus between your classes. You have some free time, so you buy a coke and look for a place to sit down. The snack bar is quite full today and there are no empty tables. You spot a table with one other person at it and decide to sit there. The other person is a guy who is having a soft drink. You have seen him before, but have never spoken to him. As you sit down at his table, he looks at you and smiles."

In this example, the therapist's description again sets the stage for the assessment interaction; the described hypothetical situation is based on material provided by the client. Because the interaction approximates a naturalistic situation, the client is being asked to role-play an interaction. However, this behavior sampling procedure is much less structured than the role-plays described in the previous section. Following the scene background narration, the client could be seated next to a conversational partner, with the partner playing the part of the male student, and the client assuming her own role as a student. For a set period of time, perhaps five minutes or ten minutes, the client and partner converse as though they were in the described snack-bar situation. The therapist again remains unobtrusive, observing but not engaged in the conversation.

Because we are assessing the client's skills, rather than those of the partner, it is useful to establish certain constraints on the partner's behavior. These constraints provide the assessment with its semistructured quality. The partner might be instructed, before the assessment session, to play the role of the other person in the interaction and to "ad lib" statements and behavior accordingly. However, the partner could also be told to follow several rules. These include always requiring the client to maintain conversational initiative by asking a question only if the client has just asked one, speaking no longer than 20 seconds at any time (such as when answering a client question), allowing any silences to last for a full 30 seconds before terminating them with a question to the client, maintaining consistently warm affect toward the client, etc. While these constraints do reduce somewhat the spontaneity of the interaction, they also ensure that the conversation will not be dominated by the partner. If that were to occur, it would not be possible to evaluate the client's skills. The client could be told, before the interaction begins, that it will be necessary to maintain the conversation until the time period for it has elapsed.

This semistructured interaction assessment approach can be modified for several types of skill-evaluation by altering the "stage-setting" description that precedes the situation. For example, to assess heterosocial date-initiation skills, the narrated background might describe à setting in which the client sees someone that he or she would like to date. The interaction partner could then be an opposite-sex person who, in this scenario, would be willing to accept a dating offer from the client. The client is instructed to interact with the partner for a set period of time, with the aim of obtaining a date, and the client's behavior while doing so is assessed.

Logistics of the Semistructured Assessment Procedure

The staff requirements for this form of skills-assessment are the same as those for more structured role-plays: a therapist who sets the stage and observes the interactions, as well as a partner with whom the client actually interacts. Partner training is also required preceding the interaction-assessment session. However, rather than having the partner deliver specific predetermined comments to the client when role-playing each situation, it is important for the partner to follow general interaction "rules" as mentioned above.

Just as it is useful to repeat structured role-play assessment on several occasions to reduce client reactivity to the procedure and establish a consistent baseline for the client's skills, it is also useful to conduct several semistructured interaction assessments. These might include varying somewhat the scene descriptions that introduce the interaction or varying the partner on different occasions. However, the interactions used to assess client skills should always be made to closely approximate actual situations that the client has difficulty in handling when they occur in the natural environment.

Unstructured Interaction Assessment Procedures

A form of social-skills assessment further removed from highly structured role-plays is the observation of client interactions under conditions of minimal structure. This method of evaluation is possible when the informal social interaction of clients with one another is being examined in a clinic or office, as well as on those occasions when it is feasible to observe the social interaction of clients in the natural environment.

Observation of Clients' Skills during Unstructured
Conversations with One Another

Let us assume that a skills-training intervention is planned to improve the everyday conversational skills of a group of clients, such as individuals confined to some residential facility. The therapist may have observed that conversations between clients appear to be infrequent and of low quality, but these observations are based on fairly global, casual therapist observations. One way to more specifically assess the clients' conversational interactions is to ask two clients to sit down with one another in a room and carry on a conversation. The therapist might provide minimal structure for the interaction assessment, such as by directing the individuals to get to know one another better. However, the basic assessment format is the relatively unstructured interaction in which the clients engage. It is not a role-play, since neither client is playing the part of someone else and because no confederate is used. Instead, the therapist is sampling the interaction skills of each client, but under circumstances somewhat more controlled than by observing them in the in-vivo setting. Control is achieved because two clients are placed in a situation, removed from other persons, and are specifically asked to interact for some general purpose (getting to know one another better, learning more about one another, or so on).

This form of skills-assessment is applicable when the aim of traning is to increase the everyday conversational skills exhibited by clients during conversations with one another. Here, the assessment situation (unstructured conversations between pairs of clients in a situation accessible to therapist observation) very closely approximates the setting and behavior being targeted for later training (unstructured conversational behavior between clients on a residential facility ward, a day treatment program, or similar setting). This procedure is also suitable when group social-skills training is planned to improve the skills exhibited by clients during their interactions with one another.

However, because this procedure is unstructured and does not attempt to create any situation other than the actual conversation that is occurring between clients, its assessment utility is correspondingly limited. Because no interaction confederate partner is used, it is not possible to closely control the conversation's content. Thus, if two clients were paired together for an unstructured assessment conversation and if one talked excessively throughout the time we observed them, it would be relatively difficult to evaluate the skills of the person who did not have an opportunity to talk.

Assessment of Client Social Skills in the Natural Environment

Earlier in this section, it was suggested that procedures such as client role-plays or semistructured extended interactions are intended to create, in a clinic setting, close approximations of interpersonal situations that a therapist cannot feasibly observe the client handling in the natural environment. Under some circumstances, however, it *is* possible for a therapist or some other skilled observer to closely scrutinize the social skills of the client during interactions in the natural setting. Direct observation of social behaviors in the natural or in-vivo environment may be possible when: (1) the client's difficulties involve interactions with other persons also in the observed environment; (2) the in-vivo setting lends itself to direct observation because the client spends a substantial amount of time in that setting and can be observed closely while in it; and (3) the particular interactions of interest to the therapist occur relatively frequently or, at least, predictably.

Tammy, the 5-year-old child who was reported to experience peer interaction problems and social isolation at school, represents a case where direct observation assessment could be conducted. Since Tammy's difficulties involved her interactions with other children at school, and because she was with other children in the confined school setting each day, it would seem feasible to directly observe how she behaved with them there. Recalling the teacher's reports, we note that Tammy appeared to have difficulty establishing cooperative social interactions during unstructured activities, such as recess or group art projects. Observation of Tammy's social behavior could be focused on such times. A therapist or other observer might visit the school at recess, free-play, or group project times, and carefully observe Tammy's social-skill behavior with other children as they interacted naturally.

A similar in-vivo assessment procedure can be applied to other settings, such as the naturally occurring conversational interactions between patients in residential facilities. Again, it is important to conduct observations at times when clients have the opportunity to interact; the situations that are assessed should be the same as those situations that will be targeted for behavior change in the forthcoming intervention. Thus, if an intervention were intended to increase the social-conversational skills of psychiatric patients while they are having dinner together, the initial assessment should be conducted by an observer who evaluates their current conversaional behavior in the dinner setting.

Direct observation of clients' social interactions during specifically identified situations in the natural environment is an appealing assessment strategy because actual in-vivo performance can be evaluated, rather than performance in contrived analogues of the troublesome situations. So long as a client's manner of handling interpersonal situations during the time of observation is representative of how that client characteristically behaves, one does not have to be concerned about the validity of the assessment. On the other hand, there are several limitations associated with direct, naturalistic assessment of social competency. One is cost-efficiency. Although a client may be in a confined, "observable" setting, such as a school or residential facility, a therapist may not have sufficient time to conduct detailed in-vivo assessments. Although it is possible for other personnel, including teachers, aides, or nurses, to observe the social skills of a client in a particular type of situation, the observational specificity needed to usefully describe a client's social-skill effectiveness requires that observers be trained rather extensively. As we will consider shortly, one must also be in a position to see and hear the client's responses to other people to assess the adequacy of skill responses; being able to monitor a client's behavior this closely in the natural environment can prove difficult and can cause clients to react to the close presence of an observer. Additionally, because the therapist is not "setting up" a situation known to be difficult for a client to handle, it may be necessary to observe clients for a considerable period of time before one can learn exactly how they are able to interact with others. For example, if we were to observe Tammy during a school recess period, we might find that she spent the entire period in solitary play, while all the other children were playing with one another. Although this would tell us that Tammy *was* isolated and noncommunicative with peers, it would not provide definite information on such important questions as whether she has the skills to initiate play with others, respond to prosocial advances from them, play cooperatively, assert herself, and so on. One way to better assess such specific capabilities is to structure peer tasks so that the social behaviors of interest can be observed more readily. This could be accomplished by arranging tasks that require the participation of the client *and* the exhibition of a certain kind of skill, such as working with several other children on a puzzle that requires social collaboration or on a project that requires cooperative behaviors (Berler, Kelly, & Romanczyk, 1980). Because the in-vivo social-skill observational-assessment techniques are quite specialized and are most often used to assess childrens' interpersonal skills, these procedures will be described more fully in Chapter 10.

To summarize, once the therapist has identified the interpersonal situations that a client appears to handle ineffectively based on interview data, a behavioral-assessment procedure can be created to observe the client's specific skill in such situations. These procedures include structured role-plays of troublesome situations (particularly useful for assertion or job-interview-skill assessment); semistructured extended social interactions (particularly suitable for conversational- or dating-skill assessment); or unstructured naturalistic observation of client behavior during everyday interactions with peers (especially suitable for some forms of conversational-skill assessment and the evaluation of children's interaction skills with peers). When an assessment procedure has been selected and a sample of the client's social-skill behavior can be obtained, it is then necessary to establish a technique to objectively evaluate the observed performance of the client and provide information on the skill behaviors that must be trained.

A Component Analysis of Social Skills

Before we can evaluate the adequacy of the skill that a client exhibits during any assessment sample interaction, we must first know what behaviors to look for. Specifically, what are the elements or behavioral components that when taken together, comprise an effective handling of the type of situations with which the client currently has difficulty?

In earlier chapters, the notion of analyzing social skills into their behavioral components was introduced briefly. The basic aim of this approach is to determine, quite objectively, what it is that socially skilled persons do when they are engaged in a certain type of interpersonal interaction. Exactly what *does* a terrific conversationalist do when meeting other people for the first time? How do successful daters go about asking other people do date them? If a personnel manager interviews a candidate and, afterward, feels that the applicant came across extremely well, what behaviors did the manager notice that led to such a positive reaction? If we can accurately and reliably determine the behaviors that skilled persons exhibit when they are in the kind of situations our client finds troublesome, it should be possible to then teach the skills-deficient client those same behaviors.

Table 3.1 presents a summary of behaviors that have been postulated to comprise various types of interpersonal skills, including refusal and commendatory assertion, conversational skills, date-initiation skills, job-interview skills, and prosocial-play interaction skills in young children. When one of these goal skills is selected as the target for intervention, the content of training focuses upon the component behaviors that constitute it. More detailed descriptions and examples of these components will be covered in our specialized chapters on each type of skills training (Chapters 7 through 10). However, several points about this table summary merit specific attention.

When a social skill is defined by the behaviors of which it is comprised, it is important that those components be identified as objectively as possible. For example, using the data reported for heterosocial skills that are summarized in Table 3.1, observers could presumably watch a client as he is engaged in an interaction with an unfamiliar opposite-sex person and reliably "see" or "count" each of the behavioral components that occur. We could determine how much time the client was speaking, the frequencies of verbally reinforcing comments made to the other person, head nods, smiles, statements disclosing information to the partner, and so on. These components of heterosocial competence are defined in a sufficiently objective, clear-cut, and behavioral manner that they can be observed and assessed unambiguously. Similarly, for other types of social skills, the component makeup of the goal "product" is also described in the most objective possible manner.

Some investigators have established that the behavioral components they cite *do* differentiate persons competent in a skill from persons judged deficient in that skill. For example, Gottman, Gonso, and Rasmussen (1975) were able to establish empirically that popular children (based on peer-nomination sociometric measures) differed from unpopular children on some of the behavioral components indicated in Table 3.1. These included popular children's

TABLE 3.1. Examples of Some Verbal and Nonverbal Behaviors Proposed to be Components of Various Types of Social Skills

COMPONENT MAKEUP OF CONVERSATIONAL SKILL

Eye contact	Percentage of speaking/listening time when client looked at the partner's eye (Stalonas & Johnson, 1979).
Appropriate affect	Client emotional tone and responsiveness appropriate to the interaction and verbal content (Urey, Laughlin, & Kelly, 1979).
Conversational questions	Questions asked by client designed to elicit information about the partner (Kelly, Wildman, Urey, & Thurman, 1979; Minkin, Braukmann, Minkin, Timbers, Timbers, Fixsen, Phillips, & Wolf, 1976).
Self-disclosing statements	Appropriate information conveyed to the partner concerning the client's interests, activities, hobbies, background, etc. (Kelly, Furman, Phillips, Hathorn, & Wilson, 1979; Urey et al., 1979).

COMPONENT MAKEUP OF HETEROSOCIAL/DATE-INITIATION SKILL

Eye contact	Same description as for conversational skill above (Bander, Steinke, Allen, & Mosher, 1975; Barlow, Abel, Blanchard, Bristow, & Young, 1977; Heimberg, Madsen, Montgomery, & McNabb, 1980).
Appropriate affect	Same description as for conversational skill above (Bander et al., 1975; Barlow et al., 1977; Heimberg et al., 1980).
Conversational questions	Same description as for conversational skill above (Heimberg et al., 1980).
Complimentary comments	Complimentary and reinforcing statements directed to the partner (Curran, 1975; Farrell, Mariotto, Conger, Curran, & Wallender, 1979; Wessberg, Mariotto, Conger, Farrell, & Conger, 1979).
Follow-up/acknowledgment statements	Comments, statements, or questions interjected in speech to express attentiveness, interest, or some reaction to what the partner is saying (Barlow et al., 1977; Heimberg et al., 1980; Kupke, Hobbs, & Cheney, 1979).
Request for a date	Specific proposal of a time, place, and activity for continuing contact with the partner on a later occasion (Curran, 1975; Curran, Gilbert, & Little, 1976).

Speech duration	Same description as for conversational skill above (Greenwald, 1977; Martinez-Diaz, & Edelstein, 1979, 1980; Zeichner, Wright, & Herman, 1977).

COMPONENT MAKEUP OF COMMENDATORY ASSERTION

Eye contact	Same description as for conversational skill above (Bellack, Hersen, & Turner, 1976; Galassi, Galassi, & Litz, 1974; Turner & Adams, 1977).
Appropriate affect	Same description as for converstional skill above (Brockway, 1976; Geller, Wildman, Kelly, & Laughlin, 1980; Kelly, Frederiksen, Fitts, & Phillips, 1978).
Speech loudness	Adequate speech loudness to be clearly heard (Bellack & Hersen, 1978; Bellack, Hersen, & Turner, 1976; Eisler, Miller & Hersen, 1973).
Praise/appreciation statement	Verbal content indicating approval or praise of the partner's good behavior (Burkhart, Green, & Harrison, 1979; Geller et al., 1980; Kelly et al., 1978; Zielinski & Williams, 1979).
Personal feeling statement	Verbal content indicating one's own positive personal feelings as a result of the partner's behavior (Brockway, 1976; Schinke, Gilchrist, Smith, & Wong, 1979; Schinke & Rose, 1976).
Reciprocal positive behavior	Verbal content offering to return or reciprocate in the future some positive act to the partner (Burkhart et al., 1979; Geller et al., 1980; Kelly et al., 1978; Skillings, Hersen, Bellack, & Becker, 1978).
Speech duration	Same description as for conversational skill above (Bellack, Hersen, & Turner, 1976; Eisler et al., 1973).

COMPONENT MAKEUP OF REFUSAL ASSERTION

Eye contact	Same description as for conversational skill above (Eisler et al., 1973; Pachman, Foy, Massey, & Eisler, 1978; Rathus, 1973).
Appropriate affect	Same description as for skill above (Hersen, Eisler, Miller, Johnson, & Pinkston, 1973; Hersen, Kazdin, Bellack, & Turner, 1979; Kelly et al., 1978).
Speech loudness	Same description as for commendatory assertion, above (Eisler et al., 1973; Hersen, Eisler, Miller, 1973; Kelly et al., 1978).

Physical gestures	Hand or arm movement, appropriate to the situation, which adds emphasis to client's remarks (Bellack, Hersen, & Turner, 1976; Hersen et al., 1979).
Understanding statement/ statement of the problem	Verbal content conveying understanding of, but not agreement with, the antagonist's position, or verbal statement of the nature of the conflict issue (Mullinix & Galassi, 1978; Woolfolk & Dever, 1979).
Noncompliance	Verbal statement specifically resisting, noncomplying or disagreeing with the antagonist (Brockway, 1976; Pachman et al., 1978; Schinke et al., 1979).
Request for new behavior/ solution proposal	Explicit request for antagonist to change his/her unacceptable behavior, or client proposal of a new solution to the conflict situation (Burkhart et al., 1979; Schinke & Rose, 1976; Zielinski & Williams, 1979).
Speech duration	Same description as for heterosocial skill above (Neitzel, Martorano, & Melnick, 1977; Pachman et al., 1978; Skillings et al., 1978).

COMPONENT MAKEUP OF JOB-INTERVIEW SKILL

Eye contact	Same description as for conversational skill above (Braukmann, Fixsen, Phillips, Wolf, & Maloney, 1974; Hollandsworth, Glazeski, & Dressel, 1978; Pinto, 1979).
Appropriate affect	Same description as for conversational skill above (Hollandsworth, Dressel, & Stevens, 1977; Hollandsworth et al., 1978; Pinto, 1979).
Speech loudness, clarity, and fluency	Client speech appropriately loud, audible, and free of dysfluencies (Hollandsworth et al., 1977, 1978; Pinto, 1979).
Positive self-statements about experience	Verbal content statement conveying positive information to the interviewer about one's work experience, training, or education (Barbee & Keil, 1973; Furman, Geller, Simon, & Kelly, 1979; Kelly, Laughlin, Claiborne, & Patterson, 1979).
Positive self-statements about hobbies, activities, and interests	Verbal content statement conveying positive information to the interviewer about one's avocational interests and pursuits (Kelly, Wildman, & Berler, 1980).
Client-generated questions	Job-relevant questions asked by the client to the interviewer (Barbee & Keil, 1973; Furman et al.,

1979; Hollandsworth et al., 1978; Kelly, Laughlin, Claiborne, & Patterson, 1979).

Verbal expressions of interest and enthusiasm	Statements conveying interest in the position or positive aspects of one's future performance if hired (Furman et al., 1979; Kelly, Urey, & Patterson (in press); Speas, 1979; Stevens & Tornatzky, 1976).
Focused responses	Concise, unambiguous statements that directly answer the interviewer's questions (Barbee & Keil, 1973; Hollandsworth et al., 1978).

COMPONENT MAKEUP OF CHILDREN'S PROSOCIAL PLAY SKILL

Social initiations	Verbal or nonverbal behaviors used to enter into play or conversational interactions with other children (Gottman, 1977; Gottman, Gonso, & Schuler, 1976; O'Connor, 1969; 1972; Strain, Shores, & Timm, 1977).
Asking questions and answering questions	When interacting with peers, eliciting information and providing information about interests, activities, and so on (Gottman et al., 1976; Gottman, Gonso, & Rasmussen, 1975).
Greeting peers	Positive verbal acknowledgments given to peers upon seeing them or entering their activities (LaGreca & Mesibov, 1979; LaGreca & Santogrossi, 1980).
Task participation/playing	Attending and participating with others while engaged in a mutual activity (Keller & Carlson, 1974; Hymel & Asher, 1977; Oden & Asher, 1977).
Proximity	Child physically near to other children and oriented to them visually (O'Connor, 1969; O'Connor, 1972; Evers & Schwarz, 1973).
Cooperation/sharing	Taking turns and sharing during play or task activities (Oden & Asher, 1977; LaGreca & Santogrossi, 1980; Strain, Shores, & Kerr, 1976; Strain, et al., 1977).
Affective responsiveness	Laughing, smiling, or touching others in a positive manner as appropriate during a social interaction (LaGreca & Santogrossi, 1980; Keller & Carlson, 1974; Hymel & Asher, 1977).
Praise to peers	Compliments directed to peers following their good performance (LaGreca & Mesibov, 1979; LaGreca & Santogrossi, 1980).

higher rate of eliciting information from their peers, disclosing information about themselves to peers, and extending social invitations to others. In similar fashion, Minkin, Braukmann, Minkin, Timbers, Timbers, Fixsen, Phillips, and Wolf (1976) compared students judged to be highly competent during conversational interactions with those judged as less competent in order to determine those behaviors related to overall conversational skill.

In other studies that have yielded information about the behavioral composition of social skills, skills-deficient clients are first taught to exhibit the behaviors that intuitively seem to be components of the goal skill. Then, more global judgments are obtained from external judges to confirm that the clients are more proficient in the goal skill when exhibiting those component behaviors than before they had learned to exhibit them. For example, Furman et al. (1979) and Kelly, Laughlin, Claiborne, and Patterson (1979) taught skills-deficient, formerly hospitalized psychiatric patients to increase their rates of such verbal behaviors as making positive statements about past employment experience, making statements conveying interest in work, and directing questions to an interviewer about a prospective position during role-played job interviews. Later, genuine personnel managers listened to audiotape recordings of the clients' role-played interviews when the clients exhibited these skills (post-training) and when they did not exhibit them (pretraining or baseline). Because the experimentally naive managers rated as higher the *overall* effectiveness of role-played interviews when these behaviors were exhibited, the authors concluded that the identified verbal behaviors were components of job-interview skill. While this procedure can establish that client use of the behavioral components is associated with higher evaluations of goal-skill competency, it does not provide information on the relative contribution of each *separate* skill component to the final competency judgment. For example, in these job-interview training studies, it may have been that only one component, rather than all of them, was responsible for the personnel managers' favorable posttraining evaluations.

In a good deal of previous social-skills training research, the behaviors proposed to be components of a skill and subsequently taught to skills-deficient individuals have been selected based only on intuitive speculation rather than on an empirically demonstrated relationship between those behaviors and external judgments of competency in the skill. Thus, therapists and researchers typically train what they *think* are the important aspects of the desired competency. Wolf and his associates (see Minkin et al., 1976; Wolf, 1978) have pointed out the need to "socially validate" the behaviors taught to clients in skills-training interventions by relating training on the behavioral components to actual improvement in handling situations that the intervention is meant to target. Further basic social validation research is needed, and skills-training therapists might regard verbal or nonverbal components felt to comprise various social skills in a somewhat preliminary light until more empirical data are obtained.

Several other issues concerning the component makeup of social skills can be briefly noted here, but will be discussed more fully when we turn our attention to training techniques in later chapters. The first is that most research has focused assessment attention on the frequency or presence of components making up a skillful response, rather than the manner in which these components are stylistically integrated with one another. As an example, Table 3.1 shows that conversational skill has been rather consistently analyzed to include such verbal behaviors as asking questions to learn more about another person, self-disclosure of information about one's own interests, providing feedback to one's conversational partner, etc. However, it would be possible for an individual to do all these things during an interaction, but to do them in an awkward, poorly paced style. If someone "shotgunned" many questions to a person he had just met and then abruptly began talking about himself, he could be exhibiting the correct components but with an inappropriate style. Therapists who teach social skills might consider both the verbal or nonverbal components of that skill *and* the manner in which they are integrated, paced, and vary in response to the behavior of the other individual in the interaction (Kelly, in press). Although little empirical attention has been given to this aspect of social-skills assessment, therapists conducting interventions should be aware of the style with which clients exhibit skill components during assessment and training.

A second, related issue involves the optimal extent or degree that even an appropriate behavior should be included in a skilled interaction. Sufficient eye contact has been identified as an important aspect of virtually all types of social skill, and interventions routinely increase the amount of client eye contact when it has been deficient. However, too much eye contact may be as unskilled as too little. There is probably an ideal rate for eye contact and, beyond that point, desirable eye contact becomes undesirable staring. This seems true for almost all of the component behaviors included in Table 3.1. While voice loudness, convincing affect, and gestures have all been proposed as appropriate nonverbal components of effective refusal assertion (see Edelstein & Eisler, 1976), each can become inappropriate if it is exhibited excessively. Similarly, appropriate verbal behaviors in a job interview (e.g., conveying positive information about one's work background or making statements conveying to an interviewer one's interest in a prospective job) can be evaluated as inappropriate if they occur too often. While social-skills assessment and training have been characteristically oriented toward increasing currently deficient component behaviors of the desired skill, it must be within the context of increasing them only to optimum levels. In some cases, a therapist may even seek to decrease behaviors that are ordinarily considered appropriate, if they occur so excessively they become inappropriate. Examples might include clients who overexhibit components such as eye contact or voice loudness, or those who excessively talk. Once again, additional research will be needed to determine the ideal occurrence rate for the appropriate component behaviors of a social skill.

Let us summarize the component-analysis approach to social-skill description: Any type of effective goal skill can be broken down into the behaviors that are felt to comprise it. This would be conceptually akin to watching an individual who is competent in a certain kind of situation, and observing those exact verbal and nonverbal behaviors that the individual exhibits. Further, a skill's makeup can be described in the most objective, behavioral manner possible by specifying the exact nature of those verbal statements and nonverbal acts that should be present in the skilled response or interaction.

When planning a treatment intervention, it is crucial for the therapist to give early attention to conceptualizing not only the type of social skill that will be taught, but also the behavioral components that make up that goal skill. Behaviors such as those included in Table 3.1 can serve to assist the therapist in defining the composition of a desired type of social skill.

Behavioral Assessment of Client Social Skill: Rating Performance in Sample Interactions

When we analyze a client's social-skill behavior sample, whether it is from a role-play, semistructured, or unstructured interaction, the aim is to locate inadequacies of performance, which can be targeted for later training. What, exactly, can tell a therapist whether a client's behavior in an assessment situation is adequate or deficient? We have already noted that any type of social skill can be broken down into its behavioral components, such as in the component analysis presented in Table 3.1. If each identified component behavior of a skill is a necessary part of that skill, it is then possible to observe whether clients exhibit each of those components in their handling of assessment role-plays, semistructured, or unstructured interactions. If a client fails to include essential behavioral components in his or her assessment interaction, those components can be identified as deficient skill behaviors, which will need to be increased. To accomplish this evaluation, a therapist objectively rates the client's observed performance on each of the component behaviors that comprise an effective skill.

Objectively rating client behavior requires that the therapist evaluate the presence, absence, or adequacy of many social-skill behavior components in the client's interactions. This can be accomplished by simply watching as the client engages in a sample interaction. However, most of the social skills described in Table 3.1 have at least six identifiable components. Because it can be somewhat difficult for a therapist to attend to many simultaneously occurring components, "permanent product" recordings of client behavior during assessment interaction sessions are often useful. In its simplest form, this can consist of audiotaping client performance during assessment role-plays or other interactions; the therapist will then be in a position not only to observe the client's "live" interaction, but also to listen to the tape recording of it after the session ends and more carefully evaluate the client's social behavior. While audiotape recordings are an economical and feasible way to generate permanent products of client performance, an obvious limitation is that the therapist cannot record information on certain nonverbal components of the client's responses, including eye contact, gestures, smiles, and so on. There are several ways to circumvent this limitation. One is for the therapist observing the interaction to evaluate nonverbal componets "live" while actually watching the client in the assessment session; verbal behaviors could be rated from a later review of an audiotape. Alternatively, the confederate partner who is interacting with the client can also observe the client and, following the session, confer with the primary therapist on the adequacy of any nonverbal behaviors of interest in the assessment. It is also possible to videotape the client's performance in the assessment session; both verbal and and nonverbal behaviors could then be rated from the videotape film at any time.

Rating Techniques

In order to fully evaluate the client's baseline skill in handling whatever situations are presented during assessment, it is necessary to compare the components present in the client's behavior with those behavioral components that will be present in ideal, skilled responses. Therefore, a first step in the skill rating procedure is to organize and list the components that the therapist will look for in the client's assessment-sample interactions. We will first consider the rating of client performance in structured role-plays, such as assertion assessment role-play interactions; rating of more extended sample interactions will then be discussed.

Figure 3.1 presents a sample form that illustrates how a therapist can rate the client's role-plays in situations requiring refusal assertiveness in response to the unreasonable comments delivered by a partner. If we compare the components included on this rating form with the behavioral components that comprise refusal assertion in Table 3.1, it is evident that the rating procedure simply determines whether the client's responses include each important skill component. Thus, a form like Figure 3.1 serves to guide the therapist in evaluating the quality or effectiveness of client role-play performance.

Whenever one evaluates or rates client social competency, there must be a defined period that constitutes the observation interval. The form presented in Figure 3.1 is used to evaluate each separate assertive response made by the client. Thus, if the assessment session consists of the client role-playing 8 different situations, and if each role-play presentation includes one comment made by the partner to which the client must respond, a total of 8 different client assertive responses can be rated. If, for each of the 8 role-play scenes, the partner directs 2 comments to the client (and the client must handle each of the partner comments with an assertive response), there would be 16 separate responses for rating, and so on. Objective rating of skill responses can

FIGURE 3.1. Sample Rating Form for Client's Refusal-Assertion Role-Plays

Client Name: _____

Date of This Interaction: _____

Type of Interaction: ____ Pretraining Assessment

                      ____ Session Practice (Training Focused on What Component?_____)

                      ____ Follow-up

Description of This Role-Play Scene: _____

COMPONENT BEHAVIORS

1. <u>Eye Contact</u> (Approximate ratio of eye contact with partner to total speaking time in this response)

0%   10%   20%   30%   40%   50%   60%   70%   80%   90%   100%

eye contact   eye contact made
never made   entire time

2. <u>Affect</u> (Emotional appropriateness/responsiveness)

             1   2   3   4   5   6   7

extremely passive   extremely firm,
nonfirm, unconvincing   convincing, appro-
                                         priate to situation,
                                         believable

3. <u>Speech Loudness</u>

             1   2   3   4   5   6   7

extremely soft-   appropriate
spoken so as to be   loudness and
inaudible   clarity

4. <u>Gestures</u> (Did the client use any observable arm or hand gestures to add emphasis to his/her response?)

                             ____ Absent

                             ____ Present

pinpoint both verbal and nonverbal inadequacies in the client's manner of handling the antagonist's comments. If we observe that a given individual maintains eye contact only about 20% of the time, speaks in a soft monotone, fails to state his or her own opinion, does not convey to the partner more acceptable future behavior, and punctuates responses with dysfluencies, each component will need to be targeted for later training.

Over a number of role-played scenes, a client may exhibit relatively consistent deficiencies on certain behavioral components, such as never maintaining sufficient eye contact, always speaking too softly, and never exhibiting one of the verbal statement components. Such consistency of deficit supports the fact

5. Understanding Statement/Statement of Problem (Did the client include in the role-play response a statement conveying the nature of the conflict problem or a statement recognizing the antagonist's position?)

    ____ Absent

    ____ Present

6. Verbal Noncompliance (Did the client include in the role-play response a statement explicitly disagreeing or noncomplying with the antagonist's unreasonable behavior?)

    ____ Absent

    ____ Present

7. Request for New Behavior/Solution Proposal (Did the client include a statement specifically requesting that the antagonist behave differently in the future or a statement proposing some more acceptable solution to the conflict?)

    ____ Absent

    ____ Present

8. Speech Duration (Length of client's role-play response, in seconds)

    ____ Seconds

9. Other Components Being Rated (or any undesirable, inappropriate behavior being examined)

Definition/Description of Behavior:

Frequency Count or Rating:

that a given component of the skill will require training. On the other hand, clients may exhibit a certain component behavior inconsistently across scenes, including it in certain responses but not in others where it also would have been appropriate. The therapist might then try to determine if the differential performance is correlated with any aspect of the scene. For example, if a male client maintained eye contact while role-playing with male partners but not with female partners, it might signify greater anxiety during opposite-sex interactions and this would need to receive attention in training. On the other hand, a behavioral component may also be exhibited inconsistently because it simply is not well-established in the client's skill repertoire; this would also suggest the importance of directing attention to it in the intervention.

In assertion role-plays, the client's responses are ordinarily somewhat brief and they follow the role-play partner's structured comments. However, other forms of social-skill assessment interactions can be more extended and complex. Role-plays of job interviews might consist of an entire series of different interview questions delivered to the client by the role-play interviewer, and the client's responses to those questions can become more elaborate. Similarly, conversational- and date-initiation-skill assessments may consist of relatively extended interactions, perhaps up to 10 minutes. Whether a client talks with a confederate in a semistructured assessment, or whether two clients are "paired" together in an unstructured evaluation of their conversational skills, the resulting sample interaction can also be rated to determine the frequency that a client exhibits identified behavioral components.

For these types of social-skill assessment, the focus of therapist observation and rating is the client's total behavior over the entire interaction. The Urey et al. (1979) and Kelly, Urey, and Patterson (1980) reports of conversational-skills training with formerly hospitalized psychiatric patients, mentioned in an earlier chapter, serve to illustrate this approach to skills rating. In these studies, each client interacted with a confederate partner for a fixed period of 8 minutes with the purpose of getting to know the partner better. The assessment followed a semistrutured interaction format. To assess the client's conversational-skill adequacy, the therapist observed and rated the entire 8-minute dialogue, tallying the total number of times a client made certain types of statements to the partner—questions directed to the partner, statements disclosing appropriate information about the client's interests or background, reinforcing comments, and so on. Once again, components that are rated in this form of assessment should be the same as the components that are felt to make up an effective performance of the goal skill, such as those included in Table 3.1. Beyond the verbal conversational statements reported in the Urey et al. (1979) and Kelly, Urey, and Patterson (1980) studies, other components of conversational skill that could also be rated in an assessment interaction include client eye contact, affect, speech loudness, and so on. By determining whether, and how frequently, such components occur over the entire interaction, it is again possible to pinpoint the extent to which a client is deficient in those specific behaviors that, taken together, comprise a desired goal skill. If the individual is found to spend most of a conversational-assessment period gazing off and talking monotonously about himself, but only rarely asks questions to elicit information from the partner or rarely offers acknowledgments and reinforcing statements to the partner, the therapist then has important information on which conversational-skill components will need special attention in later training.

Similarly, rating the performance of a client in a simulated job interview could consist of determining the frequency over the entire interview that the client exhibits each verbal skill-component (such as the total number of statements conveying positive information about past experience, to total number of times the client directs an appropriate question to the interviewer partner, and so on). Nonverbal component behaviors including eye contact, voice loudness, or affect cannot be rated by a frequency count; for each of these components, the therapist might use a rating scale format (such as a 1 to 7 scale from extremely poor to extremely good) to record the client's general exhibition of the component over the entire interaction.

The two kinds of rating procedures described here (evaluating behavioral skill-components present in client responses during structured role-play responses and determining the frequency of behavioral skill-components exhibited during more extended assessment interactions) vary in terms of the period of time when the client's behavior is rated. However, the rationale and purpose for evaluation are always the same: to determine the extent to which clients exhibit component behaviors of a social skill during the sample social interaction that the therapist observes. The components comprising one type of social skill are different than the components comprising another type of skill. Therefore, the exact behaviors that are rated by the therapist must be tailored to the kind of social skill that the assessment situations "tap" and to the type of training intervention that is anticipated (assertion, conversational, date initiation, and so on). In the later specialized chapters on these various types of social-skills training, examples will be provided of sample rating forms to measure the components associated with specific skills, and component behaviors will be defined more fully. In addition, assessment rating issues unique to each kind of skill will be discussed in their respective chapters.

Chapter 4

Social-Skills Intervention Procedures for Individual Clients and Groups

Following an initial and detailed assessment of social skills achieved through ratings of client performance during sample interactions, a therapist will next wish to give attention to the skills-training intervention itself. In this chapter, we will first consider the design and clinical utility of multiple-treatment-session interventions. Attention will then be directed toward the procedural conduct of training sessions by reviewing exactly how the previously described principles of instruction, modeling, overt practice, reinforcement, and feedback can be incorporated into sessions for clients treated individually and in groups. Clinical techniques to foster generalization of social-skills improvement to the natural (criterion) environment will also be considered. Because social-skills training with children requires somewhat different training techniques, treatment procedures for skills-deficient children will be covered separately, in Chapter 10.

Multiple-Treatment-Session Interventions: A Clinical Overview

Just as one can break down any type of social skill into its behavioral components, one can also break down a skills-training intervention into sessions, with separate sessions devoted to each of the behaviors that will be trained. For example, let us assume that a mentally retarded adolescent will receive training in conversational skills because he has great difficulty maintaining appropriate conversations with his peers. Several assessment conversations have been conducted; in each of these, the client was asked to interact with a confederate of the therapist for seven minutes. Ratings of the semistructured assessment interactions revealed that the adolescent exhibited deficits in at least five conversational component behaviors, each of which will be targeted for attention during the intervention. These behaviors included: (1) his rate of con-

64

veying information about himself; (2) his ability to elicit information from the conversational partner; (3) verbal acknowledgments of the partner's talk (such statements as "Oh," "Really," "That's interesting," "I'd like to hear more about that"); (4) his eye contact; and (5) his affect or emotional tone, which currently appears very dull and flat.

One can break down the entire intervention into sessions that sequentially give training attention to each of these behavioral components. For example, following the assessment conversations, the first training sessions can focus on teaching the client to convey information about himself to others during conversations. When he has learned to do this successfully, the next set of sessions can be devoted to a second component, such as eliciting information from others during conversations by asking them questions. When this has been mastered, the client will then be exhibiting two of the five component skills that had been initially targeted for training. Session attention can then be focused on the next identified component, and this continues until all behavioral components have been learned and are included in the client's conversational repertoire. By moving systematically and cumulatively from one behavior to the next over the course of the intervention, the client should fully master the goal skill by the end of treatment. While treatment sessions successively target each component, training is always cumulative, with the client continuing to exhibit previously trained behaviors even as new components are added.

It may be useful to present an outline that illustrates a multiple-session skills-training intervention that successively targets components of a desired social skill. We can use the conversational skills-training project with the retarded adolescent as an example, and will assume that the five behavioral components each required two training sessions.

Session 1: Behavioral assessment of baseline or initial conversational skills: semistructured conversation with partner, rated by therapist.

Session 2: Repeat same assessment conversations to establish stability of performance.

Sessions 3 & 4: Training on first component: How to convey information about oneself during a conversation.

Sessions 5 & 6: Training on second component: How to elicit information from another person in a conversation.

Sessions 7 & 8: Training on third component: How to verbally acknowledge and reinforce the talk of one's conversational partner.

Sessions 9 & 10: Training on fourth component: Maintaining eye contact when conversing.

Sessions 11 & 12: Training on fifth component: Maintaining lively, friendly emotional tone when conversing.

Sessions 13 & 14: Attention to generalizing conversational skills to natural environment.

The approach of learning the "whole" skill by successively mastering each of its "parts" can be applied to any kind of social skill. Obviously, the components that sequentially receive training attention will depend on the type of social skill being taught and the particular client deficits that were pinpointed during the behavioral assessment observations. This intervention format is well-suited for many applied settings, since it is based on multiple-session, ongoing contact with the same client. For example, the outpatient visits made by clients on a weekly or twice-weekly basis can constitute training sessions; over the course of one month with twice-weekly visits, an 8-session social-skills training intervention can take place. Similarly, since group therapy outpatient sessions usually occur on some regularly scheduled basis (such as weekly), group application of social-skills training can be adapted to the same multiple session, weekly format. The scheduling of training sessions with clients in residential facilities affords still greater flexibility, since the sessions can often be arranged on a more frequent basis.

Session Spacing and Duration of the Intervention

The duration of a social-skills training intervention is determined by a number of factors, which include the functioning level and responsiveness of the client, the complexity of the goal social skill being taught, the extent of skill deficiency exhibited by the client, and the spacing of training sessions. It is apparent that if one is teaching social skills to a relatively low-functioning person, including the mentally retarded and chronically institutionalized individual, considerably more training time may be needed before the client successfully masters a given component. On the other hand, high-functioning persons who grasp quickly the component behavior being targeted in a given session may proceed through an intervention much more quickly. As we have noted, the fact that an individual is low-functioning and severely skills-deficient does not mean that skills-training will be unsuccessful; many studies have reported successful assertive, conversational-skill, and job-interview training with chronically institutionalized and retarded populations (cf. Furman et al., 1979; Kelly, Furman, Phillips, Hathorn, & Wilson, 1979; Kelly, Wildman, Urey, & Thurman, 1979; Monti, Curran, Corriveau, DeLancy, & Hagerman, 1980; Monti, Fink, Norman, Curran, Hayes, & Caldwell, 1979). However, because it is important that a client fully and consistently exhibit a given component behavior before proceeding to the next, increased sessions for each component may be necessary for low-functioning clients. It is often difficult to predict exactly how many training sessions a client will require. For this reason, it is generally best to avoid setting, in advance, a duration for a skills-training intervention. Instead, applied interventions usually continue training a component until a level of consistent mastery has been reached (termed "training to criterion"), and only then move to the next component.

The complexity of the goal skill and the number of components on which the client is deficient initially will also determine the length of the intervention. If initial behavioral assessment reveals that a client is deficient in eight different verbal and nonverbal components of the desired skill, training will take correspondingly longer than if the client exhibits only minimal deficits.

As we noted earlier, the aim of skills-training is not simply to teach a client to exhibit socially skilled performance during rehearsal within the training session and environment. Improvement must also generalize to the natural environment. Most research appears to indicate that this generalization will not occur automatically, even when skilled behavior has been established during training (cf. Hersen, Eisler, & Miller, 1974; Kazdin, 1974; McFall & Lillesand, 1971; McFall & Marston, 1970). This means that clinical social-skills training interventions cannot simply terminate when clients have become proficient in exhibiting the goal skill during their behavior rehearsal or practice interactions. A number of additional sessions after the skills-training phase has ended are needed to encourage, plan, or "program" generalization of the improved skills into actual troublesome situations within the natural environment. Techniques for fostering generalization once training has progressed will be discussed later in this chapter.

Finally, there has been no empirical research on the optimum spacing interval between training sessions within an intervention. While some studies have reported training sessions held daily or even twice daily (Monti, Curran, Corriveau, DeLancey, & Hagerman, 1980; Monti, Fink, Norman, Curran, Hayes, & Caldwell, 1979), other interventions have successfully conducted sessions on a weekly basis (Falloon, Lindley, McDonald, & Marks, 1977; Linehan, Goldfried, & Goldfried, 1979; Ollendick & Hersen, 1979). The interval between training sessions is often determined by practical constraints, including the frequency that a client can attend sessions, the therapist's client caseload, and other factors. One therapeutic requirement that does dictate inter-session spacing is for sessions to be sufficiently frequent that clients do not forget previously trained components or demonstrate a performance decrement on a component from one session to the next. Because this training intervention model requires that clients successively "add" new behavioral components onto those that they have already mastered, it is important that performance does not diminish between sessions due to overly long intervals. One might expect that any inter-session period longer than one week would exert a deleterious influence on training; more frequent sessions appear desirable.

Is it possible to accelerate a skills-training intervention by targeting several different behavioral components of the desired goal skill in each session? Once again, there has been little empirical data on how rapidly one can cover various skill components and whether it is possible to consolidate several different components in the same session without "overloading" clients with too much new information. In general, it would appear desirable to "add" new behavioral components slowly, focusing attention on no more than one per session, or devoting several training sessions to any single component if the client has not fully mastered it. Even behaviors that seem very clear-cut and easy to exhibit, such as eye contact, speech loudness, asking a partner questions, and so on, are easy only once they have been well-established in an individual's repertoire. It is important to remember that if some element of a client's social behavior has been absent for a considerable period of time, the highest probability response is that the client will continue to exhibit behavioral deficits, almost "from habit." Covering components too rapidly or attempting to consolidate training on several components within a single session may serve to confuse clients and lead to inconsistent performance of the targeted behaviors during in-session practice. Again, the aim of training is to establish durable change in the client's skills repertoire, not transitory improvement exhibited only in a single session. It is far preferable to include additional training sessions for any component behaviors that prove difficult and thereby increase the duration of an intervention, rather than proceed so quickly that new behaviors never become firmly established or consistently exhibited in client practice performance.

Introducing the Skills-Training Intervention to Clients

One of the benefits of social-skills training intervention is that the treatment directly addresses, in a manner clear and understandable to clients, the actual interpersonal problems that have been reported or observed. Once a client is made aware that various emotional or social problems (isolation, lack of friends, inability to be offered a job after interviews, depression, social anxiety, and so on) can be a consequence of having inadequate skills to handle the troublesome situations, it usually makes a great deal of sense to the client that one way to handle situations better is to actually practice them in therapy.

Before preliminary behavioral-assessment sessions take place, clients can be told that the purpose of the assessment role-plays or contrived interactions is to permit the therapist to observe exactly how the client handles sample troublesome situations and thereby determine the type of training that will be needed. When clients are asked to monitor difficult situations by maintaining a self-monitoring diary, they can be told that they are doing this to provide the therapist with an accurate and detailed account of day-to-day interpersonal situations that create difficulty. Similarly, when the training intervention is about to be instituted, the client can and should be informed about the treatment approach: the therapist will provide specific behavioral suggestions on how the client can come across more effectively to others and, in each session, the client will be asked to actively practice using the new behaviors. The notion of "building" new skills or ways to handle difficult situations by adding one "step" (or component) at a time can be introduced, so the client understands the nature of the entire training intervention.

While many people find this explanation reasonable and high in common-sense appeal, the therapist or counselor must also recognize that social-skills training *is* different than traditional verbal therapy, and may not be the form of treatment that some clients expect. Because social-skills training requires active participation and positive expectancies by the client, additional rationales for the intervention might be provided. For example, the therapist can introduce training by pointing out how individuals can overcome discomfort in a situation by repeatedly practicing it, noting the superiority of behavioral practice of social skills beyond simply talking about interpersonal difficulties, and discussing the manner in which persons can achieve new confidence by seeing that they can now effectively handle those interpersonal situations that might have earlier caused them unhappiness or anxiety. Finally, while clients are told that they will learn and practice new ways of handling interpersonal situations in the training session, they should be made aware that benefit will ultimately be derived when they begin to use these skills in the natural environment and that this important aspect of training will also receive attention later in the intervention. However, before one can use a new skill in the natural environment, one must first learn it in the training environment.

The Social-Skills Training Session for Individually Treated Clients

Earlier, the learning theory principles of instruction, modeling, overt practice (or behavior rehearsal), reinforcement, and feedback were described as the "active ingredients" within any skills-training session. Although the behavioral components to which these principles are applied change over the course of an intervention, the training techniques within any session remain relatively constant. We will now consider how the therapist can incorporate these techniques in sessions with an individually treated client; modifications for group social-skills training will be discussed later.

Instructions, Coaching, and the Provision of a Rationale

The social-skills training session begins with a discussion, initiated by the therapist, on the component-behavior that will receive attention in that session. In this introduction, it is important for the therapist to clearly define the intended target behavior and to provide several illustrations of it. For example, in a date-initiation training session, one behavioral component might be for a male client to learn to elicit information from a female partner as he would in a casual meeting that might lead to a date.* At the beginning of the session, the client could be told that one way to exhibit this component is to ask the partner open-ended questions that will "invite" the partner to talk about her interests, hobbies, activities, background, and so on. The therapist might then present several examples of these kinds of questions ("Where is your hometown?"; "What do you like to do in your spare time?"; "What kind of music do you like?"; and so on) and then ask the client to generate his own examples of the targeted verbal component behavior. Once it has become apparent that the client understands the behavior that will receive attention in the training session, it is useful to discuss reasons *why* the behavior is beneficial or appropriate to exhibit. This discussion might suggest rationales, including the idea that asking questions enables one to learn more about someone else, permits one to learn of areas of compatibility or mutual interest, "breaks the ice" during a conversation, conveys to another person that one is interested in knowing him or her better, and probably flatters the other person, because most people seem to enjoy having the opportunity to talk about themselves. The client might be asked how *he* has felt when another person demonstrated his or her interest in him by asking questions to learn more about his interests and background.

Whenever possible, the client should be encouraged to identify reasons why a behavioral skill-component is desirable or useful to exhibit; when a client can cite the benefits associated with a certain mode of response, the behavior may have greater salience than if the client is simply told by the therapist that it is desirable to exhibit the behavior. However, if the individual appears not to understand the reasons for incorporating a specific behavior in future interactions, the therapist can prompt this recognition by pointing out the potential benefits associated with using a given component.

Identifying, discussing, and citing examples of the target component should occur at the start of every skills-training session. The amount of session time devoted to initial instruction and discussion will depend upon the complexity of the component, as well as whether the session is the first one targeting the

---

*Interestingly, date-initiation training reported in the literature has often focused its attention on teaching males to initiate dates with females; less frequently have studies taught comparable skills to females so that they could initiate dates. This probably reflects traditional sexist stereotypes and biases, since it is likely that females encounter very similar problems in minimal dating. Recent data suggest that males respond quite favorably to females who initiate dating interactions using these same component skills behaviors (Muehlenhard, 1976; Muehlenhard & McFall, in press). Therefore, similar training might be considered for both males and females who seek to increase minimal dating.

behavior or if it has already received attention in a preceding session. An instruction/discussion period of between five or ten minutes is usually sufficient, since the aim of this aspect of training is principally to define the purpose of the session.

As training progresses, it is also helpful for the therapist to use a brief period of time at the beginning of a session to review and summarize components that have been covered in earlier sessions. In the date-initiation example we are using, if the client has already received training on several component-behaviors, the therapist may wish to briefly remind the client of those behaviors and point out that the new component will be "added to" any that already had been targeted.

The Use of Modeling within Sessions

Because social-skill models can be either live or portrayed, as in videotape modeling films, the therapist can select either one for use in training sessions, depending upon the availability of technical equipment and the nature of the skill being trained. It is also possible to combine live-modeling exposure with portrayed models.

The Therapist As a Social-Skills Model

One of the most feasible modeling procedures is for the therapist to demonstrate the behaviors selected for training. In its most basic form, the therapist can verbalize examples of a targeted component. Examples of this are when a therapist verbalizes sample questions a client could ask a conversational partner, assertive statements that could be made when confronted with the unreasonable behavior of another person, or sample statements made to a job interviewer to convey interest in an employment position. Nonverbal behaviors can also be modeled informally by the therapist. For example, the therapist might interact briefly with the client, first with no eye contact and then with appropriate eye contact, to demonstrate this behavior. Speech loudness and affective components can be demonstrated in similar fashion. When the therapist acts as a skill model, the client's attention should be specifically directed to the behavior that is being demonstrated by the therapist, so that the client can benefit from this form of informal modeling.

In other cases, the therapist can serve as a live model in a somewhat more structured fashion. If a confederate is present in the room, the confederate and therapist can model a role-play demonstration interaction with the client observing it. This approach might be used in refusal-assertion training, where the confederate plays the part of an antagonist in some situation and the therapist model demonstrates an effective assertive response, paying particular attention to exhibiting clearly whatever verbal or nonverbal component is being trained in the session. The same live-modeling exposure can be used in job-interview training to illustrate responses to an interviewer's questions (with the confederate acting as an interviewer and the therapist as the applicant model), or in commendatory assertion-training. To demonstrate conversational or date-initiation skills, the therapist and confederate could simulate the appropriate kind of interaction with one another for several minutes, again with the therapist modeling the desired component-skill during the course of the modeled interaction. Compared to informal modeling, in which the therapist simply verbalizes examples of a targeted component-behavior, the more structured form of modeling offers several clinical advantages. First, the client is able to actually observe a sample interaction between the therapist and a confederate. This is likely to be more realistic than simply listening to the therapist generate examples of a component-behavior outside of the context of an actual interaction. Second, it gives the client the responsibility for closely scrutinizing someone else's effective handling of a situation. If the therapist models effective responses during simulations of the same situations that the client finds troublesome and will also later practice, this can be a highly relevant technique for observational learning. Finally, live-modeling of this sort does not require a videotape apparatus or other equipment. Prior planning of the interaction to be modeled is needed to ensure that the interaction creates the opportunity for the therapist to clearly exhibit the targeted component.

Portrayed (Videotape) Models

When videotape recording and playing equipment are available, the therapist can construct a modeling film to show the client in each training session. In an assertion-training intervention, the film might show a socially skillful model effectively handling the unreasonable behavior of others, offering disagreeing viewpoints, or so on. Conversational and date-initiation training films can be constructed to show models interacting for some period of time and exhibiting all of the behavioral components that should be present in these types of interactions. Similarly, a job-interview film could show an applicant being interviewed for a position, with the model again exhibiting all appropriate components of an effective interview.

Modeling videotape films used in social-skills training need not be elaborate and expensively produced to be effective. Narration included in the film is unnecessary, since the therapist can provide any needed comments while it is being shown. The film also need not be long; five to ten minutes would be sufficient to demonstrate almost any kind of interaction. The major requirement is that the film clearly demonstrate someone effectively handling the kind of situation that the client wishes to handle more effectively, and that the primary model (to whom the client's attention will be directed when observing the film) exhibit those skill-components that will later be taught.

When preparing a modeling film used in training, the therapist supervising its construction should ensure that the primary model to be filmed is familiar with the component makeup of the skill to be exhibited. The situation or situations that the film model handles should be very similar to those situations the client finds troublesome. Earlier, we spoke of characteristics that enhance the likelihood of imitative learning; these should be incorporated in the film whenever possible. Specifically, an ideally salient model will be of the same sex and race as the client, approximately of the same age, will appear likeable, and will achieve a positive outcome in the film.

In the case of filmed models, as well as when a therapist models a skilled interaction in the session, it is not possible to show only a single social-skill behavior component at a time. For example, one cannot readily make a realistic film or perform a live-modeling exposure that demonstrates only eye contact or only asking questions to a conversational partner, and so on. Instead, the model observed by the client usually exhibits an "entire" skilled response or is seen in an interaction demonstrating *all* the desired components. However, because only one component will receive training at a time, it is important to specifically focus the client's attention on that component whenever it occurs in the modeling exposure. Thus, if a session is targeting eye contact, the client might be instructed to observe principally how the model looks at the partner when speaking, and to disregard at present any other aspects of the model's behavior. This will prevent clients from being "overloaded" in trying to attend to many different model behaviors at one time.

The use of portrayed or filmed models in training sessions is desirable for several reasons. Once a film has been made, it can be repeated on a number of training session occasions and the therapist can remain confident that all behavioral components will be consistently exhibited in the modeling exposure. Filmed models who are highly similar to the client can be used; this might not be possible if the therapist serves as a model and differs from the client in sex, race, or age and then it would be necessary for the therapist to live-model if a film were not used. The need to have a confederate or second therapist present in the training session would also be reduced, since the primary therapist and confederate would not have to model live those interactions that are presented on film. Finally, if a videotape modeling film is shown, it is possible for the therapist and client to view it together. The therapist could then pause the film to draw the client's attention to any relevant aspect of model behavior, ask whether the client observed a behavioral component when it occurred, or even replay parts of the modeling film for added emphasis. These techniques would not be readily possible if the client were observing the therapist modeling live. However, even when live-modeling is used, the client should afterward be encouraged to spend several minutes discussing or describing how the model exhibited the component, how that component contributed to the model's effectiveness, and so on.

The Combined Use of Live and Videotape Models

It is also possible to vary the method of modeling exposure across sessions, and to provide several kinds of modeling within each session. As an example of the latter approach, the therapist might briefly model, in a live and informal manner, examples of the component that will be receiving training attention. In conversational-skill training, the therapist could ask the client to watch as he verbalized sample statements conveying information about his background and hobbies. The client could then observe a modeling film showing two people having a conversation and note how the conversational models exhibited the same behavioral component when they talked with one another. Here, modeling sources are the therapist's sample verbalizations and the film's models.

In different skills-training sessions with the same client, the method of modeling exposure can also be varied by showing a modeling videotape on some occasions; by having the therapist and confederate live-model interactions, with the client observing them on other occasions; and by having the therapist verbalize model statements that illustrate a given skill component on still other occasions. Varying the model presentation methods can avoid the possibility that a client will become bored, as might occur when the client repeatedly watched the same videotape film. Combining live-modeling by the therapist with a videotape modeling film also increases the variety of different examples of a behavioral component that can be shown, since the therapist can demonstrate different behavior samples than those shown on a single film.

Let us reiterate several of the major points concerning modeling within sessions. First, the aim of any modeling exposure is to permit the client to directly observe someone else's socially skillful response or to observe examples that illustrate a certain kind of component-behavior. This requires, in every session, that the therapist give examples of the targeted component and/or that the client observe a more formalized simulated interaction between the therapist and a confederate. Live-modeling of an actual interaction can be replaced by exposure to a modeling videotape showing a sample interaction. Any modeling portrayal must include the component that will be targeted for training in that day's session, and clients should be told to note specifically how the component is exhibited by the model. Clients should also be encouraged to discuss afterward whether and how they observed the model's use of that component. Just as the instruction/discussion segment of a training session is often relatively brief, the length of modeling exposure should not become overly long. In general, a 5- to 10-minute modeling period should be sufficient in any single session.

Behavior Rehearsal or Overt Practice within Sessions

To this point in the training session, the client has been told about the behavior being targeted, has observed it in someone else's interactions, and has discussed its rationale. The next important step is for the client to actually exhibit the component by performing it in a practice interaction. This is an extremely important and potentially difficult task for clients, since it is often much easier to verbalize and "know" how to behave in an interaction than to actually perform the new behavior. There are several ways that behavior rehearsal can be incorporated in the skills-training session. One is for the client to verbalize examples to the therapist of how the client will use the trained component. This should then be followed by a simulated or practice interaction with some other person, such as a role-play, semistructured or unstructured interaction, that can be observed by the therapist.

Verbalizing Examples

Verbalizing examples of the targeted skill-component to the therapist means, quite simply, that the client will practice saying some of the statements that he or she will make during the later and more formal practice interaction. In a date-initiation training session, if the component behavior is eliciting conversational information from a potential date, the client might generate for the therapist a number of specific, open-ended questions that he could ask. The client rehearses those questions that will be used in the forthcoming practice interaction by saying them aloud. The therapist might introduce this part of the session by telling the client:

Therapist: Today we've been talking about ways that you can get to know someone better—someone that you've just met and would like to date—by getting the other person to talk about herself. As we discussed, it's good to do this for a number of reasons: You can find out what interests the other person has (and thereby learn other things you can converse about), you can discover mutual hobbies or backgrounds, you will let the other person know you are interested in her, and you'll probably flatter her by letting her talk about herself. We've just watched a film that showed how one person does this—the kinds of open-ended questions he asks to find out more about someone else he would like to date. Now, I'd be interested in hearing some of the questions *you* yourself will ask a person that you've just met and would like to know better.

Client: I would ask her what kind of hobbies she has.

Therapist: Good. Could you say it phrased as a question?

Client: What kinds of hobbies do you have?

Therapist: Great, that's even better. Now spend a minute thinking of at least 10 more questions you would ask in a conversation of this type.

Client (after a pause): O.K. What is your major here at school? Have you started studying yet for final exams? What do you like to do in your spare time? Where were you raised? What are your favorite courses? Where do you live now? What kinds of movies do you like? . . .

In this vignette, the therapist is requiring the client to generate and verbalize examples of the targeted component by actually saying them aloud. This serves several functions. It ensures that the client understands the nature of the verbal component being trained in that session and it focuses the client's attention on specific examples of the component. If it appears that the client does not understand the behavior correctly, cannot think of examples, or uses inappropriate examples, the therapist can discuss the component further and "prompt" correct examples from the client.

A potential problem that may become apparent during rehearsal involves the client's directly copying or memorizing the exact verbal comments of a model who was observed earlier in the session. In some cases, directly copying an observed model's verbatim comments is desirable; this might be true when the client saw a modeled example of some specific verbal behavior that the client particularly liked and wishes to incorporate. However, it is also crucial for clients to grasp the general *principle* being taught (such as eliciting information from a conversational partner) and to generate their own examples of that principle. This is likely to produce more durable maintenance of a skill, with greater potential for generalization to novel situations, than when a client only tries to memorize, mimic, and directly copy a model's observed verbal comments. The therapist can encourage the "personalization" of a component-behavior by asking the client to generate and rehearse novel examples of it.

Generating examples of a target component can be used for many other kinds of verbal social-skill components. In refusal-assertion training, these might include practicing statements of opinion or requests for behavior-change from an antagonist. In conversational and date-initiation training, the client might rehearse examples of personal information statements that could be told to a partner about oneself, samples of questions to elicit information from a conversational partner, complimentary comments that can be directed to the partner, and so on. In job-interview training, the client could generate examples of specific questions to ask an interviewer, statements conveying information about past training or experience, statements conveying interest or enthusiasm about a prospective position, responses to very difficult questions from the interviewer, etc. When a training session targets a nonverbal-skill component (such as eye contact, speech characteristics, smiles, and so on), it may not be as feasible for the client to generate "examples" with the therapist, and rehearsal might then proceed directly to the more structured practice format that is described next.

Simulated or Practice Interactions

It is important that clients have the opportunity to practice using a newly learned skill-component in a simulated interpersonal practice situation within the training setting. This element of training extends beyond simply verbalizing examples of a targeted behavior and requires the client to actually exhibit the new component during a structured simulation of a difficult interpersonal interaction.

In Chapter 3, which discussed client assessment, several procedures for the "in-clinic" behavioral evaluation of social skills were described. These included using structured role-plays of troublesome situations, semistructured interactions with a confederate partner, and relatively unstructured interactions between two or more clients. Although these procedures for sampling social competency are used to assess the client's social skills before an intervention takes place and help to define the nature of the intervention, they can also serve as the vehicle for behavioral practice during the training intervention. More specifically, it is possible to incorporate role-plays, semistructured interactions, and unstructured interactions within treatment sessions, giving the client an opportunity to exhibit the component-behavior that is receiving training attention in that session. Let us examine how this can be accomplished.

Structured Role-Plays in Training Sessions

We earlier noted that structured role-play forms of assessment are useful when the client is being taught to respond to the relatively structured, discrete comments of another person (such as in refusal assertion, commendatory assertion, or job-interview training). Role-playing can also serve as a useful procedure for in-session behavior rehearsal for these forms of social-skills training.

In the case of refusal-assertion training, a typical session might include the treatment aspects we have already described—instruction and rationale for that day's targeted component, observation of an assertion model who exhibits the component, and, possibly, client-generated examples of the behavior. At that point, the client can be presented with the opportunity to use the behavior during an actual role-play with another person. The therapist might select one of the role-play situations that had been used in the earlier assessment and that had been constructed to approximate an actual situation that the client reported to be troublesome. The role-play scene is presented to the client in the same manner as it was in the initial assessment; the therapist narrates the background description of the situation and another person, the role-play partner, delivers one or more comments to the client, each of which requires an assertive response. However, in contrast to the assessment role-plays, the client is now specifically instructed to exhibit the targeted component during his or her assertive responses to the partner. If the session's targeted component is eye contact, the client specifically maintains a high degree of eye contact during the role-play; when other components have already been targeted in preceding sessions, the client is asked to also include those behaviors in each role-played scene. When intensive social-skills training is being conducted, the client can rehearse several different role-play scenes in each session. These scenes might be from the "pool" of situations that had been used in the initial role-play assessment, or they might be novel situations that the client reported as troublesome since the time that the initial assessment was conducted.

The number of role-play scenes that should be practiced in any session is largely determined by the client's level of performance on each scene. If the targeted component is exhibited correctly and consistently over several different role-play practice scenes in the same session, and if it is evident to both the therapist and the client that the behavior has been incorporated into the client's behavioral repertoire, practice on it can terminate. If the client does not exhibit the behavior consistently, comfortably, or correctly in role-plays, additional practice scenes should continue.

The role of the primary therapist is observer of the client's role-play interactions, just as it had been during the assessment role-plays. However, it is expanded in several ways. First, the therapist specifically evaluates whether the client is using the component-behavior that is receiving training attention in that session, as well as any components that had been trained previously. Second, following each role-play scene, the therapist provides feedback, reinforcement, or additional instruction to the client on the component-behavior before continuing with the next scene. This feedback aspect of the therapist's role will be considered in more detail shortly.

In the case of job-interview training sessions, rehearsal role-plays may be somewhat longer. Practice might entail the client's responses to a series of questions delivered by the role-play interviewer, either using the entire job-interview script (as during initial assessment), or using some more abbreviated set of interview questions. Some job-interview component skills do not occur only in response to a specific interview question delivered by the partner. For example, statements conveying information about one's past experience, interest statements, or job-related questions directed by the client to the interviewer can appropriately occur at various points throughout the role-play interview; therefore, clients can be instructed to use these components as often as possible throughout the entire practice interview. The therapist observing the role-play would then determine how frequently the client exhibited the target component throughout the complete practice interview. This might be by counting the frequency of occurrence for various targeted verbal behaviors, estimating the client's overall percentage of eye contact, and so on. Feedback, reinforcement, and further instruction can then be provided to the client, and the practice interview might be repeated.

As we have just described it, role-play practice in training sessions requires the presence of a third person—the practice partner—who interacts with the client. This is an ideal arrangement, since it frees the therapist to devote full attention to observation of the client's responses. However, it is not always possible to locate some other person who can serve as the confederate practice partner in training sessions. In these cases, the therapist can also act as the practice partner and role-play situations with the client. For example, after narrating an assertive-training scene description, the therapist then "changes roles" and delivers the partner's comments directly to the client, concurrently observing the adequacy of the client's response. In job-interview training, the therapist can act as a role-play interviewer for the behavior-rehearsal portion of the session.

Semistructured Interactions in Training Sessions

Some social skills do not readily lend themselves to the structured role-play format, for either assessment or behavioral practice. Earlier, it was suggested that conversational and date-initiation situations can be better approximated using semistructured interactions in which the client converses with a partner for a predetermined period of time. Although the client and partner both assume some situational role (meeting at a snack bar, being together at a party, or so on), the interaction is structured only to the extent that individuals interact as though they were in that situation, and the partner follows some general conversational "rules" established by the therapist to avoid partner dominance in the interaction. The same semistructured interaction format that was used in conversational or date-initiation assessment can also be followed for behavioral practice in training sessions.

The client can be seated next to the interaction partner while the therapist narrates a short description of the situation on which the interaction will be centered. The format is, once again, identical to the assessment-interaction procedure, except that the client now gives particular attention to exhibiting the behavioral component that is receiving training attention. For example, if the target behavior is "asking conversational questions," the client is directed to exhibit this behavior frequently during the course of the simulted interaction with the confederate. Nonverbal components, including eye contact, speech loudness, affect, or smiles, are practiced similarly.

The therapist acts as observer of the client's simulated conversation with the partner, and ordinarily does not take part in the interaction. However, the therapist does evaluate the client's performance with respect to the component-behavior under attention. This could include counting the number of times that the client correctly exhibited a specific verbal component (asked a question, made a comment to the partner conveying information about his or her own interests, explicitly asked for a date, etc.). It is also possible for the observer-therapist to evaluate the presence of any nonverbal components that are receiving training attention in the session. It is most desirable if a therapist confederate partner is available to interact with the client during any practice conversations. However, when a second person is unavailable to serve as the practice confederate, the therapist can function in the role of interaction partner and actually engage in a conversation with the client. When this alternate procedure is used, the therapist has two tasks during the practice period: to serve as interaction partner *and* to observe and evaluate the client's behavior during the interaction. At the conclusion of the simulated conversation, the therapist reviews the client's performance and provides appropriate feedback, reinforcement, and any further instructions that appear indicated.

Although it is desirable for clients to have several opportunities for behavioral practice within the same session, this may not always be feasible. Semistructured but extended interactions (5 to 10 minutes) with a confederate partner for behavioral practice require more time than, for example, each structured role-play used in assertive-training. In order to keep session duration within reasonable limits, and to avoid the possibility of client fatigue, it may sometimes be necessary to use only one semistructured practice interaction. On these occasions, the session would terminate with the therapist's feedback and reinforcement following the practice interaction.

Unstructured Interactions in Training Sessions

These can be handled in similar fashion to semistructured behavioral practice. Let us assume that a conversational training intervention is being conducted with several institutionalized clients and one aim of the project is to increase the everyday conversational behavior between them. Group skills-training techniques will be discussed in detail later in this chapter; let us note here that one approach for behavior-rehearsal within the training session setting would be to "pair" clients with one another for their practice conversations. Here, a confederate partner is not used and each client in the conversation is directed to exhibit the component behavior that is under attention in that session. For example, if eye contact is the targeted behavioral component, the therapist would instruct both conversational partners to exhibit increased eye contact with one another. The therapist would also provide general directions to the clients concerning the purpose of the practice interaction (trying to get to know one another better, discussing mutual interests, and so on). As the unstructured conversation itself takes place, the therapist observes the behavior of each client and evaluates the extent to which both individuals successfully utilize the trained component throughout the interaction. At the conclusion of the conversational interval, feedback and reinforcement are once again provided to the members of the dyad.

Is it possible to eliminate behavioral practice within the training-session environment and, instead, ask clients to utilize the trained skill immediately after the session concludes? For example, if the client is in a residential setting or aftercare–partial-hospitalization program, could the therapist instruct the individual to seek out and engage in a conversation with some other client in the facility and, during that interaction, particularly exhibit the component being trained? This approach is potentially useful, since behavioral practice would occur within the natural environment for which training is intended. Whether this natural environment form of behavior-rehearsal can prove effective depends on several factors. The first is whether the therapist will be in a position to closely observe the client's performance in the natural-setting practice. It is essential that immediately after any practice interaction, a client receive detailed feedback from the therapist. A second consideration is whether or not the practice interaction can actually take place immediately after the format training session ends. If a client leaves a session, goes to a ward dayroom, and attempts to initiate a conversation with another client, that other client must also be willing to talk for some period of time. Otherwise, the practice interaction will not occur and the client receiving treatment may actually be socially punished for attempting to initiate the practice conversation. If natural-environment behavioral practice situations are not under therapist control, their effectiveness as a practice modality may be reduced. Additionally, when a client is first mastering the skills to handle a situation more effectively, he or she may still have difficulty coming across well to others. This could lead to negative reactions from others, even in situations that are intended as nonthreatening practice. It would be more desirable for the client to initially rehearse a skill under situations staged or controlled by the therapist, and seek out naturalistic opportunities for behavioral practice only when the skill has first been mastered in the more controlled practice environment.

To summarize, the aim of behavior-rehearsal or overt practice in training sessions is to provide the client with an opportunity to actually exhibit a social-skill component during an interaction with another person. The staged social interactions used in behavioral practice should correspond as closely as possible to the actual situations that a client has difficulty handling or would like to handle better. In assertion-training, practice might center on role-plays approximating troublesome situations the client has encountered, perhaps including the same role-played situations that had been used earlier for behavioral assessment. In conversational or date-initiation training, the practice situations should simulate the circumstances of actual opportunities the client has to meet other people; again, the interactions used in training sessions might well be the same as those presented during pretreatment behavioral assessment, except that the client is now being "equipped" with the behaviors needed to handle those interactions more effectively. Similarly, job-interview practice entails having the client actually rehearse responses to role-play interviewer's questions. The more closely that both assessment and practice situations can be made to approximate troublesome interactions in the natural environment, the more likely it is that the client will learn to handle those interactions effectively outside of training.

Therapist Feedback and Reinforcement Following Client Behavior Rehearsal

While behavioral practice of social skills is a necessary part of training, repeated practice alone is probably insufficient to produce behavior change for clients. In most social-skills training studies, there appears to be relatively little improvement in client performance when it is observed over repeated baseline assessment interactions (cf. Foy, Massey, Duer, Ross, & Wooten, 1979; Frederiksen, Jenkins, Foy, & Eisler, 1976), confirming that practice alone is unlikely to produce improved skills. The treatment aspects reviewed to this point all precede client behavior-rehearsal in a session and enhance rehearsal's effectiveness. Additionally, the treatment procedures that follow the rehearsal or practice period determine the success of training. These procedures include therapist-provided feedback, reinforcement, and shaping.

When a client has completed a practice interaction and has attempted to exhibit an identified behavioral component, the therapist observing the interaction should immediately provide performance feedback to the client. Characteristics of effective verbal feedback provided by a therapist are immediacy, specificity, presentation emphasizing positive aspects of the client's performance, and the provision of corrective information, if it is needed. The therapist should provide a client with performance feedback as soon as possible following any behavioral practice; it is unlikely that a client will substantially benefit, for example, from feedback provided on practice that had occurred in a training session from the preceding week. Instead, feedback on rehearsal performance should occur in the same session. When several brief role-plays constitute practice, feedback should follow each. If only one practice interaction occurs in a session, feedback should follow it.

As we noted in Chapter 2, verbal feedback should always be "attached" to specific observed aspects of the client's behavior in the practice interaction. Beyond simply telling a client that he or she did "well" during a practice interaction, the therapist should point out what the client did well, citing specific examples of how the client appropriately exhibited the behaviors targeted for attention in that practice. It is often useful to provide the client with information on the degree of change the therapist has noted in behavioral practice. If a client made eye contact only about 10% of the time in assessment, but increases it to about 50% in the first training session on that component, this can be directly pointed out to the client. The greater the detail or specificity of feedback, the more likely a client will be to understand how performance was improved; this enhances the likelihood that the target behavior will be more durably incorporated in the individual's skills repertoire. Feedback should, in most cases, be limited to the component-behavior being trained in that session, as well as to any behaviors that have already been taught in preceding sessions. A therapist would not ordinarily comment on an aspect of the client's practice performance until it has become the target of training. However, because behavioral components are to be successively "added" across sessions, it is appropriate for the trainer to provide feedback on all components that have received attention to that point. This is particularly important if a previously trained behavior appears to be "dropping off" in practice after it had been established and exhibited earlier.

Feedback can be provided verbally by the therapist in a highly satisfactory manner. However, if videotaping equipment is available in the training setting, it is possible to videotape the client's behavior during the rehearsal or practice period and then to play back the film for the client's self-observation when the therapist reviews the performance. This form of direct self-observation-mediated feedback has been utilized in date-initiation training (see Melnick, 1973) and job-interview training (Barbee & Keil, 1973; Furman et al., 1979) to show clients elements of their practice performance immediately after it has occurred. The use of videotape self-observation also permits the client to critique his or her own performance and, if the tape replay is stopped at appropriate times, the client can practice generating alternative responses. In these ways, feedback that includes videotape self-observation is a useful training technique if suitable equipment is available.

When feedback provides positive recognition of some aspect of a client's practice performance, it probably operates as a positive social reinforcer. Assuming that therapist praise does function as an effective reinforcer for a given client, it will serve to strengthen the probability that the individual will continue to exhibit the behavior being praised. This raises the issue of how to provide post-practice feedback when a client does not demonstrate noticeable improvement on a behavior that had just been trained. When a new behavior is being initially acquired, it often does not show immediate, high-level improvement on the first trial or practice attempt. Instead, performance often improves more gradually, yielding what would be plotted as a slowly ascending curve across practice sessions. Therefore, a number of sessions may be needed to train more difficult behavioral skill-components. Exceptions to this pattern are "one-trial" learning, in which performance shows dramatic improvement after one training session. This would be expected for relatively clear-cut and discrete behaviors (e.g., those responses that can be performed quickly following modeling exposure), or behavioral components that the client already had previously learned but simply did not exhibit until specifically instructed to do so.

When a client fails to appropriately exhibit a trained component during behavioral practice, or fails to exhibit it at rates higher than in sessions before it had been trained, feedback still begins with the therapist citing *some* positive aspects of the client's performance (occasions when the component was observed, albeit infrequently, by the therapist; commendation of the client for attempting to use the behavior, even if the attempt was unsuccessful; and so on). Post-rehearsal feedback provided by the therapist always should first focus on something the client did well, if it was only continuing to rehearse a situation that was very difficult. However, attention should then be turned to the component-behavior that remained deficient in practice. The therapist might attempt to ascertain why the client did not exhibit the behavior: Was it forgotten? Did the client have difficulty thinking of examples of the component, such as might be the case in conversational questions or other verbal skills? Was the client uncertain when in the practice interaction to exhibit the behavior and, therefore, did not perform it at all? Did the client feel uncomfortable or awkward making certain verbal comments or engaging in nonverbal acts? All of these are plausible reasons why a client may fail to exhibit some aspect of a socially skilled response, especially when the component is a new addition to the individual's behavioral repertoire. Feedback might then lead to additional instruction from the therapist, as well as training that includes further rationales for the target behavior, examples presented by the therapist, examples generated by the client to the therapist, and so on. If time permits, another opportunity to practice or rehearse the interpersonal situation (through a role-play or other interaction) should be provided.

When the client continues to have difficulty exhibiting a component during practice interactions, it may be useful for the therapist who observes the rehearsal to intercede in the practice by "prompting" correct responses from the client. In an extremely difficult case, the therapist might be seated near the client while the client is interacting with a partner. The therapist could then prompt responses by whispering suggestions to the client while the client interacts with the partner. These might include reminders ("Be sure to talk loud enough"; "Keep up your eye contact") or suggested statements ("Ask where he goes to school"; "Tell her something about your hobbies now"). In later practice sessions, therapist prompts should be gradually withdrawn as the client becomes able to exhibit the correct behaviors without them.

Finally, the therapist must remain cognizant of the appropriateness of client style or flow of interaction, especially during later stages of the intervention when a number of behaviors have already been taught. As described earlier, the manner in which components are integrated is important. If the therapist finds that a client is exhibiting the correct verbal or nonverbal behaviors but in an inappropriate manner, feedback and instruction should be given. Examples of such misapplications include a client "shotgunning" questions or other comments to the practice partner all at one time, talking too loud when speech had previously been overly soft, gesturing excessively or at incorrect times, or maintaining too much eye contact. In general, issues dealing with the integration or style of responses might be introduced in training after the basic components have been mastered.

To summarize, the conduct of a training session includes four treatment steps: (1) identification, instruction, and rationale for that day's target component; (2) modeling exposure; (3) rehearsal or overt practice with a partner; and (4) feedback, reinforcement, and additional instruction following the practice interaction. While the intervention progresses from one skill component to the next, the basic training format of any given session remains relatively consistent. By the conclusion of treatment, all requisite components will have been mastered and the client's overall handling of the practice interactions should be considered skillful.

Training for Generalization of Skill Enhancement to the Natural Environment

One of the most critical aspects of any skills-training intervention is bringing about generalization of skill improvement to the natural environment. This issue is certainly not unique to social-skills training, since generalization or carryover of effects from therapy sessions to relevant situations in the extratherapy environment is a requirement for any treatment program, regardless of its orientation.

There are a number of clinical techniques and procedures that can facilitate generalization across time (follow-up maintenance of skill improvement), across setting (from the training environment to the natural environment), and across specific situations (so the client can effectively handle situations different than those used in practice, but which require the same type of social skill). Attention to generalization of training effects should be intensified toward the conclusion of an intervention when the client is already making skilled responses during in-session practice. If clients are strongly encouraged to approach difficult situations in the natural environment before they have been able to master effective responses for handling those situations, they may encounter further punishment and lack of success, and become frustrated. It is important to reiterate that an applied training intervention does not terminate when clients have become proficient in all components of their behavioral practice. Treatment concludes when the client has been able to generalize new skills to critical situations in the environment. This often means including a number of additional sessions, even after the formal training period ends, to focus on generalization enhancement. Let us review several procedures that can help bring about generalization.

Presentation of Novel Practice Situations in Training Sessions

During behavior-rehearsal in training sessions, clients practice their responses around certain interpersonal situations. However, the aim of training is to teach clients how to handle not only those situations that are actually practiced in training, but any situation that requires the same skilled response. For example, will a previously unassertive client be able to make assertive responses to situations somewhat different than those actually practiced and mastered in training?

One procedure for evaluating this is to present the client with novel practice situations. Novelty can be achieved in assertion role-plays by varying the narrated scene description to provide different background circumstances for the practice interaction, by varying the role-play partner with whom the client interacts, or by varying the role-play comments made by the partner to the client. In other forms of skills-training, novel stimuli or practice situations can also be incorporated in later phases of training. In job-interview-training role-plays, the client might be presented with novel questions to which he or she must respond. Different role-play interviewers can be used to approximate different styles of interacting (a pleasant interviewer, a more abrupt interviewer, one who asks many questions or few questions). The sex of the interviewer might be varied. In conversational or date-initiation training, different practice partners can also be used.

The therapist, by observing how these practice variations are handled, will be in a position to know whether the client is able to apply newly developed skills under stimulus conditions somewhat different from those that were usually presented in training-session practice. Although this will require the primary therapist to locate additional practice partners or construct slightly different sample interactions for rehearsal, the therapist will also be able to feel more confident that the client can generalize new skills to these novel situations. If deficits are noted in the novel situation performance, "brush-up" training is indicated.

"Booster" or Follow-Up Training Sessions

Following the conclusion of a training intervention, it is often useful to provide periodic "booster" sessions to ensure that social-skill gains are maintained. This can be accomplished by presenting the client with practice interactions in follow-up sessions. The format of follow-up interactions could be similar to those used in the intervention (role-plays, semistructered interactions, etc.), presenting both novel and formerly practiced situations. The therapist observing the follow-up practice can provide feedback and additional training on any skill aspects that have diminished and appear to require it. Follow-up or booster sessions might be planned for various time intervals after completion of the primary intervention (e.g., each month). They are especially important if the client has had little opportunity to use the newly developed skills in the natural environment or continues to report difficulty handling in-vivo situations that should have benefited from training.

Focusing Client Attention on Natural Environment Situations
Where Newly Acquired Skills Can Be Used

It is important that clients be explicitly made aware that the purpose of social-skills training is to improve the way they handle interpersonal situations outside of treatment. One way to draw attention to this is by asking clients to describe opportunities they have to use their new skills in genuine interactions and to increasingly place themselves in those situations, even if they had previously avoided them. In the case of skills that facilitate the development of relationships or serve similar purposes (including conversational, job-interview, dating, and commendatory-assertion skills), the therapist and client can discuss specific occasions of when and where the client might interact with others to "try out" the new behaviors. When, in the individual's day-to-day life, can the person meet others to engage them in conversation, interact with people who might be potential dates, or go on job interviews? Are there currently existing opportunities to enter into these social situations that the client may not be perceiving, or perceives but has not acted upon? Or, alternatively, will it be necessary to work with the client to increasingly "place" him or her in natural settings where there will be more frequent opportunities to meet other people? If an individual has acquired new conversational skills, but spends almost all of his or her time alone, it will be necessary to assist that client in spending more time near others before those skills can be used. This aspect of treatment might include discussion of such possibilities as a client's greater involvement in hobby groups, social clubs, church social activities, neighborhood activities, or attendance at parties. Discussion of these activities could also be followed with "homework" assignments to gradually increase the client's level of participation in them.

When attention is focused on using new skills in the natural environment, it is desirable to ask that the client self-monitor interactions where the skill could have been used, as well as how the client actually handled the situation. This technique is similar to the self-monitoring diary that was kept in the initial assessment phase, but, rather than recording only the circumstances of troublesome interpersonal situations, the client is now also detailing more successful attempts to handle interactions effectively. Clients can be encouraged to write down brief comments each day describing any situations in which they had an opportunity to use their skill, the location where the interaction took place, how they behaved and whether they felt they exhibited the trained components, and what outcome was achieved. By making the client more cognizant of environmental opportunities to use newly trained skills, and by asking the client to attend explicity to his or her own behavior in those interactions, it is possible to increase the "connection" between training practice and the natural environment.

Therapist Reinforcement When Clients Report Skill Usage

As the client brings to the session information about in-vivo situations in which the newly learned skill could have been used and describes how those situations were actually handled, the therapist will have an opportunity to verbally reinforce any client-reported attempts to exhibit the skill. For example, a previously date-anxious individual might tell the therapist about a situation in which a heterosocial interaction was attempted. The therapist should inquire to determine how the client behaved and, specifically, whether trained skill-components were attempted or used. The client can be specifically and directly commended for any efforts to use newly trained skills in situations that were formerly troublesome. It is important for several reasons that the therapist strongly and consistently reinforce client reports of social-skill attempts towards the end of the training intervention. This is likely to be a time when the client is still uncertain concerning his or her performance in the natural setting, and it is helpful for the therapist to assure the client that new skills can be used in that environment. Additionally, early social-skill attempts may not always be successful. The newly assertive person may find that others do not respond well to this behavior; the formerly date-anxious person may not get dates immediately after training; the previously shy individual may not develop friendships as a result of early conversational attempts. Thus, there is often a period of time when the new skill is not consistently reinforced in the in-vivo setting. Because new behaviors are maintained best when each attempt is reinforced, the therapist can provide reinforcement to counter the failures most clients will periodically experience in their early attempts at socially skilled functioning in difficult situations. If a client reports encountering a situation that was not handled well, it would be useful for the therapist to provide review, practice, and otherwise "brush up" on strategies to use, should a similar interaction recur.

When the individual receiving skills-training is in some setting where he or she can be observed by the therapist or other treatment staff, it is often possible to reinforce the client's skill behavior directly, rather than simply reinforcing the client's reports of behavior. For example, if institutionalized patients are taught more effective conversational skills, those residential staff who are in a position to observe the patients' everyday social interactions can be told what behaviors the patients have learned and are attempting to use. The staff can then note whenever a patient exhibits those conversational behaviors, either during informal interactions with other patients or with staff, and can direct specific praise to the individual for exhibiting them. Once again, the aim is to intensify and make more consistent the reinforcement consequences for socially skilled behavior in the natural environment.

Finally, the client's own capacity for self-reinforcement should not be overlooked. Many socially deficient persons seem to develop a pattern of habitually criticizing and punishing themselves for their perceived or actual shortcomings in social interactions ("Why didn't I speak up just then?"; "I wanted to go over and talk to her, but I waited too long and missed the chance"; "I really handled that badly"; and so on). In addition to the therapist or staff praising a client's use of more effective social skills, the client should also be instructed to praise himself or herself when new skills are attempted in the natural environment. Further, self-reinforcement following skill use should occur regardless of whether a positive outcome was actually achieved, since the client is to be commended for applying the skill and cannot entirely control how another person in the interaction will respond. Thus, when a previously unassertive woman expresses her opinions in a meeting, she should praise herself afterward, whether or not her suggestions were actually adopted; when the formerly date-anxious individual initiates a heterosocial interaction, that initiation should be self-reinforced, even if the other person declined the date request.

Cognitive Strategies for Decreasing Behavioral Inhibition

Cognitively mediated inhibitions often prevent clients from exhibiting social behaviors that they, in fact, know how to perform. Persons may suppress even appropriate assertive responses, fearing negative evaluations from others, the possibility of being disliked, or believing that their opinions are unimportant. Individuals may suppress the initiation of social interactions such as dates or conversations because they believe themselves to be uninteresting and unattractive, or because of fears of rejection. The basic model underlying most skills-training interventions is that these cognitive fears and detrimental attributions follow past failure to handle situations well; by equipping clients with more effective social behaviors, the cognitions will also change. This often appears to be the case. However, in many instances, it is also important to incorporate cognitive modification techniques within treatment. If clients have learned to master practice interactions but seem unable to handle similar in-vivo situations, or if they report anticipatory fears, evaluative anxieties, and inhibition associated with the in-vivo interactions, cognitive modification should be considered.

Repeated behavioral practice in training sessions, when accompanied by therapist feedback that stresses positive change in the client's practice performance, serves to increase confidence. The therapist can also use other cognitively oriented techniques that will particularly enhance generalization. Clients might be asked to verbally identify with the therapist, and actually list all the positive consequences associated with using their new skills in the natural environment. For example, an individual who has completed refusal-assertion training could be asked to identify the benefits of handling situations assertively: being able to express your own views; showing others that you have opinions; behaving more forcefully and changing inequities in the way some people might otherwise act towards you; not feeling exploited or taken advantage of; being noticed; influencing others' decisions; coming across as a leader; and so on. As much as possible, the client should be encouraged to actively identify those benefits, with the therapist assisting and guiding the discussion.

At the same time, there are certain "risks" that clients probably feel and that should also be discussed. No matter how appropriate, reasonable, and nonhostile an assertive response is, some people will not like an assertive individual; this may be particularly true when the assertive person is a female (Kelly, Kern, Kirkley, Patterson, & Keane, 1980). The individual who is attempting to initiate dates will not always be successful and may be rejected even when he or she makes highly appropriate approach responses. The person who has developed effective conversational skills will encounter people who simply do not want to reciprocate conversation, and even the skilled job interviewee will not always be offered a job. Many clients who have previously been skills-deficient remain oversensitive to the possibility and significance of such negative outcomes, and discussion of these issues is important in later phases of training. The therapist might assist the client in "weighing" the many benefits associated with the use of new social skills in relevant situations against the possibilities of occasional rejection, not being liked by everyone, and so on. The cognitive-oriented techniques advocated by Ellis (see Ellis, 1962; Ellis & Grieger, 1977) may be useful in reducing excessive worries and evaluative social anxiety toward the end of the skills-training intervention.

It is also possible to teach clients to directly modify their own negative or anxiety-maintaining cognitions, particularly when these cognitions occur before a client enters a social interaction and when they might otherwise lead the client to avoid that situation or perform poorly in it. An example of negative cognitions is the job applicant who has learned effective interview skills but still experiences great anticipatory anxiety and many failure-related thoughts before an interview. Another case is the individual who has learned appropriate social-interaction skills in training, but worries excessively prior to initiating a conversation or a date request in the natural environment. Meichenbaum and his colleagues (Meichenbaum, 1977; Meichenbaum & Cameron, 1974) have demonstrated the clinical utility of identifying the fear-related self-statements in which the client engages prior to the critical in-vivo situation. This can be accomplished by asking the client what he or she thinks about, worries about, or fears as the critical situation is approached. If the individual is unable to report specific examples of these self-statements, it may be necessary to ask the client to closely attend to his or her own thinking during some in-vivo interactions and record the self-statements that were noted. These self-monitoring records or notes can be brought to the next session and reviewed with the therapist.

The client can then be taught to modify anxiety-related cognitions. As outlined by Meichenbaum (1977), an individual must first learn to identify when negative cognitions or self-statements begin to occur in the natural environment. It would appear likely this might be at the time the client realizes a difficult situation is forthcoming, when the client first decides to enter into the interaction, or as the interaction is approached or initiated. As soon as the client is able to detect or recognize the existence of potentially detrimental statements, or as soon as anticipatory anxiety is noted, the client begins generating positive, success-oriented, and anxiety-reducing self-statements in place of the negative cognitions. Thus, the individual is taught to cognitively relabel situations and describe them in less-threatening terms, to generate positive anticipations of performance, and to focus on the potential for beneficial social outcomes.

It is not sufficient to simply admonish a client to "think positively" when approaching difficult situations. Time in later training sessions must be spent teaching the client to identify potentially detrimental cognitions or self-statements. Then, attention in sessions can be given to assisting the client in actually practicing, by overt verbalization, new and more positive self-statements. Examples of such statements might include, depending on the nature of training and of the client's current maladaptive cognitions: "Just stay calm"; "I've got a lot of interesting things I can tell this person"; "I'm going to speak clearly and will be understood"; "It's really going to be fun for me to meet this person"; "I'm going to handle this well"; etc. The client might practice generating a number of positive self-statements aloud in the session, with the therapist listening and providing reinforcement. However, it will be necessary for the client to learn to think them covertly before an in-vivo situation, rather than say them aloud. Therefore, after the client has practiced saying a list of effective anxiety-reducing or performance-facilitating statements, the therapist can ask the client to fade out saying them aloud and practice thinking them, by saying each in thought. The final, and most important step, is for the client to actually use these new and more positive cognitive self-statements when approaching potentially difficult social interactions in the natural environment. In essence, modification of one's own thoughts is itself a skill that can be practiced in training and then applied in genuine interactions, just as behavioral social skills are first practiced and then used in-vivo.

The treatment approach of cognitive modification has been detailed by Meichenbaum (1977) and appears to be a very useful component in social-skills training, especially with respect to enhancing the generalization of training to the natural environment by decreasing cognitively mediated behavioral inhibition. However, it is crucial that clients have *first* learned more adaptive social-skill behavior; if the individual lacks the objective skill behaviors in his or her repertoire to handle an interpersonal situation effectively, it is unlikely that the person will be able to actually achieve positive social outcomes, and new self-statements will be insufficient to produce enduring behavior change.

To summarize the issue of generalization, it is probably unwarranted for a therapist to simply assume that once clients have learned new social skills in the training setting, clients will then "automatically" use them in the natural environment. As a training intervention is being planned, an important preliminary step to ensure the environmental relevance of training is to construct behavioral-assessment situations that closely approximate the actual situations a client would like to handle more effectively. Further, training and behavioral-practice situations should also be "tailored" to the exact interactions that the client finds troublesome or difficult to handle.

As the intervention concludes, and as we then want the client to actually use new skills in the natural environment, additional treatment steps are needed. These include: follow-up or booster practice sessions; presentation of novel practice situations to ensure that the individual can handle interactions similar to (but not identical with) those that had already been practiced; focusing client attention on actual opportunities in the natural environment when the use of their new skills would be appropriate; reinforcing client efforts to use new skills in those in-vivo situations; and utilizing cognitive modification approaches to decrease behavioral inhibition. In most instances, treatment attention to generalization should occur after the client has begun to master the goal social-skill in practice; it is important that the individual be equipped with the behavioral abilities to handle difficult situations well before being placed in those situations. Sessions focusing on generalization enhancement can often conclude the skills-training intervention with the individually treated client.

The Social-Skills Training Group

There are several reasons why a therapist might wish to conduct a social-skills training group, rather than working with just a single individual. One of the foremost is cost and time-effectiveness. As we will see, social-skills group interventions often require little more time than single-client treatment, both in session length and in the duration of the entire intervention. Thus, a group of clients can be treated with only slightly greater expenditure of therapist time than is needed for one client. In addition, because a number of clients will be present for each session, clients can often serve as behavioral practice partners for one another, reducing the need for therapist confederates to function as partners in role-plays, semistructured interactions, and so on. Many of the learning principles for social-skills training may operate even better in a group environment than in single-client treatment: clients can serve as live skill-models for one another during sessions; they can provide feedback, reinforcement, and suggestions to one another, rather than the therapist's always having to do this; and clients' discussions with one another can provide mutual support and encouragement. Finally, because training is conducted in a group setting, the session itself is a social interaction or event; this may serve a useful function for many isolated or socially anxious individuals.

One major requirement for group-administered training is that there exist a number of clients with similar social-skill deficits, all of whom could benefit from the same type of intervention. Thus, training could be conducted with a group of unassertive persons, a group of date-anxious individuals, or with a number of clients who can benefit from comparable training in conversational skills. However, this also raises one of the limitations of group-administered training: When training is conducted in a group, an individual with highly unique social-skills training needs, or an individual who responds to training much more slowly than the others in the group, may not be able to derive as much benefit from treatment oriented towards the group's pace as from an intervention tailored specifically for that individual client. However, because of its efficiency in applied settings, as well as the peer-mediated treatment influences made possible in a group, this format of skills-training is often desirable and practical.

There has been very little empirical attention given to the ideal size or client composition for a skills-training group. A number of investigators have reported successful interventions with client groups ranging in size from three to twelve (see Kelly, Urey, & Patterson, 1980; Hersen, Kazdin, Bellack, & Turner, 1979). One limiting factor on the uppermost number of clients in the group involves the time needed for behavioral practice in sessions. As we will see, it is often possible to have the group break up into practice pairs during the behavior-rehearsal portion of each training session. If this practice format is used, clients can rehearse or practice their skills simultaneously with one another, and it is not necessary to have each client practice individually and successively. This reduces the session's length. However, there still must be sufficient time in the group itself for each client to verbalize personal examples of the targeted behavioral component, comment on the behavior of a model, and discuss the rationale for specific skill behaviors. If the skills-training group is too large, there will either be insufficient time for each client's active participation in the session, or sessions will need to be very long. An optimal size group, in this light, might consist of four to eight clients.

With respect to client composition of the skills-training group, it would appear desirable not only for all members to have similar types of skills deficits (such as assertiveness, date-initiation, and job-interview), but also to be approximately comparable in the degree of skill deficiency. It is neither practical nor essential to require that all clients exhibit deficits on the same behavioral components of the goal skill; it does seem desirable for all members to be approximately comparable in their extent of social-skill impairment, overall functioning level, and probable response to training. If clients differ from one another too greatly on these kinds of criteria, it may be difficult for the therapist to conduct and pace the group such that all clients benefit from training. For example, let us assume that one client can master each component on the very first occasion that it is targeted for attention, while all other clients require much more repeated practice and training. If training is paced for the slower clients, the highest-functioning clients may become bored; conversely, low-functioning participants would derive little benefit from a group geared to the advanced clients' more rapid skill-acquisition level. To some degree, variability in skill-acquisition rate will always occur and can be handled by assigning special roles to the more advanced clients, such as being live models or providers of feedback to slower-paced clients during sessions. However, relatively initial homogeneity of client pretraining skill level appears to be desirable in most cases.

Just as an ideal format for individual client social-skills training involves ongoing, multiple-treatment sessions, the same format is useful for group-administered interventions. Following behavioral assessment of each client's social competency, group training-sessions can successively and cumulatively direct attention to each of the behavioral components that together comprise the final goal social skill. By moving from one component behavior to the next over the course of the intervention, the desired skill will have been successively shaped in each client at the end of training. The number of group sessions needed for the entire training intervention again depends on the complexity of the goal skill (particularly, the number of different components that comprise it and that will need to be taught), as well as clients' functioning level and the time required for them to master each component. Then, just as in single-client interventions, treatment attention can be directed more intensively to increasing generalization of each client's skill-improvement to the natural environment.

Behavioral Assessment Preceding the Training Intervention

Just as it is important for behavioral social-skills assessment to precede an individual client's training intervention, it is useful to assess each group member's skills before group training itself begins. The purpose of assessment remains the same: to pinpoint those behavioral components of an effective skill response that are deficient and require training attention. When an individual client is treated, performance in pretreatment assessment interaction determines the exact components that will later receive training. In the case of a group of clients, it is unlikely that all members will exhibit deficits on the same components. However, each client's performance during individual sample interactions still provides important data on training needs. For example, in a job-interview training intervention with five persons, we might observe and rate the performance of each during a pretraining job-interview assessment role-play. The therapist may find that all of the clients exhibit adequate eye contact with their interview partner, that none of the five conveys very much specific information about past experience to the interviewer, and that two of the five ask the interviewer a number of appropriate questions but three do not. The therapist could then conclude that, of these three component behaviors, eye contact will probably not require any training attention, a good deal of session time will be needed to teach clients to convey appropriate information about their work or educational experience, and asking job-related questions of an interviewer will require some attention in training sessions, so that the several clients deficient in asking questions can learn to do so. The behavioral components of the goal skill targeted during this intervention, then, will be those in which any group member is deficient, with the greatest attention being focused on the behaviors with which most of the group's clients have difficulty.

The client-assessment procedures for a group social-skills training intervention are similar to those used with individually treated clients, as described in Chapter 3. It is often useful to meet with the group on several occasions for the purpose of identifying specific examples of troublesome situations for each client. For example, in a refusal-assertion training group, one female client may report difficulty asserting herself with male co-workers in the office setting. A second client may also experience assertiveness difficulties, but principally in the context of social relationships with neighbors and family members. A third client may have trouble expressing personal opinions in work conferences and meetings. Thus, while all have trouble asserting themselves, the situations in which this deficit manifests itself are different for each. The aim of one or more preliminary group discussion sessions might be for each client to generate descriptions of a number of specific problematic situations that he or she has encountered. The therapist conducting the session takes notes of these descriptions and uses the information to later construct role-play assessment scenes, just as scenes would be constructed from the situation reports of an individually treated client. When individualized scenes have been constructed for each client, that group member would then role-play his or her own scenes for behavioral-assessment purposes, as well as for practice in subsequent training. If group members have difficulty generating detailed examples of situations they find troublesome, the self-monitoring diary recording procedure can be used by clients, and daily information on troublesome situations can be brought to the therapist at the time of the next session. From this information, additional personalized role-play scenes for each client can be constructed by the therapist.

In some cases, it may not be necessary to develop different and unique assessment sample-interactions for each client. For example, in a job-interview training group that consists of clients who will be seeking similar types or levels of work (all high school graduates, all college graduates, all persons seeking labor employment), the therapist may be able to construct a single interview question script that will be used for the assessment interview of each participant (cf. Hollandsworth et al., 1977; Kelly, Laughlin, Claiborne, & Patterson, 1979). This would be justified if it appears likely that all clients will face similar questions in their genuine job interviews. In heterosocial or conversational assessment, the same interaction format can be used to assess the skill of each client (e.g., an 8-minute semistructured or unstructured interaction); only the background narrative description preceding it need be tailored to the individual client's situation. Thus, in assessment interactions preceding a group heterosocial-skills-training project, a client who is a student might be told to imagine that she is interacting with another student at a campus dance, while a heterosocially deficient individual who has opportunities to meet others at a local bar might be told to imagine that the assessment interaction is taking place at that setting. However, the actual sample interaction will be identical for the two clients.

When social-skills assessment is being conducted with an individually treated client, it is often necessary to use a therapist confederate to serve as the partner in the client's sample interactions. This can also be done in group interventions. For example, one of the early group meetings can be devoted to behavioral assessments, and the therapist can tell the group that each member will be engaging in his or her sample interactions on that day. Then, the therapist can escort clients to separate locations for their individual assessment interactions. These locations can be offices, areas of the clinic, or even different parts of a large room. Each client then meets his or her partner and engages in the assessment interaction apart from the other clients. In assertive-training, each client-partner dyad might be role-playing the individual scenes that had been identified as problematic for that client. In job-interview training, each client might be role-playing a standard job interview with the partner. In conversational or date-initiation training, each client would interact with his or her partner for some predetermined period of time. Thus, while training will later be conducted in a group, each client is assessed in individual sample interactions with a confederate partner; there could be as many assessment interactions taking place at one time as there are clients in the group or partners who can serve as interaction confederates.

For the evaluations to provide useful treatment information, the therapist who leads the group must obtain specific information on each client's perform-ance in the assessment interactions. This includes information on how ade-quately each client exhibits the goal skill's component-behaviors during the sample interactions. If the number of clients who are being assessed is suffi-ciently small, the therapist may be able to circulate and observe each client-partner interaction pair to evaluate each person's performance on those compo-nent-behaviors that comprise an effective social skill. Whenever one or more clients are observed to exhibit deficits in a skill component, that component can be noted so that it will later be targeted in group training sessions. Alternative-ly, if the therapist cannot directly observe all clients in their assessment interactions, audiotape recordings can be made of each client-partner pair and later they can be evaluated by the therapist to determine training needs. A final performance-rating strategy is for the confederates to function both as interac-tion partners and as raters of the client's skill behavior. This requires that the partners be given information on the specific behavioral components that they are to observe. Each partner can then report information to the therapist on the exact behavior of the client with whom he or she was paired during the sample interactions, and the therapist can in turn target those components for later training. For this to be effective, the partners must receive some training on identifying the component-behaviors they will be expected to rate. This might include estimating the quality of client nonverbal behaviors such as eye con-tact, loudness, or affect; using rating scales; and determining the presence or frequency with which verbal components are exhibited by the client.

A practical problem involves the availability of confederates who can serve as partners for each client. Even a small training group consisting of, perhaps, five clients requires five other persons, who can also serve as partners. It is possible to reduce this support staff by conducting clients' assessment interac-tions at different times and "reusing" the same partners for several clients. However, another approach that is less costly in staff time is to have clients serve as interaction partners with one another. Let us consider how this approach of pairing clients with one another for their sample interactions might be used in several types of skills-training.

Assertive-training. All clients who will be in the training group can be assigned into pairs or "buddies." During the assessment role-plays, one member of each dyad can first play the part of the antagonist. The situations that will be role-played are those that the client who is being assessed reports as troublesome. A script for each role-play scene is prepared in advance by the therapist; the client who will play the antagonist directs comments from a role-play script to the client who is being assessed. The client being assessed, in turn, responds to the partner's comments while the therapist observes and evaluates the quality of the assertive responses. This system functions in exactly the same manner as do assertive role-plays with a therapist confederate, except that another client serves as the partner. When all the first client's role-play scenes have been completed, the two clients reverse roles. They then role-play the scenes for the other member of the dyad.

Job-interview training. Clients again can be assigned into role-play pairs. Here, one member of the pair can play the part of a job interviewer and follow a written script of questions to ask the client, who is playing the role of the employment applicant. When they have finished the role-play interview, the two clients reverse roles, with the former applicant acting as interviewer and following the same interview script.

Conversational-skills training. A similar procedure can be used with the two members of each pair, directed by the therapist to interact with one another for a set period of time. Depending upon the assessment aims, the conversational interaction can be semistructured or unstructured. If it is semistructured, the "partner" member of the dyad can follow certain conversational rules established by the therapist, just as the therapist confederate partner would. These might include not monopolizing the conversation (by asking a question only if asked one by the other client), never talking for more than 20 consecutive seconds, remaining noncontingently warm, allowing the other person to "break" all silences, and so on. If the interaction is intended to be unstructured, neither client would be given instructions other than to talk for some period of time, to get to know one another better, etc. Once again, the assessment procedures are identical to those when a confederate partner is used, except that here another client serves as the interaction partner.

Using clients as partners for one another's assessment interactions presents practical advantages when other staff are unavailable to serve as interaction partners. However, it is necessary to explain to clients how they are to behave in the sample interactions, particularly when one client plays the structured role of a partner—a role-play antagonist, a job interviewer, for example. It also remains necessary for the therapist to closely scrutinize the skill performance of each client during his or her interactions to assess areas of deficit. However, as we will see, utilizing clients as partners with one another can be helpful not only in pretraining assessment, but also for behavioral practice or rehearsal when training begins.

Group Training Sessions

Social-skills group training sessions utilize the same learning principles as does individual training. Instruction and rationale for that day's targeted component-skill behavior, modeling, rehearsal or practice, and reinforcement and feedback are always incorporated in the group session. Let us consider how these principles are modified for group-administered training.

Instruction, Coaching, and Provision of Rationale

Individual client skills-training sessions begin with the therapist identifying that day's target component, providing examples of it, and discussing reasons for the importance of the behaviors. In a skills-training group, a similar procedure can be followed, except that the discussion also involves input and comment from all group members. The therapist can solicit from the group members their opinions about why a particular behavior is an important part of the goal skill, and ask how each client would feel when interacting with another person who exhibited that behavior (or did not exhibit it). In addition to providing clear examples and instruction on the behavior, the group leader encourages clients to verbalize rationales for its importance.

Modeling Exposure in the Skills-Training Group

In the training of individual clients, modeling can be accomplished when the therapist informally verbalizes examples of the target behavior, models an interaction live before the client and exhibits the behavior, or shows a modeling film in which skilled models can be observed by the client. These procedures are applicable in the skills-training group as well.

It is also possible for clients to function as social-skill models for other clients in the group session. One way for this to occur is by having a relatively proficient group member verbalize examples of a target component during the group session and thereby be observed by the other clients. In a conversational-skills group, a session might be focusing on the behavioral component of self-disclosing appropriate information about oneself in conversations. The therapist could ask one client to explain what specific things he might tell a conversational partner about himself. The client then verbalizes specific information he would convey in a conversation, perhaps concerning his hobbies, interests, where he went to school, his favorite television shows, music that he likes, and so on. As the client lists these self-disclosure topics, the other clients will be benefitting from his modeled examples. In turn, the therapist can ask other clients to verbally generate their own examples of the target behavior, again providing a live-modeling experience for others in the group. Thus, one client's rehearsal or practice serves as a modeling source for the other clients who observe it.

Client practice and modeling may also be combined by having clients actually rehearse an interaction in the presence of other group members. For example, in a job-interview training group, a client might be asked to play the part of an applicant during a role-play interview in front of the group; the client would be instructed to particularly exhibit whatever behavior is receiving attention in that day's session. The interviewer in the role-play can be either a therapist or another client. As the client practices the interaction, that client will be benefitting from behavior rehearsal of the skill; as other clients observe the role-play and see the behavioral component exhibited, they will be benefitting from another modeling influence. Similar client-modeling can be incorporated in other types of skills-training groups by having selected clients role-play assertive responses, brief conversations, or date-initiation styles in the presence of the other members.

Client-modeling is a useful adjunct source of imitative learning in social-skills training groups. However, even if the therapist always selects a client who is felt likely to be a good skill model, that client may not exhibit the targeted behavior in its most correct, clear form. For that reason, the group leader may wish to combine several modeling sources within the same session. The therapist might first verbalize examples of the behavior, then live-model a short interaction demonstrating its use in a social context or show a modeling videotape, and only then ask one of the more proficient group members to rehearse an interaction that demonstrates the behavior, while the other clients observe the practice.

Rehearsal, Feedback, and Reinforcement in the Skills-Training Group

Practicing sample interactions before the group affords the opportunity for behavior rehearsal and for modeling; it is also possible for the other clients, who just observed the "model" client, to provide performance feedback to their peer. After the in-group practice, the therapist can ask various members of the group to comment and offer feedback on the adequacy of the client practice they watched. Just as when feedback and reinforcement are provided by the therapist, other clients should be encouraged to: (1) comment specifically on the behavioral component(s) that have already been targeted for training, and not comment on yet-untrained aspects of the performance; (2) always provide positive or commendatory feedback first on what their peer did well; (3) make any corrective feedback comments concerning the component-behavior's exhibition that are warranted; and (4) offer specific instruction or suggestions, if they are needed. In essence, the therapist teaches clients to provide specific, constructive behavioral feedback and reinforcement of the other client's practice or rehearsal performance in the session. If it was evident that a client's in-group rehearsal was inadequate, the group leader should have the client repeat it again before the other group members until it becomes more effective and the target component reaches proficient levels. At that point, a different client can practice a simulated interaction in front of the group, providing still another modeling exposure source for the other clients and an opportunity for more client-administered feedback, reinforcement, or suggestions. This can rotate among all group members, or as many clients as session-time permits.

Finally, depending on the nature of training and the amount of behavior rehearsal that the therapist wishes to incorporate in the session, the group can be broken up to permit clients further individual practice opportunity. If therapist confederate partners are available, each client might be assigned to his or her partner and asked to practice a sample interaction with that partner. This practice is identical to that used in the pre-intervention behavioral assessment, except that each client is now asked to particularly exhibit the trained behavioral component during the practice. If confederate partners are unavailable, clients can be paired with one another for skill rehearsal, again in the same manner that was described earlier in this chapter. The group leader's role is to determine how adequately each client or client-pair engages in the component during individual behavior rehearsal; perhaps the leader can do this by circulating among the dyads and observing client performance. An even more efficient procedure is to break the group up into practice triads. Here, two clients engage in the practice interaction, while the third serves as a "surrogate trainer" and offers feedback, reinforcement, and suggestions following their practice. The members of the triad then change roles, so that each has the opportunity to practice, be a practice partner, and be an observer-trainer. If it is evident after practice that clients have not yet mastered the behavior, the next group session will need to give it still more attention. When most clients are able to exhibit the component consistently and successfully in their rehearsal, the subsequent group session can focus attention on the next behavioral skill-component to be trained in the intervention. As group sessions move from one component to the next, clients' overall performance of the goal skill will be successively improving. By the conclusion of formal training sessions, each client should have mastered the skill and should be demonstrating effective performance in all practice interactions.

When clients have demonstrated improvement in their handling of practice interactions, treatment can then focus on skills-generalization to the natural environment. All of the techniques described earlier for fostering generalization are applicable in the skills-training group. Clients can be exposed to novel rehearsal interactions by varying the partners (confederates or other clients) with whom they interact, the exact situations that are practiced, and so on. Clients might be asked to self-monitor significant daily interactions that occur between group sessions; group time can be spent discussing each participant's reports of in-vivo situations where the newly acquired skills were used. While the therapist actively reinforces such reports of skill usage, it is even more powerful for clients to actively praise, encourage, and offer suggestions to one another. As group members discuss situations where they successfully used appropriate social skills in the natural environment, their successful reports serve as a modeling influence on other persons in the group. Finally, cognitive modification procedures, including the identification of negative cognitions, the practice of overt and then covert positive self-statements regarding performance in social interactions, and other cognitive restructuring techniques, are all useful in group social-skills treatment.

The treatment techniques reviewed in this chapter represent suggested training procedures. Depending upon the setting in which training is conducted, the staff and equipment resources, and the nature of the client population, the therapist in an applied setting may find it necessary to modify some of the procedures, or to evolve techniques or treatment emphases other than those described here. Perhaps the two most important questions that should always guide the skills-training practitioner are, first, whether a given training technique represents a logical application of learning principles and, second, whether the training intervention is effective. The question of intervention effectiveness and evaluation will be considered in Chapter 5. With respect to the first issue, it is evident that there are many different ways to incorporate learning-theory principles into training sessions. For example, modeling can be accomplished using a number of different procedures: therapist verbalizations of examples of a component behavior; therapist live-modeling of a simulated interaction; modeling videotapes; client practice that serves as a model for other clients; and so on. The important point is that any of these techniques can be used to represent the incorporation of imitative learning principles in the session. Similarly, whatever formats are used for instruction, discussion and rationale presentation, behavioral practice or rehearsal, and feedback/reinforcement, it appears essential that some application of each of these principles occur in every session.

Social-Skills Training in a Workshop-Format Intervention

There may be occasions when a practitioner is called upon to conduct some form of social-skills training in a workshop-like format. By this, we mean that training is to be conducted with a group of participants in one or perhaps two extended sessions lasting at least several hours. Training is therefore group-administered, but does not take place in multiple, ongoing sessions and must be concentrated in a much more brief period of time.

From almost all perspectives, this is not an ideal method for teaching social skills to any clinical population of interpersonally deficient persons. When training is compressed into a single, long session, it is extremely difficult to provide adequate attention to individual component-behaviors of the goal skill, to provide sufficient opportunities for behavioral practice, or to give adequate individual attention to those persons who require it. Similarly, techniques that foster the generalization of training from the workshop setting to critical events in the natural environment can be incorporated in only cursory fashion, since it would usually not be possible to have periodic but regular contact with clients to monitor whether they are using the new skills, to reinforce reported skill usage in the natural environment, to deal with cognitive inhibitions adequately, and so on. This means that workshop-format training is almost certainly unsuitable to teach general assertion skills, conversational skills, date-initiation skills, or job-interview skills to persons with substantial deficits in these competencies. When a therapist is asked to conduct workshop-format or single-session social-skills training for almost any clinical population, one of the best initial strategies might be to convince the requesting party of the need for multiple, ongoing session training. Then, the intervention would become much more a social-skills training group, permitting sufficient time for thorough training and generalization attention.

However, under certain circumstances, concentrated workshop-format training can be useful. These circumstances might occur when: (1) the persons to receive training are relatively high-functioning under most circumstances and are not a "clinical" population in the usual sense; (2) training is intended to assist them in better handling very specific situations in the environment; and (3) a longer multiple-session intervention cannot be undertaken. An instance when a one- to two-session, workshop-format training project might be useful is training to enhance the ability of graduating high school or college students to successfully handle job interviews (cf. Hollandsworth et al., 1977; Hollandsworth & Sandifer, 1979). Here, the clients who receive training are likely to be relatively high-functioning and able to derive some benefit from even a brief intervention. In contrast, it appears unlikely that more seriously skills-deficient clients, such as formerly hospitalized psychiatric patients, vocational rehabilitation clients, or the chronically unemployed, could benefit from a workshop in interview training. Instead, they would require more intensive training in this area. A similar example is workshop-format social-skills training to increase the ability of high-functioning persons to handle very specific work-related situations. A group of hospital nurses might be provided with workshop training for the appropriate handling of unreasonable demands from patients;

factory supervisors could be given training in commendatory or refusal skills for use with their employees; retail-store salespersons might be provided with social-skills workshop training to assist them in approaching potential customers; and so on. Again, each of these applications is characterized by a relatively specific intended use of the goal skill, and the recipients of training presumably are not seriously skills-deficient, but instead wish to further enhance their behavior in a specific situation.

The major task of the group leader who conducts a workshop-format intervention is to incorporate basic treatment principles into a much shorter period of time. The leader who conducts the session first must objectively define the end-product goal skill, identifying those behavioral components that comprise an effective handling of the target situation. If the purpose of the workshop-type intervention is to teach a specialized application of one of the goal skills we have already discussed (e.g., job-interview training for employment-seeking students, or assertiveness for supervisory employees), skill components such as those outlined in Chapter 3 and the later specialized-skills chapters are probably relevant. On the other hand, if the workshop is intended to target some other, perhaps unusual, kind of social skill (such as the social skills needed for salespersons to effectively approach potential customers), it will be necessary for the therapist to first investigate what behaviors constitute an effective example of that skill. When the trainer has determined the specific verbal and nonverbal behaviors comprising the goal skill, the aim of the workshop will be the same as any other form of social-skills training: to teach the participants to exhibit those components in their behavior within the targeted situations.

One aspect of a social-skills training intervention that may have to be eliminated or curtailed due to time constraints is pretraining, individualized behavioral assessment of each participant. If training is to be conducted in a single and extended session, it may simply not be possible to have each client role-play individual assessment interactions or otherwise participate in an observed-behavior sample assessment. This creates a situation of uncertainty for the workshop leader, since the leader will be unaware of which behavioral components are missing in most clients' baseline performance and, therefore, which behavioral components of the goal skill will require training. If it is ever necessary for the therapist to eliminate or curtail pretraining behavioral assessment of each client, it is probably best for the therapist to assume that at least some clients will be deficient in each component that makes up the goal skill. Consequently, training attention in the workshop focuses on all components of the skill, with greatest attention and time devoted to those components deemed most critical to effective handling of the interpersonal situation in question.

When planning the workshop intervention itself, the therapist will wish to incorporate the same learning principles that characterize any other kind of social-skills training. One way to do this is to conceptualize the session in terms of time segments, and to assign attention to several of the behavioral components in each time segment. Let us consider a possible training format for a workshop intended to teach effective interview skills to job-seeking students who will soon be graduating from school. Let's further assume that the workshop is large, with 50 participants, and is conducted in a relatively short single session (2 to 3 hours), to illustrate how these principles can be used under nonoptimal conditions.

The session might begin with the leader identifying the purpose of the workshop and listing all the interview components that will receive training that day. The leader could then "group" the components into several categories. One might be "talking about oneself"; it might include such separate component behaviors as conveying detailed information about work experience, conveying information about education or training background, and conveying information about more personal interests, hobbies, and so on. A second category could be "sounding interested"; it might include the behaviors of asking relevant questions to one's interviewer, making statements that convey interest in the position, and so on. A final component category might be "nonverbal style"; it might include eye contact, posture, affect, and speech characteristics. This categorization procedure consolidates many different components, which could not be individually trained in a short period of time, into a more manageable set of three behavior classes. The first time-period of the workshop can focus explicitly on one set of behaviors, with the second period of time devoted to the next category, and so on. In essence, a category of components in this workshop is being treated as a single component would be treated in a more intensive, ongoing intervention.

Within each time-segment, the therapist can apply learning principles to the entire set of behaviors being targeted in that segment. For example, the leader might list, identify, and instruct the group in each of the separate behaviors that make up the first category. This includes providing examples of statements conveying detailed information about one's work experience, education, and interests; instructing the participants in ways to answer interviewer questions on these matters, or in how to spontaneously offer this information to the interviewer even if it is not specifically requested; focusing on reasons why it is important to convey these kinds of information in an interview; and so on. This part of the workshop corresponds to the provisions of the instruction/rationale portion of the social-skills training sessions discussed previously.

Next, the leader provides modeling exposure for the participants, using either a live-model interview or a videotape modeling film of an ideal interview. Clients are asked to note how the model exhibits not just a single behavioral component, but each of the components in the category receiving attention in that portion of the workshop. Other modeling techniques described earlier might also be incorporated at this point of the session.

Behavior rehearsal must also be included in workshop training to permit each participant the opportunity to practice the category of components being targeted at that time. Since it is improbable that a single session-leader or even several leaders can observe or interact with all clients in a large workshop, participants might be grouped in threes for behavior rehearsal. As we discussed earlier, one member of each triad can serve as interviewer in a role-play job interview, following a list of standard interview questions from a written script provided by the therapist. A second person can act as the applicant; it will be this client who is actually practicing the skill behavior. The third member of the triad can function as observer of the role-play and provide feedback, reinforcement, or suggestions to the role-play applicant following the practice interview. Members of the triad rotate roles during the rehearsal phase, perhaps with the therapist circulating among all triads to join in the practice observation and judge when most clients have mastered the category of behaviors under attention.

When this phase of the workshop session is completed, the leader can reconvene the entire group and move on to the next category of components, training these in the same way as the first category (with instruction/rationale, modeling, breaking the group down for triad rehearsal with feedback, and so on).

The reader may note that this procedure is not fundamentally different from the individual and group training models described previously. All involve training identified behavioral components of the goal skill in cumulative fashion and all involve the application of the same learning principles to accomplish this aim. Workshop-format training does so in a more consolidated, compressed fashion, often with relatively less attention given to the assessment of each individual client. Whenever possible, workshop interventions should also include attention to skills generalization, since the requirement that clients generalize their skills to the natural setting is as important here as in any other form of social-skills training.

To summarize, accelerating skills-training into one or two sessions, although time-efficient, has limited utility. It is not a training method of choice for enhancing the interpersonal repertoire of most skills-deficient persons such as clinical populations, mental health center clients, unassertive persons, extremely shy and socially anxious individuals, or those needing individualized training. It may be a suitable format for teaching very situationally specific skills to high-functioning groups when more ongoing and intensive training cannot feasibly be conducted.

Chapter 5

Assessing the Effect of Social-Skills Interventions

The 1980s have been termed "the decade of the empirical clinician" (Association for the Advancement of Behavior Therapy, 1980). In part, this designation points out the need for therapists to objectively assess the effectiveness of their treatment interventions. Certainly, most behavioral practitioners who conduct social-skills training are interested in empirically scrutinizing the impact of this training. However, there has often been a schism between the research literature on a treatment method, which includes very heavy reliance on experimental control and precise measurement, and clinical applications of the same treatment, under conditions where there may be only minimal attention to objective evaluation. There are a number of practical reasons why empirical, controlled treatment assessment is made difficult in applied or direct-service settings. These may include the policies of the setting, which often stress service-provision but do not have clinical research as an agency priority; an absence of the staff support or staff time needed to carefully evaluate treatment effectiveness; a lack of clients to serve as members of a control group for group treatment evaluation; and setting policies that prohibit the assignment of any client to a control or comparison group. For these as well as other reasons, therapists in applied settings often come to think of any systematic treatment evaluation as research, and of research as something that they cannot do.

On the other hand, virtually no practitioner consistently utilizes any form of treatment in the absence of information at least *suggesting* that the treatment works. In its most basic form, a data source upon which most therapists rely is client verbal self-report. If a client reports difficulty in some life area early in treatment, but then in later treatment reports that those difficulties have abated, the therapist is using one data source, client verbal reports, pretreatment and posttreatment to infer that behavior change has occurred. The therapist often further infers that the intervening treatment was responsible for client reports of improvement, and the therapist's own use of the treatment technique is reinforced by the reported improvement in client functioning. This sort of rudimentary, casual treatment evaluation is used by virtually all practitioners, regardless of orientation, during the course of their applied interventions. Unfortunately, there are a large number of limiting factors associated with casual treatment evaluations. For example, the data source is limited to the client's subjective reports, which may not be behaviorally accurate and are very susceptible to bias. If, indeed, improvement has occurred, it may be due to events other than treatment that interceded between the early and late client reports (Campbell & Stanley, 1963).

There are a wide range of more objective methods for assessing the impact of a social-skills training intervention, either with a single client or with a group of clients. The choice of treatment evaluation method depends largely on the aims of the therapist. In some instances, a therapist may simply be interested in answering the question: "Is my client now better in handling interpersonal situations than he or she was before the intervention?" In other instances, the therapist may wish to elaborate this question to answer both whether the client is more interpersonally skilled following an intervention *and* whether this improvement is definitely the result of the training intervention itself. Either of these evaluation questions can be dealt with in an objective fashion in any social-skills training project, often without the need for extensive expenditures of staff time, equipment, or special resources. In addition, treatment assessment procedures are available that can permit a therapist to rigorously evaluate the effectiveness of individual or group social-skills training without the need for untreated control groups.

In this chapter, we will consider two major topics relevant to evaluating the effectiveness of social-skills training: measures or sources of data that convey objective information on client social functioning, and methods for interpreting these data to answer treatment evaluation questions. In all cases, it will be assumed that training occurs in an applied setting, and the intervention-assessment procedures to be described will be those that can most feasibly be incorporated in applied training.

Measures from Which the Outcome of the Training Intervention Can Be Determined

In any form of treatment-effectiveness evaluation, it is necessary to assess the quality of client social behavior on multiple occasions. As we will see later in this chapter, one of the simplest, although least rigorous, assessment methods is simply to compare clients' pretraining social-skill behavior with their social effectiveness subsequent to training. In other intervention-assessment designs, social-skill measures are taken at different points during the intervention period. However, regardless of the kind of intervention evaluation and its rigor or stringency, it is always necessary to obtain measures of the client's social-skill behavior at various points in time. If the therapist can establish that client change indicative of more effective social-skill functioning has occurred, the therapist will be in a position to know conclusively that the client's interpersonal skill repertoire has been enhanced.

A number of data sources can provide the therapist with important information on change in client social skills as a result of treatment. These include: (1) objective ratings of client performance during sample interactions in the training setting; (2) global ratings of overall social competence during sample interactions; (3) paper-and-pencil self-report inventories completed by the client, which describe his or her comfort and behavior during social interactions; (4) detailed self-monitoring information provided by the client on social behavior outside the therapy setting; and (5) direct observation of the effectiveness of client social behavior in the natural environment. The reader may note that a number of these measures were discussed earlier in Chapter 3, when we considered initial assessment of the skills-deficient client. This is because many of the same measures used in pretraining client assessment can be repeated at later times to evaluate the client's response to the intervention package. Let us now consider each of these measures and how they can be used to evaluate client response to a training intervention.

Objective Ratings of Client Performance During Sample Interactions in the Training Setting

Behavioral assessment of a client's social skills during role-plays of troublesome situations and during semistructured or unstructured sample interactions was suggested earlier as a desirable clinical method for evaluating specific deficits in the way a client interacts with other people. The purpose of initial or pretraining assessment was to identify behavioral skill-components that the client failed to exhibit, or failed to exhibit appropriately, during the observed sample interactions. Further, the role of the therapist was to rate the client's performance in these sample interactions, and to specifically and objectively evaluate the degree to which the client exhibited each behavioral component that contributes to an effective, skilled response.

One direct way to assess the impact of the training intervention is to repeat the same sample interactions at later times, and to thereby determine whether the client now exhibits those behaviors that had previously been deficient. Utilizing client performance in contrived or sample interactions requires that several conditions be met. The assessment situations used later in the intervention must be comparable to those used before the intervention began in order for client skill-change to be meaningfully evaluated. For example, if eight role-play scenes are used during initial pretraining client assessment, the therapist will want to use the same role-play scenes, or scenes comparable to those initially used, for later assessment. If client behavior during a semistructured 5-minute conversation is used during the initial assessment phase, the same interaction format would be undertaken later to evaluate change in conversational skills.

A second requirement for using client simulated-interaction performance as a dependent measure to assess an intervention's effect is that the same behavioral components be objectively measured on each occasion that the interaction is evaluated. This can be accomplished by rating the client's interactions for the presence or frequency of each behavioral component; rating forms such as those presented in Chapter 3 and in Chapters 6–10 are suitable for this purpose. If the therapist rates a baseline (or pretreatment) assessment interaction on eight component behaviors, and later in the intervention rates client performance in comparable interactions on the same eight components, it is possible to objectively identify change on any of them. For example, the therapist would be able to report that on one occasion, a client made eye contact with the partner approximately 10% of his speaking time. By rating the same component in a later interaction, the therapist could determine that eye contact was now 80%. In an initial assessment of job-interview role-play, the therapist might find that a skills-deficient client made three statements conveying information about her work background to the interviewer partner; when the same role-play interview is repeated later, fourteen such statements might be tallied over the course of the interaction. A similar behavior-change analysis can be conducted on virtually any other social-skill component, provided it can be rated from the client's performance.

It is often unnecessary to plan special and extra times when client performance in sample interactions will be conducted to obtain this information. One very feasible way to incorporate objective evaluation of skills competency into an ongoing intervention is by rating client performance during the behavior-rehearsal or practice interactions that are already a part of each training session. Evaluating client use of behavioral skill-components during client "in-session" rehearsal has been an approach widely used in the social-skills training research literature. For example, Frederiksen, Jenkins, Foy, and Eisler (1976) taught appropriate assertion skills to two individually treated psychiatric patients who were deficient in this capability. In each training session, clients received instruction, modeling exposure, feedback, and reinforcement in a manner similar to that outlined in Chapter 4. The form of behavior-rehearsal used in each session was having the client role-play assertive responses with a confederate, who played the part of an antagonist; a group of the same role-play scenes were used in all sessions. By objectively rating the client's practice performance each day on all component behaviors under study, Frederiksen et al. were able to objectively determine that the client improved on such components as eye contact, making appropriate behavior-change requests to the antagonist, and so on. Because role-play practice was an important clinical aspect of each training session, the only added "cost" to obtain this objective information on the intervention's success was having an observer rate the client's practice in each session.

A similar approach has been used to obtain treatment-effectiveness data for other types of skills-training interventions. For example, Furman et al. (1979) conducted job-interview skills-training and, as part of every session, had each client practice a standard role-play job interview. Thus, the role-play interview represented the practice or rehearsal "ingredient" of each training session. These investigators audiotaped the practice interviews and were then able to count the frequency that the clients exhibited each component-behavior in their practice on various occasions throughout training. Once again, the clients did not have to do anything out of the ordinary during the session for the purpose of obtaining this data; all that was required was for the therapist to develop a procedure to objectively rate the client's role-play job-interview performance in each session. By keeping notes, completing a component-behavior rating-form while observing the client's live practice, or tape-recording the practice performance of clients during their rehearsal interactions, the therapist can combine client rehearsal with objective assessment of the quality of that rehearsal. Specific data on client behavior-change can thereby be obtained as part of the natural course of a skills-training intervention.

Global Ratings of Overall Social Competence During Sample Interactions

By rating a client's practice during simulated role-plays and semistructured or unstructured interactions, it is possible for the therapist to objectively determine whether a client exhibits those specific, individual component behaviors that comprise a socially skilled handling of the practice interaction. At the end of an entire conversational skills-training intervention, the therapist might rate the behavior of a client during an 8-minute conversation with a partner and determine that all trained components are present in the client's interaction: good eye contact (about 80%) is present, the client's rated affect and frequency of smiles are relatively high, the client directs 14 appropriate conversational questions to her partner, makes 28 statements conveying appropriate personal information to the partner, and so on. All of these are much higher than they were during comparable 8-minute assessment conversations that had been conducted before training took place. Does this confirm that the client is now a skilled conversationalist, at least in the practice setting?

In preceding chapters, we noted that social-skills interventions train a final desired goal skill by teaching each of the behaviors of which it is comprised. Therefore, one would expect that when a client exhibits all necessary behavioral components of that goal skill in his or her handling of an interaction, the client would be judged favorably on the global skill as well. However, this is an assumption whose validity must be empirically checked. Wolf and his colleagues (Minkin et al., 1976; Wolf, 1978), as well as Kazdin (1977) have pointed out the importance of socially validating the outcome of behavioral-treatment interventions. One aspect of the validation process is demonstrating that when an individual engages in a set of trained behaviors, that person is then more proficient in the global or overall skill that was the original purpose of training. In essence, this aspect of evaluation seeks to relate change in specific behaviors to corresponding change in overall social impact. Without such confirmation, there is the potential risk that an intervention might change certain discrete behaviors, but leave the client fundamentally unchanged in the overall skill that was the original target for intervention.

In an applied training intervention, data on the social validity of treatment can be obtained by establishing that clients are more proficient in the goal skill based upon improved global, subjective judgments of their social competency. In the assertion-training literature, investigators have often asked an observer not only to rate the occurrence or frequency of specific behavioral skill-components during client rehearsal, but also to evaluate how assertive the client behaved based on a global judgment. Whenever possible, this judgment should be made by someone other than the therapist, since the therapist's global judgment of client overall competency in a practice interaction will likely be biased. A number of skills-training interventions have had the practice partner, with whom a client actually interacts during behavior rehearsal in sessions, rate the overall skill shown by the client during the interaction they just completed (cf. Goldsmith & McFall, 1975; Falloon, Lindley, McDonald, & Marks, 1977; Argyle, Trower, & Bryant, 1974). These ratings can be made by asking the confederate partner to complete rating scales, such as an anchored 7-point scale, to describe the client's effectiveness in the interaction. In a conversational training project, partners could be asked to rate the client's *overall* performance (from *1 = extremely poor* to *7 = extremely good*) on such dimensions as conversational pleasantness, ease of interaction, the amount of interest shown by the client in the partner, and overall conversational ability of the client as assessed by the partner. For other types of social skills, different appropriate global criteria can be utilized.

It may be possible to have outside judges evaluate the client's global performance during selected practice interactions. For example, in the Urey et al. (1979) heterosocial-skills training project, male clients were taught how to appropriately meet and interact with unfamiliar females. To establish the social validity of the training outcome, different female judges were asked to listen to audiotape recordings of each client's pretreatment assessment interactions with the partner, as well as later posttraining conversations when clients were exhibiting the component behaviors that had been taught to them. The female judges who listened to the tapes were nonprofessional staff unaware of the purpose of training; thus, their subjective evaluations of client social skill were unbiased and approximated the way a naive female observer might respond to the client's behavior. The judges were asked to complete several global skill-evaluation questions using 7-point scales, to rate the client's overall skill, the interest-value of the interaction, how eager the judge might be to herself talk to the male heard on the tape (who was the client), and so on. Because the judges consistently rated posttraining tapes more positively on these subjective dimensions than pretraining tapes, the investigators obtained information confirming that clients not only engaged in objective heterosocial-skill component behaviors more often after training, but that they also were seen as "better" conversationalists in a more global, subjective sense. A very similar global assessment procedure has been used in studies on job-interview training (Furman et al., 1979; Kelly, Laughlin, Claiborne, & Patterson, 1979; Kelly, Wildman, & Berler, 1980). Here, tape recordings of clients' pretraining and posttraining role-played practice job interviews were presented to genuine personnel managers for their evaluation. The managers rated such dimensions as the candidate's (client's) overall quality of work experience, the vocational ambitiousness of the client, the enthusiasm shown by the client in working, and whether the manager listening to the role-play would actually hire this person based on the interview. Whenever the therapist uses outside or naive judges to evaluate global or subjective aspects of a client's skill, it is of course essential that the client give permission for a person uninvolved in treatment to hear or observe the interaction, so as not to violate client confidentiality.

Up to this point, we have always stressed the need for social-skills interventions to assess and train very objective, "molecular" behavioral components of the goal skills. Here we turn our attention back to the "molar" aspects of socially skilled behavior and ask whether, in a global and subjective sense, the client appears more proficient in the overall goal skill that was the target for training. If so, the social validity and applied impact of the treatment intervention will be better substantiated.

Paper-and-Pencil Self-Report Inventories of Social Skill

When client pretraining assessment techniques were discussed in Chapter 3, it was noted that most paper-and-pencil client self-report inventories of social skill yield only general information on the individual's behavior in interpersonal situations. For example, it is essentially impossible to learn from self-report inventory scores what exact situations are troublesome for a given client or how that client objectively behaves in those situations. Thus, they are of limited utility in planning the exact social-skills training that a client will require or the precise skill behaviors that will need to be covered in the intervention. Further, social-skill self-report inventories yield information on how the client feels in social interactions or how the client reports behaving, not on how the individual objectively acts.

For some of the same reasons that self-report measures of social skills do not yield extremely specific data on the training requirements of skills-deficient clients, they can be a useful ancillary data source for the overall evaluation of an intervention. This is the case for reasons similar to those that we just discussed in the section on global, subjective evaluations of social competence. With global evaluations of interpersonal competence, a subjective judgment of the client's overall handling of a practice interaction is being made by some external, observing judge—the confederate partner, a naive observer, someone naive to the treatment but "expert" in evaluating that social skill, such as a personnel interviewer rating role-played job interview performance, etc. When client self-report measures of social skill are administered, we are asking the client to subjectively evaluate his or her own handling of interpersonal situations. Ordinarily, self-report inventories do not require the client to detail behavior in one particular situation, but instead "tap" the respondent's perceptions of how a certain kind of situation is usually handled or how he or she ordinarily feels in that kind of situation.

It is important to note that while paper-and-pencil inventories of social skill may be scored or quantified in an objective manner, the data source is actually the client's self-perception or description of his characteristic behavior. Self-report scores may not always correspond, for example, to objective observations of component skill behaviors made by the therapist observing practice interactions or even with global, subjective judgments of social competency made by an external observer (see Mischel, 1968). However, inventories can provide the therapist with very useful, albeit generalized, data on a client's cognitive evaluation or personal perception of his own typical behavior in certain types of situations, such as interactions requiring assertiveness, or social initiation. Since treatment assumes that clients' self-appraisals will become more positive as the result of their developing new behavioral skills and as the result of direct cognitive-modification aspects of training, this perceptual change should be reflected by more positive self-report inventory scores.

A variety of social-skills self-report inventories have been developed and reported in the clinical research literature during the past several years. Table 5.1 lists some of these scales, their publication sources, and brief descriptions of each. Chapters 6, 7, and 8, which respectively concern conversational-skills training, date-initiation, and assertion-training, include reprinted copies of several of these inventories. In general, self-report inventories focus upon: (1) the respondent's description of his or her current behavior in a certain kind of situation, such as the Wolpe-Lazarus Assertiveness Questionnaire or the Rathus Assertiveness Schedule, both of which measure reported behavior in situations where assertive responses are appropriate; or (2) reported feelings, cognitions, or fears in certain kinds of interpersonal interactions, such as the Fear of Negative Evaluations Inventory or the Social Avoidance and Distress Scale. The therapist could select scales that appear to most closely tap those dimensions of interest in the treatment invervention evaluation.

Self-Monitoring of Social Behavior Data

When we considered the initial client assessment that occurs in the planning stages of a social-skills training intervention, as well as the generalization programming that occurs late in treatment, the utility of client self-monitoring data was noted. Self-monitoring information differs from self-report inventory measures in several ways. First, monitoring data are more behaviorally specific; the client is asked to record and briefly describe specific social interactions that actually occur in the natural environment. These might be occasions when the client behaved assertively (or wanted to), initiated a conversation with a member of the opposite sex (or wanted to), and so on. Usually, other specific situational information is obtained for each recorded incident, including where it occurred, who the other person was, how the client behaved or felt, and what outcome was achieved. A second difference between self-report inventories and self-monitoring data involves the manner and time-frame for which the client provides information. An inventory is completed in one sitting and the respondent retrospectively describes how he or she usually behaves, but over a generally unspecified period of time. On the hand, the self-monitoring data are completed in an ongoing or continual manner. The individual can be asked to make entries concerning each day's social situations in a self-monitoring diary at the end of that day, or can even be asked to carry a note pad for recording information about relevant situations immediately after they have been encountered. For these reasons, self-monitoring data are both specific in terms of the situations recorded and the time interval over which they occur.

An important reason for the therapist to collect and keep client self-monitoring records is to better assess whether the individual's social interactions in the natural environment have changed over the course of the intervention. In some respects, this may be the single most significant measure of treatment effectiveness that can be obtained, since it provides relatively specific behavioral data from the natural environment and, except when it is possible for the therapist to directly observe client social behavior outside of the training setting, it can be the best source of available in-vivo behavior-change information. Self-monitoring data can be analyzed in several ways, depending on the specificity of records kept by the client and the aims of the therapist. When

TABLE 5.1. Self-Report Inventories Commonly Used in Social-Skills Training

Inventory Name & Reference Source	Brief Description
Social Avoidance and Distress Scale (SAD)[a]—Watson & Friend, 1969	Assesses the respondent's negative emotions in social interactions (tension, anxiety), and tendency to avoid those interactions.
Fear of Negative Evaluations Scale (FNE)—Watson & Friend, 1969	Assesses the respondent's fear or oversensitivity to the opinions and evaluations of others.
The Situation Questionnaire—Rehm & Marston, 1968	Assesses the respondent's degree of discomfort in date-related social interactions; item content makes it suitable for males only.
Survey of Heterosexual Interactions (SHI)[b]—Twentyman & McFall, 1975	Assesses the respondent's degree of discomfort in date-related social interactions; item content makes it suitable for males only.
Survey of Heterosexual Interactions for Females (SHI–F)—Williams & Ciminero, 1978	Similar to SHI, but item content makes it appropriate for females only.
Assertion Inventory—Gambrill & Richey, 1975	Assesses the respondent's refusal and commendatory assertive skills; separate scales to evaluate discomfort when behaving assertively and avoidance of situations requiring assertiveness.
Rathus Assertiveness Schedule (RAS)—Rathus, 1973	Assesses the respondent's refusal assertive skill; does not tap expression of commendatory assertiveness.
College Self-Expression Scale (CSES)—Galassi, Deleo, Galassi, & Bastien, 1974	Assesses the respondent's assertive skill along with three dimensions: refusal skill, commendatory skill, and "self-denial" (overapologizing, excessive concern for how others feel, etc.).
Wolpe-Lazarus Assertiveness Questionnaire—Wolpe & Lazarus, 1966	Assesses the respondent's refusal- and commendatory-assertive skill.

[a]The Social Avoidance and Distress Scale (SAD) is reproduced as Figure 6.2 in this book (p. 146).

[b]The Survey of Heterosexual Interactions (SHI) is reproduced as Figure 7.2 in this book (p. 161).

training is intended to increase the frequency with which a client initiates positive social interactions in the natural environment, such as date-related or conversational initiations, the number of times that these interactions take place can be examined by the therapist. For example, the therapist might find that early in treatment, a heterosocially deficient client monitored both date-initiations and actual dates over a 2-week period. The records indicated that one date-initiation attempt took place, but no actual dates occurred. At some point late in the intervention, over a comparable 2-week period, the client brings in self-monitoring records showing that five initiations occurred and resulted in four actual dates. Thus, the therapist has obtained self-monitoring information indicative of more successful in-vivo dating behavior, both in terms of dating-related social approaches and actual dates.

Another type of self-monitoring data analysis takes into account the number of occasions when a trained skill was successfully used in proportion to the total number of occasions when the client reported wanting to use the skill. An example of this in an assertion-training intervention is having the client record all situations when he or she wanted to behave assertively, along with a description of how each of those situations was actually handled. During a one-week period prior to or early in training, a skills-deficient client might bring in self-monitoring records showing six different times when the individual felt the need to be assertive, but no occasions when assertive responses were made (yielding a total of zero). During a comparable time interval subsequent to training, the therapist might determine from self-monitoring data that the amount of assertive responses in situations deemed by the client to require assertiveness increased to 75%.

For self-monitoring data to be systematically used in treatment evaluation, the therapist must have the client bring recording forms to training sessions. This, in turn, requires that the client diligently make self-monitoring record entries on a daily basis for whatever time intervals the therapist is examining (e.g., one week before training and one week at the conclusion of formal training; for two weeks before and two weeks after the training intervention; continuously throughout the intervention). However, client record-keeping of this type can present practical difficulties. One of the primary problems is that self-monitoring of day-to-day social interactions over an extended period of time can be hard for even well-motivated clients to perform. Client compliance in gathering self-monitoring information can be enhanced by providing them with forms on which to record their social interactions, by asking clients to keep only necessary details in the monitoring notes, by stressing that these records are an important part of treatment, and by directly reinforcing clients for bringing accurately completed self-monitoring forms to the session. Even with these steps taken, the therapist should be aware that self-monitoring of in-vivo social interactions is high in "response cost" to the client; for practical reasons it may be necessary to limit the use of this data source to selected time phases, such as pretraining and posttraining, rather than use it continuously throughout the intervention.

Self-monitoring-based data are susceptible to several forms of bias. Over time, some clients may become "fatigued" and devote less attention to recording the occurrence or details of in-vivo social interactions than they had early in the self-monitoring phase. This can result in their "missing" certain interactions that would have been recorded previously. On the other hand, clients can also become more proficient in self-monitoring critical in-vivo events as they acquire more experience in this procedure, artifactually inflating the number and nature of the entries in their records as time progresses. Additionally, altered client perception of social interactions or of their own performance in those interactions is likely to accompany social-skills training, and may bias the objective accuracy of self-monitored reports of behavior. For example, at the conclusion of training, the therapist and client devote substantial time to the discussion of in-vivo situations in which the trained skill can be applied. This treatment attention to applications of the skill, and perhaps a desire to please the therapist, could affect the client's accuracy of self-monitoring. However, in spite of these limitations, data derived from client self-monitoring records may represent one of the most viable ways for the therapist to evaluate the impact and generalization of the training intervention.

Direct Observation of Client Social Behavior in the Natural Environment

Self-monitoring of data utilizes the client as observer of his or her own social behavior when it is impossible for the therapist or other external observer to function in this day-to-day role. When we considered client pretraining assessment methods, we noted that client social behavior in the natural environment can also be directly observed when: (1) the natural environment is observationally accessible; (2) the social interactions of interest are naturally occurring at either a high rate or on a predictable basis, so that the observer will be in a position to monitor them; (3) the staff trained to conduct such social-skill observations are available. These criteria are usually met most successfully within residential settings or schools.

If it is logistically possible to conduct in-vivo behavioral observations of client social skills in the natural environment as a part of initial pretraining assessment, it should also be possible to repeat the observational methodology later to determine behavior-change in the same setting. Gutride, Goldstein, and Hunter (1973) and Jaffe and Carlson (1976) observed the social behavior of institutionalized psychiatric patients during mealtimes in the residential setting as an in-vivo dependent measure of training effectiveness. In these studies, trained observers evaluated the presence or absence of specific conversational skill component-behaviors during every 30-second interval (Gutride et al., 1973) or 10-second interval (Jaffe & Carlson, 1976), while the client was seated at the dinner table with other clients. The investigators were able to associate training with increased rates of such behaviors as conversational verbal content, eye contact, forward learning, and initiations of dialogue within the natural environment.

When they can be accomplished, direct and quantified observations of client social behavior in the natural setting represent an ideal source of information on the effectiveness of training. Provided that specific observations are reliably made by trained observers, the therapist can gain information about whether the client is actually exhibiting new skill behaviors in the intended natural environment. The in-vivo observational assessment procedures described in Chapter 3 are also applicable when using this technique as a data source for evaluating the intervention's success. In addition, several other procedural points must be emphasized when in-vivo observations are repeated on multiple occasions for treatment evaluation purposes. The first involves setting or situational comparability whenever in-vivo observations are made. If a client's social interactions are observed in a specific setting, such as at mealtime or during on-ward free time, on one set of occasions before training occurs, any later set of observations must also be made under the same situational conditions. The more dissimilar the situational conditions in terms of location, activity, other persons present in the observational setting, time of day, and so on, from one set of observations to the next, the less will be any potential for interpreting behavior-change across those different periods.

A second important factor when conducting repeated in-vivo observations involves the client reacting to the person observing the social interactions. Let us assume that a therapist plans to observe an inpatient's conversational behavior in a ward dayroom setting before, and again following, a conversational-skills training intervention, to determine any change in the nature and frequency of the individual's interactions. One of the therapists is present in the dayroom setting each afternoon from 3:30–4:00 p.m. when the client is there, and the observer rates various behavioral components present in the client's interactions during this period. The measure is obtained daily for one week before, and again one week after, the training intervention. As much as is possible, all conditions within the dayroom setting are comparable during pretraining and posttraining in-vivo assessment. However, during the post-training observation phase, the client may notice the therapist in one part of the dayroom and, because of the therapist's presence alone, will be "reminded" to engage in the behavior. Presumably, the observer here serves as a cue for the client to engage in the trained skills; if the observer were not present in the setting, the client might not use the newly trained skills. In this case, the observer functions as a discriminative stimulus, and it is the observer's presence in the setting that governs whether or not the individual will exhibit socially skilled behavior. This phenomenon might lead to distorted and artifactual evidence of improved posttreatment social skills. Ways to minimize this problem include surreptitious observation so that the client is unaware that he or she is being watched, or observation conducted by some person other than a therapist involved in the training procedure itself, who is therefore less likely to serve as a discriminative stimulus for skill behavior.

The use of direct observation procedures in the natural environment to measure socially skilled behavior-change accompanying a treatment intervention is a highly desirable information source when these data can be feasibly collected. The reader unfamiliar with in-vivo observational rating procedures who plans to utilize such data to evaluate training may wish to consult a specialized reference source that describes direct observation methodology (see Cone & Hawkins, 1977; Hersen & Bellack, 1976; Keefe, Kopel, & Gordon, 1978).

The Desirability of Multiple Measures to Evaluate Social-Skills Training Effects

There is an old Indian fable concerning six blind men who came upon a strange beast which, in fact, was an elephant. Each of the men had heard of elephants, but none had actually seen one. In order to understand what this large animal was like, the men approached the elephant and each one grasped part of it.

The first blind man put out his hand and touched the side of the elephant. "How smooth! An elephant is like a wall."

The second blind man put out his hand and touched the trunk of the elephant. "How round! An elephant is like a snake."

The third blind man put out his hand and touched the tusk of the elephant. "How sharp! An elephant is like a spear."

The fourth blind man put out his hand and touched the leg of the elephant. "How tall! The elephant is like a tree."

The fifth blind man reached out his hand and touched the ear of the elephant. "How wide! An elephant is like a fan."

The sixth blind man put out his hand and touched the tail of the elephant. "How thin! An elephant is like a rope."

Shortly, the six men began quarreling over the appearance of an elephant and attracted the attention of a wise Rajah who then spoke to them:

"The elephant is a big animal. Each man touched only one part. You must put all the parts together to find out what an elephant is like."*

A similar set of circumstances confronts the therapist who wants to obtain information on the effectiveness of a social-skills training intervention. Because any form of social competency is a complex phenomenon, there is no single measure from which the therapist can infer that significant behavior-change has occurred. Objectively rating the presence of exhibited skill-component behaviors during a client's practice interactions is desirable because of its "molecular" orientation; the therapist can see whether or not the client exhibits those discrete components that had been taught in the intervention. However, it is limited because it is based on behavior sampled in the training setting and also because it does not directly evaluate the global adequacy of the client's skill. Obtaining judgments of overall client social competence during practice interactions can provide subjective, global evidence of improvement, but does not relate this to specific client social behaviors, and is still a measure based on performance in the practice setting rather than the natural environment. Self-report inventories usefully tap a client's self-perception, description, and feelings about his or her social behavior, but are subject to behavioral inaccuracy and situational nonspecificity. Self-monitoring data and direct observation of client skills in the natural environment are excellent in-vivo measures, but require considerable effort on the part of the client in self-monitoring or the treatment staff in direct observation; additionally, direct in-vivo observation procedures may be almost impossible to conduct when the client is not in a confined setting of some kind.

Ideally, the therapist examining the effectiveness of an intervention will select several types of measures to use in treatment evaluation and thereby be able to detect changes in clients' specific behavioral repertoire during practice interactions, their global improvement in practice as evaluated by impartial observers, their inventory-based self-reports of social functioning, and improved skill during troublesome situations in the natural environment based on self-monitoring or observational data. To the extent that these different types of measures are incorporated in treatment evaluation and, taken together, confirm improved social skills, the therapist can be confident that the intervention was successful. Further, this confidence will be based on empirical data from a variety of measurement sources.

*From Quigley, L. *The Blind Men and the Elephant*. New York: Charles Scribner's Sons, 1959. Copyright 1959 by Charles Scribner's Sons. Reprinted by permission.

On the other hand, it is possible that measures such as those described in this section will yield contradictory information on client improvement. This can also be quite useful, since it provides important treatment information on areas requiring further training attention that would never have been detected if careful evaluation of training effectiveness were not conducted. One set of inconsistencies might exist between objective ratings of component-behaviors present in a client's practice interactions and more global, subjective evaluation of overall skill competency. For example, let us assume that late in a conversational-skills training intervention, the therapist evaluates a client's 8-minute practice conversation and determines that all the component-behaviors targeted in treatment are being exhibited correctly and at reasonable rates during the interaction. The therapist might then ask an impartial observer, such as another staff person at the center where training takes place, to evaluate an audiotape of the client's performance on more subjective criteria, in the manner described earlier in this chapter. The therapist finds that the global evaluation is not extremely positive and does not validate the proposition that the client's performance reflects skilled behavior. Assuming that the judge's global evaluation is reliable and nonidiosyncratic (which could be determined by having additional judges also rate the tape recording), it would suggest that some elements of the client's conversational behavior still need training attention. If this occurred, the therapist might seek to determine what aspects of the conversation or what behaviors by the client led to the negative overall-competence evaluation by the external judges. Additional training attention could then be focused upon those aspects.

Another type of outcome data inconsistency that might occur is between self-monitoring records or direct in-vivo observations and the client's proficiency during behavioral practice in the training setting. If it is apparent that the client can effectively handle in-session practice interactions, but data from the natural environment indicate that troublesome situations are still avoided or handled ineffectively, this would suggest to the therapist that more attention to generalization is needed.

The important point in each of these examples is that careful attention to intervention-assessment serves much more than abstract "research" purposes. *It provides the therapist with empirical information of clinical importance on the success of training and on trouble-points that still may require additional attention.* Without treatment-evaluation measures, it is unlikely that the therapist would be in a position to accurately gauge the impact of the intervention.

Treatment Evaluation Designs for Applied Settings

To this point, we have considered measures that can provide information on social-skill behavior. However, planning the evaluation of a training intervention involves not only selecting appropriate sources of data, but also determining when data will be obtained. In large part, the times when social-skill data are collected determine the rigor of the treatment-evaluation design and the questions that can be answered on client behavior-change as a result of the intervention. We will now turn our attention to several treatment-evaluation designs that can be used in applied settings, both for individually treated clients and for group social-skills training interventions. There are, of course, an extremely large number of experimental research designs capable of analyzing the effect of social-skills training. In this chapter, only a limited number of evaluation strategies will be presented. Those discussed here will be strategies that seem most feasible within applied or direct-service settings, since that is the scope of this book. Experimental designs that require several control groups, untreated groups of clients, and treatment withdrawal or reversal procedures will not be stressed, even though they often provide superior experimental control.

Treatment Evaluation Designs for Individually Treated Clients

Three procedures that can be used to evaluate the effect of social-skills training with individually treated clients in most applied settings are: (1) pretraining and posttraining assessment on the same repeated measures; (2) the time series analysis (Campbell & Stanley, 1963); and (3) the multiple-baseline analysis (see Hersen & Barlow, 1976). The first two approaches provide the therapist with information on client behavior-change across time, but are not experimental designs and therefore cannot be used to attribute client change to the intervention itself. The single-subject multiple baseline, a more rigorous treatment evaluation methodology, does permit the attribution of client behavior-change to the intervention, for reasons we will discuss.

One-Client Pretraining and Posttraining Assessment

This represents perhaps the easiest approach to intervention assessment, because all social-skill measures are taken at only two points in time: before and again subsequent to the training. The same measures can be used on each occasion. An example of this approach might be to objectively rate client performance in the initial assessment interactions, which precede social-skills training (role-play performance, semistructured or unstructured contrived interactions), on whatever component behaviors are of interest. Subjective or global evaluations of competency in the practice interaction could be obtained. Also, the client can be asked to complete relevant self-report inventories, to self-monitor targeted social interactions in the natural environment for some period of time, and so on. All of the obtained pretraining measures are then scored or quantified. No further assessment takes place until the conclusion of training, when the same measures are re-administered and self-monitoring data are again collected by the client for an interval of time comparable to that in the pretraining period. All posttraining data sources are quantified or scored, and it is possible for the therapist to compute change on each of them. The therapist can then determine pretraining-to-posttraining changes on every component-behavior that was rated during the client's sample interactions, on global numeric ratings of overall skill in these sample interactions, on self-report measures, and on data derived from the client's self-monitoring records.

The advantages of this evaluation approach rest with its simplicity and the low amount of time and effort it requires by the therapist and the client. It also provides the therapist with objective information on client behavior change from one point in time compared with another. However, as noted by Campbell and Stanley (1963), it does not tell the therapist *why* change has occurred. Improvement may have been due to the intervention, but might also be attributed to practice effects (unrelated to the specific treatment approach), "history" or specific events outside of treatment that account for improvement (e.g., the establishment of new relationships); maturation of the client; and other factors unrelated to the intervention per se (Campbell & Stanley, 1963). Also, pretraining-to-posttraining changes for one client cannot be examined statistically for significance, so data obtained in this fashion cannot be rigorously analyzed and must be considered as essentially descriptive. While not a controlled research design, examining pretraining-to-posttraining change on social-skill measures can provide descriptive, quantified information on client behavior-change over time.

Time Series Analysis

Campbell & Stanley (1963) have described a treatment-evaluation approach for groups that can be used for an individual client as well. Termed the "time series experiment," this procedure is essentially a modification of the pretraining-to-posttraining assessment except that all measures are obtained on a number of different spaced occasions before and after the intervention. This can be represented in diagrammatic fashion as:

$$0_1 \quad 0_2 \quad 0_3 \quad 0_4 \quad X \quad 0_5 \quad 0_6 \quad 0_7 \quad 0_8$$

where each "0" or observation indicates a time when social-skills measures are taken (01–04 are all repetitions of the pretest; 05–08 are all repetitions of the posttest) and the "X" indicates the treatment intervention itself. In practice, this approach might be used when a client is assessed on each measure once weekly for four weeks before training starts and, again, once weekly for four weeks upon conclusion of the intervention.

As Campbell and Stanley point out, this approach improves upon the "one-time" pretraining and posttraining assessment method in a number of ways. Improvement due to practice alone could be detected, because it would be evident if performance improved from one pretraining assessment to another in the absence of training. However, the time series analysis still cannot rule out the possibility that external events that temporally coincide with treatment are responsible for any improvement seen in the posttraining assessments. Also, although statistical analyses of time series measures for individually treated clients have been described (Gottman, McFall, & Barnett, 1969; Kazdin, 1976), this statistical approach ordinarily requires that measures be taken on a great number of occasions, in excess of what would be practical in most applied settings. However, the therapist who wishes to evaluate skills-training intervention with somewhat greater rigor than is possible with the simple pretraining-posttraining assessment may wish to consider the time series analysis.

Multiple Baseline Analysis Across Skill-Component Behaviors

The treatment evaluation strategy known as the multiple baseline has become an extremely popular method for analyzing the effect of applied behavioral interventions, including social-skills training with individually treated clients. Originally described by Baer, Wolf, and Risley (1968), potential uses of this evaluation technique have been elaborated by other investigators (see Barlow & Hersen, 1973; Hersen & Barlow, 1976; Wolf & Risley, 1971) and have seen wide application in the skills-training literature. Several reasons for the multiple baseline's popularity are its suitability for single-client interventions, its ability to clearly establish that client behavior-change is a consequence of training, and the fact that the methodology does not require any aspect of clinical treatment to be sacrificed for experimental control purposes. Let us consider in detail an example to illustrate how this procedure can be used.

Bornstein, Bellack, and Hersen (1977) individually treated several child clients who were described as exceedingly passive, shy, and unassertive, especially when confronted with unreasonable behavior from others. Based on interview information, a number of specific interpersonal problem-situations were defined. Following techniques such as those elaborated in Chapter 3, role-play assessment scenes were constructed to approximate each potentially troublesome situation. Each role-play described a different situation and required the client to respond to antagonistic or unreasonable comments delivered by the role-play partner as though the client were actually in that situation. Client performance in the assessment role-plays was videotape recorded and rated to determine those component-behaviors of effective refusal assertiveness that were deficient. The rating procedure consisted of having an observer watch each client's role-plays and, using a rating form that listed all components of effective assertion, indicate the degree to which each behavioral component was present for each role-play scene. Major deficits were found on such components as eye contact while speaking to the partner, loudness of speech, and requesting more acceptable future behaviors from the antagonist partner. Over the next two sessions, the same assessment procedure was repeated, with each client role-playing how he or she would handle the same set of scenes. These additional assessment role-plays were also rated to determine whether the clients' responses included the refusal-assertion components. As might be expected, the same components remained deficient across all three separate assessment sessions. This demonstrated that (1) the identified components were consistently deficient in assertive responses; (2) a stable pretraining (baseline) rate could be established for each of these component deficits; and (3) the client's role-play performance did not improve over time as a result of repeated practice alone.

After the three separate role-play assessment sessions, Bornstein et al. first directed attention toward teaching one of the clients to maintain eye contact with the partner whenever speaking to him. Training sessions always included instruction, modeling, rehearsal, reinforcement, and feedback in much the same manner as described in Chapter 4. For the behavior rehearsal portion of each session, the client role-played each of six scenes that had been used in the initial assessment role-plays. If training was successful on the first day that eye contact received training attention, one would expect to find that the client more frequently exhibited this behavior during the session's role-plays. To assess this, the investigators rated each of the practice or rehearsal role-plays from the first training session and found that the targeted eye contact component had increased. During initial assessment role-plays, the client's ratio of eye contact to speech duration was zero; the client never looked at the partner during any of the six role-played scenes on the three occasions when the scenes were presented. On the first training day, ratings of the client's eye contact revealed an immediate and striking eye contact increase to 100% of speech duration time. Further, when the other deficient components were rated from role-play responses on the first training day when eye contact was targeted, it was found that they remained as deficient as they had been during pretraining assessment.

With this finding rests the essential rationale for a multiple baseline analysis. Over the course of pretraining-assessment role-plays, a stable (albeit deficient) baseline level is established for each of the component-behaviors that will later require treatment attention. In this case, the components were eye contact, speech loudness, and requests for new behavior from the partner. When training on one component is introduced, the therapist expects that an increase in this targeted component should be evident in the client's practice that day. Since other component behaviors do not receive training attention in the same session, the therapist expects (or predicts) that they will be unchanged in that session's role-plays. Further, the next component to be trained should increase in the client's practice only at the time it receives specific attention in the intervention. The third component is predicted to improve contingent upon specific training, and so forth.

Figure 5.1 is a graphed presentation of the role-play performance for one client in the Bornstein et al. (1977) project throughout the entire intervention. Each separate graph in the vertical series represents a different behavior that was to be trained. The uppermost graph is the first component to be trained, the graph below it is the second component behavior, and so on. Across the horizontal axis are sessions; the vertical axis for each separate graph indicates the range of that component behavior over the six role-played scenes. the vertical dotted line through each graph indicates the first session in which that component-behavior was specifically targeted for training. For example, in the uppermost graph, the first 3 data points are from the pretraining assessment role-plays. When training was introduced on eye contact (session 4, and actually the first training day after assessment sessions), the ratio of eye contact to speech duration increased from zero to 1.00 or 100% eye contact while speaking to the partner. Thus, the first component improved, but only contingent upon specific training in that day's session. The next two sessions continued to focus on eye contact in order to establish it even more firmly. The second skill behavior, speech loudness, was first trained in session 7, as indicated by the broken vertical line in the next lower graph. Inspecting the graph for speech loudness, we find that ratings revealed deficiency throughout its own baseline (or the entire interval until treatment attention was targeted to it), at which point this component also improved.

The multiple baseline rationale, in this case, is that when a global skill is broken down into separate and independent component-behaviors, each component should increase, but only contingent upon the introduction of specific training for it. If all components improved at the same time when only one of them was being trained, it would suggest that improvement was not due to treatment, since only one aspect of the goal skill was receiving attention. Conversely, if a component failed to increase when training was specifically targeted toward it, this would suggest that the treatment was ineffective in that session.

Now, let us consider how this evaluation design "meshes" with the skills-training intervention model described earlier. It was suggested that a final-goal social skill be broken into behavioral components and that each component sequentially receive training attention across sessions. If a relatively standard practice-interaction is included in each training session, the procedure necessary to perform a multiple baseline analysis is in place. All that is then required is for the therapist or some other observer to rate the client's performance in each session's practice interaction. This should ordinarily occur in training

FIGURE 5.1. Multiple-Baseline Analysis of Child's Role-Play Performance Before, During, and After Assertiveness Training[a]

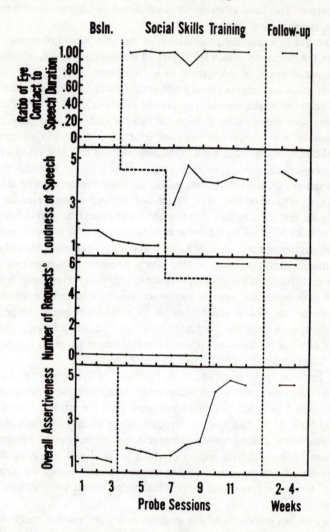

[a]From Bornstein, M. R., Bellack, A. S., & Hersen, M. "Social skills training for unassertive children: A multiple baseline analysis," *Journal of Applied Behavior Analysis*, 1977, *10*, 189. Copyright 1977 by the Society for the Experimental Analysis of Behavior, Inc. Reprinted by permission.

[b]Number of requests for more acceptable future behaviors from the antagonist partner.

sessions, since the therapist must observe the practice interaction and evaluate the presence of any targeted component-behaviors in order to provide feedback to the client. However, a quantitative observation procedure is needed in order to graph the client's performance with respect to each component-behavior in every session's practice. This can be accomplished by using a rating form such as that utilized in the evaluation of initial assessment interaction before the training phase of the intervention began.

It is noteworthy that the multiple baseline analysis used in this way only requires the therapist to objectively rate or count, and then graph, the client's practice performance in each session. Thus, it is an evaluation design well-suited to applied settings, since it does not require outside control groups, removal of any treatment, or elaborate costs in time or support. There are a number of issues related to multiple baseline methodology concerning such questions as the independence of component-behaviors, the number of training sessions per component-behavior necessary to conclusively establish its improvement, and so forth. For example, a multiple baseline analysis of this kind assumes that the component-behaviors that are separately trained are independent of one another, or uncorrelated. If two components are correlated, such as voice tone and affect ratings might be, we would expect that training on one would also cause the other to change, even when the second component was not directly treated. When conducting a multiple baseline analysis across social-skill components, it is desirable to train each behavior for several sessions. This would establish more conclusively that the targeted component demonstratably improves, while the as-yet untreated components do not improve. Additionally, while most multiple baseline data graphs are inspected visually to determine whether improvement occurred, statistical analyses for single-subject designs can be conducted. The reader interested in these issues might consult a source such as Hersen and Barlow (1976).

Finally, it is possible to combine a multiple baseline analysis of client performance during each session's practice interactions with other measures administered at the beginning and the conclusion of the entire intervention. These pretraining and posttraining measures might include self-report inventories, global evaluations of overall social competency, or self-monitoring records.

Treatment Evaluation Designs for Group Social-Skills Training

The kind of evaluation procedure used to assess the impact of a group social-skills training intervention is determined by both the degree of evaluative rigor sought by the therapist and the availability of a control group. Three of the intervention-evaluation procedures we will consider are group modifications of the pretraining-posttraining, time series analysis, and multiple-baseline-across-skill-component behavior designs just described. None of these requires control groups. Several designs that require a control group will be briefly considered.

One-Group Pretraining and Posttraining Assessment

For individually treated clients, the most rudimentary form of objective assessment is achieved by administering all skill measures—behavioral, global competency judgments, inventories, and self-monitoring records—before and again after training. This procedure can be used for all members of the social-skills training group (Campbell & Stanley, 1963). Depending on the nature of the sample social interactions used, the performance of all clients in the group might be individually observed in pretraining and posttraining interactions, such as a standard role-play job-interview or semistructured interaction. Alternatively, each client might be asked to repeat the sample interactions that had been constructed specifically for him or her, such as individualized assertion role-plays, both before and after training.

The benefits and limitations of the single-group pretraining-posttraining assessment are the same as the single-client pretraining-posttraining assessment. This procedure is time-efficient and does provide objective data on client social-behavior-change. It does not provide experimental control, since the therapist cannot determine that any observed change is a function of the treatment intervention rather than extraneous or nonspecific factors that also occurred between pretraining and posttraining assessments (Campbell & Stanley, 1963).

Time Series Analysis for Group Interventions

The time series evaluation approach of conducting a series of assessments both before and subsequent to the training intervention phase can be used for all members of a group. Here, each client who will be in the group is individually assessed on a number of occasions (e.g., weekly) on all social-skill measures. Then, after the training intervention, each client again is repeatedly assessed on the same measures that had been administered before treatment. This evaluation strategy is commended by its relatively low requirements of staff and client time and effort. Its major limitation involves the fact that observed client behavior-change, even if consistently low when sampled across all pretraining occasions and then consistently high across all posttraining occasions, still cannot be conclusively attributed to the interceding training (Campbell & Stanley, 1963).

Multiple Baseline Analysis Across Skill-Component Behaviors
When Training Is Group-Administered

The multiple baseline assessment of an individually treated client is achieved when that client's behavioral performance in a sample social interaction is observed during or following each training session. It must be demonstrated that the specific skill-component receiving training attention on a given day improves in that day's behavioral practice relative to its levels before receiving attention, while components that have not yet been targeted for treatment do not improve in practice interactions until they are specifically trained. The same multiple baseline rationale can be used to evaluate the behavior-change of individual clients when each of those clients is a member of the same social-skills training group (Kelly, 1980). This treatment evaluation approach was used in studies that were previously described. For example, in one group conversational-skills training project (Kelly, Urey, & Patterson, 1980), each client engaged in a fixed-length, semistructured conversation immediately following every group training session. In the conversations, clients were instructed to focus on exhibiting the component behavior that had received training in the immediately preceding group session. By audiotaping each client's conversation following every session, the therapist could rate the interactions for all verbal components and determine how frequently each occurred. As predicted, components always increased in the post-group conversations contingent on specific training. A similar approach has been used in group job-interview training interventions (see Kelly, Laughlin, Claiborne, & Patterson, 1979; Kelly, Wildman, & Berler, 1980). Here, the frequency with which group members exhibited verbal components during their individual, standardized job-interview role-plays after each group session was evaluated. Figure 5.2 presents a graph of the role-play interview performance of clients in the Kelly, Laughlin, Claiborne, and Patterson (1979) project. The graphic presentation shows a multiple baseline across three component-behaviors, with group training sequentially targeting: (1) directing job-related questions to an interviewer; (2) making statements conveying positive information about experience and training during an interview; and (3) verbally conveying interest or enthusiasm in the prospective position. Each line on the graph represents the performance of a given client. The target components shown in this figure generally increased during each client's individual practice role-play interviews following group training sessions, but improvement always occurred when the component was specifically given treatment attention in the group. This use of the multiple baseline is quite similar to that in individual client applications; here, treatment is administered to a group of clients rather than just one. Each client is individually assessed during his or her practice interaction during or immediately after every group session. The therapist must observe the interactions, either directly or by making recordings of them, which can be rated later. The ratings are then quantified to yield frequencies of occurrence for each component under study, so that these data can be graphed for each client. If most clients improve in their individual practice following training on the component that received group attention, the effectiveness of the intervention can be conclusively established without the need for external control groups (Kelly, 1980).

Control-Group Designs to Assess an Intervention's Effectiveness

A very wide range of rigorous intervention-evaluation designs is available to the therapist who has access to control groups against which to evaluate the performance of clients in the social-skills training group. While an exhaustive discussion of "between-groups" designs suitable for evaluating social-skills interventions is beyond the scope of this book, we might consider two of the basic control-group evaluation strategies, described by Campbell & Stanley (1963), which are feasible in some applied settings.

Nonequivalent Control-Group Design

The nonequivalent control group design requires the presence of two groups of clients, one of which will receive the social-skills training intervention and one of which will serve as the control group. In this evaluation design, clients are not randomly assigned to the skills-training or control group. Thus, if a group of individuals has been selected to receive skills-training and some other, similar group of clients already exists in the treatment setting, the latter group can serve as controls. As noted by Campbell and Stanley, it is desirable for skills-training and control-group clients to resemble or be matched with one another as closely as possible on any characteristics that might affect their social functioning. However, because clients are not randomly assigned to the two groups, the design is not as rigorous as when random assignment is used. Its chief virtue is that this is a control-group treatment-evaluation design that can represent a reasonable compromise between true experimental control and the practical realities that often operate in applied treatment settings.

In this evaluation strategy, all clients in both the skills-training and control group are administered all skill measures before the intervention takes place. These measures might include assessment role-plays, sample interactions, self-report inventories, data achieved through self-monitoring or direct in-vivo observations, and so on. Then, clients in the skills-training group receive their entire intervention while clients in the control group receive either no training or some other form of non-social-skills treatment. At the conclusion of this phase, all clients from both groups are re-administered each of the same

FIGURE 5.2. Multiple-Baseline Analysis of Performance in Role-Played Job Interviews[a]

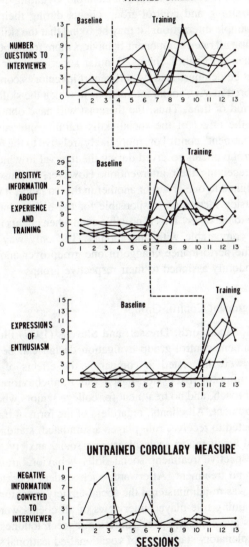

[a]From Kelly, J. A., Laughlin, C., Claiborne, M., & Patterson, J. "A group procedure for teaching job interviewing skills to formerly hospitalized psychiatric patients," *Behavior Therapy*, 1979, *10*, 306. Reprinted by permission.

measures that had been used at pretest. Based upon statistically analyzed changes on each measure for both the skills-training and control groups, the therapist will be in a position to evaluate skill-improvement in the treatment group relative to the control group. For example, by rating the performance of social-skills training and control-group clients during their pretraining and posttraining sample interactions, it may be found that the skills-training group members exhibit all rated component-behaviors more frequently at posttraining assessment than do control clients. Similar superiority for the social-skills training might be demonstrated by self-report inventory scores or frequencies of self-monitored in-vivo social interactions in which the skill was used over a one-week period of time. Thus, the therapist will have obtained information documenting the effect of the social-skills training intervention relative to either a "no-treatment" control or, more likely, relative to the form of treatment that control-group clients received during the interval in which skills-training clients were receiving their intervention. However, because clients are not randomly assigned to one group or another in this strategy, it remains possible that some outside factors are responsible for the differential change of one group relative to the other. This is possible even when clients in the two groups appear to be comparable with one another. The only way to conclusively demonstrate the performance change of one group over another is if clients have been randomly assigned to their respective groups.

Random-Assignment Control Group

A study by Hollandsworth, Dressel, and Stevens (1977) illustrates how the random-assignment control-group evaluation design can be used. Hollandsworth et al. were interested in comparing the effects of behavioral job-interview training, a discussion-based but nonbehavioral job-interview counseling approach, and no treatment for college seniors who would soon be seeking employment. All clients, regardless of the form of training they were randomly selected to receive, role-played a simulated, standard job interview and completed a self-report scale measuring social anxiety. Clients then received their respective treatment: social-skills–behavioral training, traditional discussion, or no treatment. Afterward, each student repeated the role-play interview and was re-administered the social-anxiety inventory. The pretraining and posttraining role-played interviews of all clients were rated on such components as eye contact, speech duration, speech loudness, positive self-statements, explanatory statements of vocational-educational skill, etc. Statistical analyses, which compared mean-change scores of client performance in the three groups, were conducted on each measure. Because Hollandsworth et al. (1977) found that discussion and behavioral-skills training were each associated with improvement on different measures when compared to the no-training control group, the investigators suggest combining behavioral and discussion modes of treatment within job-interview training.

Designs for Evaluating Treatment: A Summary

In this section, we have sampled several approaches that can be used to evaluate social-skills training interventions. The particular evaluation method selected will depend on the kind of question the therapist would like to answer, the degree to which the therapist wishes to rigorously establish that training was responsible for observed social-skill improvement, the resources or support that an applied setting can devote to intervention assessment, and the time constraints or interests of the therapist. In many cases, simple pretraining and posttraining assessment of clients of social-skills measures may yield all the information that the therapist seeks on the success of his or her social-skills training. In other cases, more controlled evaluation strategies such as time series analysis, multiple baseline analysis, or "between-groups" designs can be used to provide treatment outcome information.

There are no intrinsically "right" or "wrong" intervention-assessment strategies, although some approaches do provide more specific and conclusive information than others. Perhaps the most important point is that the therapist not take any intervention's outcome for granted, no matter how well the intervention is thought out. Instead, planning an applied intervention should also include the planning of objective mechanisms by which that intervention's clinical success can also be gauged. By incorporating treatment-evaluation measures into skills-training, the therapist will be in a position to gain objective information on whether or not clients improve. If objective measures indicate there has not been improvement, the therapist will be in a position to provide the client with additional training. If objective measures do demonstrate improvement, the therapist's confidence in the success of his or her own interventions will be substantiated by empirical data.

Chapter 6

Conversational-Skills Training

The term "conversational skills" refers to the ability to successfully initiate and then maintain informal conversations with other people. An effective conversational repertoire not only permits an individual to come across well during informal interactions, but is also a likely precursor to the development of longer-range relationships such as friendships, because forming those relationships first requires that the individual successfully interact with other people in conversation. In contrast to other types of social skills that serve relatively circumscribed purposes, such as refusal-assertion or job-interview skills, conversational competence is needed across a wide variety of everyday interpersonal situations. Date-initiation behavior, which will be considered in the next chapter, represents the specialized kind of conversational skill that is used when the purpose of the interaction is specifically to obtain a date.

When teaching conversational skills, the therapist is assisting the client in learning new verbal, nonverbal, and stylistic behaviors to use when conversing with other people. The training seeks to build those behavioral competencies that permit a client to obtain the goal of meeting and conversing with others in an effective manner; training also seeks to increase the client's own reinforcement value to others so that they find the client to be a reinforcing social agent and they are then more likely to reciprocate or maintain interactions with him.

Client Populations for Whom Conversational-Skills Training Has Been Used

Within the social-skills training literature, conversational training has been used most extensively with four distinct client populations: persons who are or who have been institutionalized in psychiatric facilities; mentally retarded citizens; adolescents; and college students reporting difficulties or discomfort in conversations with others.

As we briefly noted in Chapter 1, individuals who have been confined in

136

institutional settings often exhibit pervasive social-skill deficits, including the inability to initiate and maintain appropriate conversations with others. During recent years, there has been a significant trend away from institutionalization and toward community-based treatment for persons who have been previously confined to institutional psychiatric settings. This has resulted in the discharge of many long-term psychiatric patients to community settings—halfway houses, day hospital programs, mental health aftercare, and so on. Similarly, mentally retarded persons are increasingly placed in nonresidential environments, as shown by increased attention to educational mainstreaming, vocational training, and placement in cooperative apartment housing and halfway houses in the community.

A number of investigators have pointed out that institutionalized or formerly institutionalized persons who lack appropriate everyday conversational skills will not be in a position to establish social relationships in the community because they come across to others as peculiar, dull, unrewarding, or even threatening (Bellack & Hersen, 1978; Kelly, Urey, & Patterson, 1980; Kelly, Wildman, Urey, & Thurman, 1979; Urey et al., 1979). In essence, as long as an individual appears to others to be a "former psychiatric patient" or "retarded," it is unlikely that other people will be eager to develop everyday relationships with that individual. This social avoidance serves to ensure continued isolation; the absence of relationship supports in the community may, in turn, be associated with poor adjustment outside the institution and increased recidivism (re-admission) rates (Phillips, 1968; Zigler & Phillips, 1962). The aim of conversational-skills training for institutionalized, aftercare, or mentally retarded clients is to equip them with appropriate competencies they can use in the course of everyday, informal interactions.

Other investigators have applied conversational-skills training procedures to higher-functioning clients who exhibit either deficiencies in their conversational ability or discomfort during such interactions. For example, Minkin et al. (1976) successfully provided conversational-skills training to four adolescent delinquent girls who were unable to communicate effectively and were unlikely to develop successful peer relationships with others as a result of their conversational deficits. A similar project, intended to teach predelinquent adolescents to converse more effectively with adults, was reported by Maloney, Harper, Braukmann, Fixsen, Phillips, and Wolf (1976). Still other investigators have described the successful results of conversational-skills training interventions for college students experiencing social anxiety and problems in interpersonal communication (cf. Arbes & Hubbell, 1973).

In general, it appears that training in conversational skills is indicated for both residential or outpatient populations when: (1) the client currently exhibits deficient performance during informal conversations with others; (2) the client is unable to establish friendships or other relationships because he or she lacks the skills repertoire to meet others, converse with them, and be a socially rewarding agent; or (3) the client currently avoids conversations with other people due to anxiety associated with these interactions, fear of negative evaluation from others, etc.

Conversational-Skill Assessment

In this section, we will first examine and define those behavioral components that have been related to overall conversational skill. Attention will then be given to procedures for rating clients' practice conversations to assess the presence of those component behaviors. Finally, several self-report inventories, which can be used as supplemental data sources to evaluate the effectiveness of a conversational-skills training intervention, will be considered.

Behavioral Definitions of Components of Conversational Skill

In Chapter 3, the component makeup of various types of social skills was discussed. As we then noted, behaviors that have been postulated as components of conversational skill include: eye contact; affect; speech duration; conversational questions; self-disclosing statements; and reinforcing or complimentary comments. For a therapist to reliably assess the presence of these behaviors in a client's conversations (such as during pretraining-assessment conversations or practice conversations during the course of training) or to convey to the client how to exhibit them during interactions, it is necessary to define all component behaviors in an objective fashion. As we might expect, investigators of conversational skills have not always used identical definitions even for the same component. For example, some investigators have measured eye contact as the amount of time the client looks at the interaction partner; other investigators have measured the amount of time that the client looks at the partner and the partner also looks back. These procedural discrepancies notwithstanding, let us consider component definitions that the therapist can use when evaluating client conversations or when training conversational skills.

Eye contact. Eye contact can be behaviorally defined as the percentage of time when the client is speaking or listening to the conversational partner that the client also looks directly at the partner's face. If the client spends a total of 6 minutes actively conversing with a partner, and if the therapist observes eye contact to be made for 3 of those minutes, client eye contact can be estimated to be 50%.

If extremely precise measurement of eye contact is sought, the therapist can separately "time" the client's speaking and listening duration and the duration of this period when client eye contact is also observed. By dividing the eye contact time by the speaking and listening time, the exact percentage of client eye contact can be ascertained. However, it is also possible for a therapist to rate eye contact less formally, by estimating the appropriate percentage of conversation time when eye contact is observed (0, 10%, 20%, 30%, and so on).

Affect. Affect represents the degree to which the client's emotional tone is judged to be appropriate to the situation in which he or she is interacting. Affect is usually measured as a single component, although external judgments of conversational affect are based on such cues as the client's observed voice tone, facial expression, and voice modulation or loudness. An affect-rating is often made by the observer using an anchored rating scale; one example of this is a scale from *1 = extremely appropriate affect* to *7 = extremely inappropriate affect*. The client's overall behavior throughout the entire observed conversation is the basis for the affect judgment.

Because affective appropriateness is linked to the situation in which one observes a client, the particular emotional tone that is considered appropriate will necessarily vary. For example, affect in a conversation is generally appropriate if the client appears warm, friendly, interested in and responsive to the partner, lively, and so on. However, if a conversational partner at some point tells the client about a very unfortunate or unhappy event, we would expect the client's emotion to change and be more subdued, sympathetic, or consoling.

A form of inappropriate conversational affect that is seen in some clients is an absence or flatness of emotional tone. Schizophrenic patients often exhibit a dullness of affect, which makes them appear both very disinterested in others and uninteresting to others. Here, the patient's affect would be considered inappropriate because of its absence, rather than because it is mismatched with the content of a conversation.

Speech duration. The duration of a client's total speaking time in a conversation has been associated with conversational competence by a number of investigators (see Kelly, Furman, Phillips, Hathorn, & Wilson, 1979; Minkin et al., 1976). Speech duration is generally targeted for assessment and training attention among clients who provide very little verbal input during their conversations with others. On the other hand, some clients talk excessively during conversations; here, the aim of training might be achieving a reduction in their speech duration. Duration of speech is usually measured by the therapist activating a stopwatch whenever the client speaks during a conversation.

Speech-duration measurement provides the therapist with information on the quantity of verbal input by a client during his or her conversations. However, speech duration alone does not provide information on the qualitative or content aspects of that client's conversation. For this reason, low speech duration during pretraining assessment interactions is often treated by teaching the client to increase the frequency of other verbal conversational component behaviors, such as asking questions, or making self-disclosing statements. When these verbal behaviors are increased, speech-duration ratings will also increase, since the client will then be talking more.

Conversational questions. A conversational question can be defined as any question asked by the client that results in the partner's disclosure of some information. Conversational questions can be direct requests for information, such as: "Where do you go to school?"; "What do you like to do in your spare time?"; or "Do you ever go fishing?" Questions might also include statements that function to elicit information from a conversational partner, even if they are not phrased directly as interrogative comments. Examples of indirect questions might include: "Tell me more about that"; "Oh, really?"; or "So you are in school" (Minkin et al., 1976). The crucial element is that a conversational question asked by the client leads the partner to disclose information.

Conversational questions, like the other verbal content behaviors we will discuss in this section, can most easily be rated by tallying the number of times they occur throughout the entire conversation. The therapist observing an assessment or practice interaction can simply count the total frequency of questions asked by the client to the partner for a conversation of some fixed duration.

Self-disclosing statements. Another content component of conversational skill involves the client's verbalization of statements that convey appropriate information about himself or herself to the partner in the interaction (Kelly, Urey, & Patterson, 1980). A self-disclosing statement is any "piece" of information that conveys self-disclosing information. Examples of self-disclosing statements include: "I like to water ski in the summer"; "I come from a large family"; "My favorite television program is *Lou Grant*"; or "I really hated that test." Each of these statements discloses something of the interests, hobbies, background, preferences, or opinions of the speaker and thereby permits the other person to get to know the speaker more thoroughly.

Although this component has been termed self-disclosure, the label does not imply the revelation of highly personal information, deep feeling-statements, or an individual's secrets. Indeed, disclosing overly personal information in a conversation with a relative stranger can probably be viewed as undesirable and socially unskilled, since it may make the partner ill-at-ease. Similarly, statements that convey negative personal information are not counted as appropriate self-disclosure statements. Such undesirable disclosures might include references to loneliness, treatment for emotional problems, self-deprecating statements, and so on.

Self-disclosing statements can be feasibly rated in a client's sample conversations by using a frequency count system and tallying the total number of such statements throughout an entire interaction. The therapist will need to determine how self-disclosure "facts" that are linked together in a client's conversation will be rated. For example, if a client tells the partner "I like to go swimming in the summer, but prefer to read in the winter," the single sentence could be rated as two separate disclosures since two different pieces of information are conveyed.

Reinforcing or complimentary components. Reinforcing or complimentary comments (Kelly, Urey, & Patterson, 1980) or positive conversational feedback (Minkin et al., 1976) can be defined as verbalizations made by the client that directly compliment the partner or reinforce the partner's speech by acknowledging that the client approves, concurs, or understands what the partner just said. We can include in this component category such direct compliments as "That's very nice"; "I enjoy talking to you"; or "You must be good at tennis." At the same time, a variety of less-direct statements also serve to convey the client's interest in the other conversant, and thereby reinforce the other person's speech. These might include such acknowledgments as "I know"; "Good"; "Hmm"; or "Right!" The frequency of such reinforcing comments can be rated by counting the number of times they are emitted by the client during an entire sample conversation.

Rating Client Conversation for the Presence of Skill-Components

As we noted earlier, the client's assessment conversations are observed by the therapist before the skills-training intervention begins, in order to pinpoint those components that are deficient and that will need specific training. During the course of the intervention, client practice conversations are also observed and rated to determine whether the individual now exhibits any conversational skill components that were previously deficient. To accomplish this behavioral assessment of conversational skills, the therapist can use a rating form to summarize information on the client's exhibition of all relevant component-behaviors during an observed interaction. A sample rating form for conversational-skills assessment is presented as Figure 6.1.

Let us assume that we are conducting an initial pretraining or baseline skill-evaluation and that we will observe a client's conversational behavior during a semistructured or unstructured interaction, as outlined in Chapter 3. The client and conversational partner, perhaps a therapist confederate, are seated together and are asked to get to know one another better for a fixed 8-minute period of time. The therapist or some other observer is located unobtrusively, but is able to see and hear the interaction; as discussed in the chapter on assessment, variations in this observational system also include audiotaping or videotaping the interaction so that it can be rated later, or asking

FIGURE 6.1. Sample Rating Form for Conversational Skills

```
Client Name:_____

Date of This Conversation:_____

Type of Interaction:

                    _____ Pretraining Assessment

                    _____ Session Practice (Training Focused on

                    What Component?_____)

                    _____ Follow-up

Length of Interaction:_____minutes
```

COMPONENT BEHAVIORS

1. Eye Contact (Approximate ratio of eye contact to total time
             that client was actively conversing)

```
   0%   10%   20%   30%   40%   50%   60%   70%   80%   90%   100%

   eye contact                                          eye contact
   never made                                           made entire
                                                        time
```

2. Affect (Emotional appropriateness/responsiveness)

```
      1         2         3         4         5         6         7

   extremely                    average                extremely
   inappropriate                                       appropriate
   or affective                                        and affect-
   responsiveness                                      ively respon-
   absent during                                       sive during
   interaction                                         interaction
```

3. Client Speech Duration (Measured in seconds throughout entire
                    conversation)

```
             _____seconds
```

4. Conversational Questions (The total number of times that client
                    directed a conversational question to
                    partner)

```
   Tally:_____  Total:_____
```

5. Self-Disclosing Statements (The total number of times that
                    client made a statement disclosing
                    appropriate information to partner)

```
   Tally:_____  Total:_____
```

6. Reinforcing/Complimentary Comments (The total number of times
                    that client made a rein-
                    forcing/complimentary
                    comment to partner)

```
   Tally:_____  Total:_____
```

Other Components Being Rated (or any undesirable, inappropriate
                    behaviors being examined)

Definition/Description of Behavior: Frequency Count or Rating:

the conversational partner to make some component ratings while interacting with the client.

As the conversation begins, the therapist makes a notation on the rating form when any of the verbal component behaviors occurs. A tally-mark is placed in the appropriate category whenever the client directs a conversational question to the partner, makes a self-disclosing statement, or makes a reinforcing or complimentary comment. The therapist can also attend to those skill-components that are not discrete, "countable" behaviors, such as the percentage of time when eye contact is made and the client's affective appropriateness; ratings for each of these components can be marked on the form at the end of the conversation. Total client speech-duration, timed by activating a stopwatch whenever the client is speaking, might also be determined for the entire conversation. By the conversation's end, the therapist will have a quantified record of the client's performance with respect to each rated component. An identical procedure can be used to rate sample conversations at any point in the intervention, including at the time of pretreatment assessment, during conversational practice associated with individual training sessions, or at the conclusion of the intervention.

Ratings of Other Conversational Skill-Components.

The component-behaviors included in the sample rating-form are based on conversational skill research; however, it is important to note that there are undoubtedly other desirable behaviors that contribute to overall conversational skill. Certainly, this component rating-list does not exhaust all the behaviors that skilled persons exhibit in conversation. The therapist conducting a skills-training intervention should bear in mind that additional verbal or nonverbal behaviors can be examined or rated in client-assessment conversations and later trained in the intervention. For example, a given client might sit in a "wooden" manner and never gesture during interactions. A posture and gesturing component might then be added to the list of assesssment and training components for that individual client. Whenever a "new" component is examined, it is important that the therapist also determine some way to objectively measure and later teach that behavior. For example, body posture or flexibility could be behaviorally defined in terms of frequency of observed arm and hand movements or gestures throughout a sample conversation, or it could be defined in terms of some numerical rating (e.g., from 1 to 7) to describe the client's overall rigidity or flexibility of posture.

It is also possible that certain clients may exhibit undesirable or inappropriate behaviors during conversation. For example, Urey et al. (1979) found that one client persistently made negative comments about himself during assessment conversations, including talking about his "nerve trouble" with strangers.

Similarly, Stalonas and Johnson (1979) reported that a client made frequent "disclaimers" by compulsively overqualifying routine statements she made to others during everyday conversations. Other clients' conversational performance may be disrupted by speech dysfluencies, unusual mannerisms, or verbal content repetition. The therapist assessing a client whose conversations include the presence of inappropriate behaviors can adapt the rating-form to permit the scoring of them also. Because inappropriate conversational behaviors may spontaneously decrease as new, more appropriate skills become learned, ratings of these behaviors can serve as an ancillary measure of training-effectiveness. On the other hand, if a client continues to exhibit undesirable or inappropriate behaviors in practice conversations over the course of training, specific attention towards reducing them will also be needed.

Assessing Deficiency Levels of Conversational Skills

What observed frequency or rating for a conversational skill-component constitutes a deficiency? In Chapter 3, on client assessment, we noted that although research has established relationships between specific component behaviors and overall competence in a social skill, little attention has been given to the optimal rates of occurrence for various components over the course of an interaction. As an example, let us ask what percentage of eye contact *do* most people maintain in a conversation? Over an 8-minute conversation with a stranger, how many questions does a skilled conversationalist ask, or how many statements of self-disclosure does that person make? Unfortunately, there have been few normative studies to address these issues.

It is evident that when a client is extremely deficient on any social-skill component, and when that component's presence is known to be related to overall social competence, the behavior should then be targeted for training. These include cases of little or no eye contact, very poor affect, and very low-frequency verbal skill behaviors. In less extreme instances, and in the absence of normative or empirical data on ideal rates for conversational skill-components, the therapist may need to rely on more subjective impressions to determine whether or not a component behavior's presence is at a sufficiently low level to merit attention in training.

Similarly, the therapist will have to consider when to stop training a given behavior. If a client exhibits very low eye contact during pretraining assessment conversations, and if this behavior is then selected for later training, how much eye contact do we wish the client to learn to maintain? If the client maintained no eye contact during several pretrained conversations, but later demonstrated 50% eye contact during a practice conversation after it had received attention, should the therapist assume that it was at an ideal (or "criterion") level? Once again, these are important questions since too much of an otherwise appropriate conversational behavior (eye contact, animated affect, questions, self-disclosures, or compliments) may cause the client to be perceived as inappropriate. The therapist's subjective judgment is often required at this point; additionally, having an outside observer judge or rate the client's global conversational competence during a sample interaction may provide useful information on the person's overall social impact.

Self-Report Inventories and Conversational Skill

Self-report inventories do not provide the detailed information necessary to plan and conduct a social-skills training intervention, for reasons such as those considered in Chapter 5; however, they can provide a useful adjunctive source of information on an intervention's success. There have been no published self-report inventories specifically for conversational skill or conversational anxiety. However, Watson and Friend (1969) have developed two scales relevant to the assessment of client-reported anxiety during informal social interactions with others. They are the Social Avoidance and Distress (SAD) Scale and the Fear of Negative Evaluation (FNE). Items comprising the Social Avoidance and Distress Scale are presented in Figure 6.2.

The SAD focuses upon the respondent's feelings or behavior along two dimensions: social avoidance, or the tendency to avoid and escape from interactions, and social distress, which consists of negative emotions such as tension or anxiety during social interactions. The 28 items comprising the SAD are keyed to control for acquiescent response sets and the scale's authors have provided data supporting the validity and reliability of the inventory (Watson & Friend, 1969). High scores indicate greater social anxiety; the authors report normative college students scale means of 11.20 for males and 8.2 for females (out of a possible 28). However, Watson and Friend also note that the most frequent or modal SAD score based upon a normal college student sample was zero; consequently, high scores on this measure appear to demonstrate very severe social avoidance or discomfort.

Applied conversational-skills training interventions might use an inventory such as the SAD to evaluate whether changes in a client's generalized self-reports of social avoidance accompany skill-improvement over the course of treatment. If training is successful, the therapist would expect that the individual's reported social discomfort would decrease as the person begins to use newly trained behaviors during everyday conversational interactions. Because SAD-like inventories do tap generalized feelings, rather than specific social performance, and because it is likely that self-perception of improvement or reduced discomfort follows improved behavioral performance, one would not expect SAD scores to necessarily change from one session to the next. However, for those clients who provide reports of elevated social anxiety before an intervention, there should be a reduction in SAD scores following conversational-skills training.

A second inventory that may be appropriate for conversational-skills training projects is the Fear of Negative Evaluation (FNE), which can be found in Watson and Friend (1969). The FNE is a 30-item true-false measure, constructed in similar fashion to the SAD. However, the FNE is intended to measure a client's concern, apprehension, and worry about the way that others evaluate him or her, and it thereby taps a social-evaluative fear dimension. The item content of the FNE does not concern specific social or conversational situations; sample items include: "I rarely worry about seeming foolish to others"; "I am afraid that people will find fault with me"; and "I often worry that I will say or do the wrong thing." Because FNE items are not tied to a given form of social situation, the scale could be used for various types of skills-training interventions, including conversational skills. At the same time, the generality of item content makes the scale a very global and nonspecific assessment measure.

FIGURE 6.2. Social Avoidance and Distress Scale[a]

1. I feel relaxed even in unfamiliar social situations. (F)
2. I try to avoid situations which force me to be very sociable. (T)
3. It is easy for me to relax when I am with strangers. (F)
4. I have no particular desire to avoid people. (F)
5. I often find social occasions upsetting. (T)
6. I usually feel calm and comfortable at social occasions. (F)
7. I am usually at ease when talking to someone of the opposite sex. (F)
8. I try to avoid talking to people unless I know them well. (T)
9. If the chance comes to meet new people, I often take it. (F)
10. I often feel nervous or tense in casual get-togethers in which both sexes are present. (T)
11. I am usually nervous with people unless I know them well. (T)
12. I usually feel relaxed when I am with a group of people. (F)
13. I often want to get away from people. (T)
14. I usually feel uncomfortable when I am in a group of people I don't know. (T)
15. I usually feel relaxed when I meet someone for the first time.(F)
16. Being introduced to people makes me tense and nervous. (T)
17. Even though a room is full of strangers, I may enter it anyway. (F)
18. I would avoid walking up and joining a large group of people. (T)
19. When my superiors want to talk with me, I talk willingly. (F)
20. I often feel on edge when I am with a group of people. (T)
21. I tend to withdraw from people. (T)
22. I don't mind talking to people at parties or social gatherings. (F)
23. I am seldom at ease in a large group of people. (T)
24. I often think up excuses in order to avoid social engagements.(T)
25. I sometimes take the responsibility for introducing people to each other. (F)
26. I try to avoid formal social occasions. (T)
27. I usually go to whatever social engagements I have. (F)
28. I find it easy to relax with other people. (F)

[a]From Watson, D., & Friend, R. "Measurement of Social-evaluative anxiety," *Journal of Consulting and Clinical Psychology,* 1969, *33,* 450. Copyright 1969 by the American Psychological Association. Reprinted by permission.

Representative Conversational-Skills Training Interventions

In this section, several representative studies of training in conversational skills will be reviewed. Because our main focus will be on applied treatment interventions, analogue research and studies that utilized very brief treatment will not be considered.

Conversational-Skills Training with Individually Treated Clients

Urey et al. (1979), in a project noted in Chapter 3, conducted conversational-skills training with two formerly hospitalized male psychiatric patients. Both were enrolled in a mental health center's aftercare program and both had been diagnosed as schizophrenic. The program staff recognized that the two clients appeared unable to maintain appropriate conversations with others, one because he appeared quite inappropriate in conversational conduct, and the other because of affective and social unresponsiveness. Because the clients reported experiencing the greatest difficulty during everyday interactions with females, training was targeted toward their conversational behavior with women.

Pretreatment semistructured conversational assessment was conducted by rating 5-minute interactions between each client and a female conversational partner. Assessment conversations were repeated on three different days, were always videotaped, and were rated by the therapists to determine which component behaviors were deficient. Across all three assessments, each client consistently asked his partner few conversational questions (0 to 4 per 5-minute conversation), made few self-disclosures of appropriate personal information (0 to 6 such statements per conversation), and rarely offered any verbal acknowledgments or compliments (0 to 2). One client exhibited extremely flat affect (rated as a 1 on a 7-point scale); the other verbalized as many as 14 different disclosures of negative personal information in the 5-minute conversations.

For one client, 9 individual training sessions were conducted; the other required 13 training sessions, due to his slower rate of skill-acquisition. The training sessions were themselves conducted in a manner almost identical to that described in Chapter 4, with several sessions devoted to each behavior that had been deficient in the assessment interactions. Brief instruction, examples, and a rationale for the component behavior were described; then, a modeling videotape was shown. The film portrayed two skilled persons interacting in conversation as though they had never previously met one another. Immediately after the modeling exposure, the client engaged in a 5-minute semistructured practice conversation, which was videotaped. Feedback and verbal reinforcement were provided as the therapist and client together reviewed the videotape of the client's just-completed practice conversation. In order to objectively assess whether the client exhibited the targeted component in his practice interaction, each practice conversation was always rated for all behavioral components. This provided a multiple-baseline analysis of treatment effects for each client.

In addition to demonstrating that each client substantially increased his frequency of previously deficient skill-components, Urey et al. (1979) also videotaped conversations between each client and unfamiliar partners whom the client had never met before training; the videotapes were made immediately after the intervention and at 1- and 6-month follow-ups. Since clients exhibited the skill-components at higher than baseline rates in their conversations with novel partners on each posttraining occasion, generalization of training to novel partners was shown. To further socially validate the effect of treatment, the novel conversational partners who interacted with each client during pretraining, posttraining, and at the follow-ups subjectively rated the client's global conversational skill on dimensions including interest shown in her, genuineness of affect, eye contact, personal appearance, how interesting the client was during the conversation, etc. These confederate-partner ratings were made using 10-point scales immediately after each generalization conversation. Because the novel partners who made these ratings were aware that clients had received training between the pretraining and posttraining conversations and, consequently, may have been biased, other nonprofessional judges evaluated videotapes of each client's pretraining and posttraining conversational competencies on the same global dimensions, using 10-point rating scales. These judges were naive as to whether a given videotaped conversation was before or after the intervention. Both the partners and the naive external judges always rated the posttreatment interactions higher on subjective, global indices of skill, thereby providing social validation of the training outcome.

Kelly, Furman, Phillips, Hathorn, and Wilson (1979) reported the results of conversational-skills training with two moderately retarded adolescents, ages 13 and 20, with I.Q. scores of 37 and 57, respectively. In this project, a somewhat different pretraining conversational-assessment procedure was employed. The partner who participated in the assessment interactions was a nonretarded adolescent. However, conversations were relatively structured, with the partner always including a set of 13 comments directed to the client in each conversation (for example, "What did you do at school today?"; "You seem like a nice person"; and "There are a lot of games I like to play"). Although the partner's behavior was not confined to only these 13 comments, the standard comments were included in each conversation to ensure that the client always had an opportunity to ask the partner conversational questions, or to self-disclose information about his own background and interests in response to the standard partner comments. Based upon two assessment conversations, which were videotaped and rated by the therapist for the presence of appropriate component-behaviors, training was conducted to increase the rate of clients' statements disclosing personal information about themselves (termed "informational facts"), conversational questions, and "social invitations." Social invitations were defined as statements suggesting that the partner join the client in some shared activity (e.g., "Do you want to play baseball sometime?"). This component was derived from research on social competence showing that social invitations are related to peer popularity among children (Gottman, Gonso, & Rasmussen, 1975); it was trained because the two clients were in a school setting.

Individual training sessions consisted of exposure to a modeling videotape, which showed two adolescents engaging in a conversation that included the same 13 standard comments that occurred in each client's own practice conversations. The models exhibited all components that were to receive training attention. An adult therapist then coached the client in how to exhibit the behavior that was receiving attention in that session. Then the therapist left the room and the adolescent partner came in. The partner and the client had a practice conversation identical to that used in pretraining assessment. Ratings of each session's practice conversation demonstrated that the clients more frequently exhibited the component in that day's practice interaction. Additionally, in-vivo observations of the clients' free-time behavior conducted during recess at the school indicated that they increased the amount of time spent talking with others and playing with others after the intervention.

Group Training of Conversational Skills

Only a limited number of group conversational-skills training studies have been reported in the clinical research literature. Those include projects by Minkin et al. (1976); Kelly, Wildman, Urey, & Thurman (1979); and Kelly, Urey, & Patterson (1980).

Minkin et al. (1976) taught a small group of delinquent female adolescents to exhibit two verbal components of conversational skill: directing appropriate questions to the other person in an interaction and providing "positive conversational feedback" (verbal acknowledgments or reinforcing comments) to the partner. These component behaviors were selected because each had been associated with global judgments of conversational competence among a normative sample of nondelinquent junior high school to college-age girls (Minkin et al., 1976).

Prior to group training, clients individually engaged in several assessment conversations with previously unknown adult partners. Each conversation was unstructured, with both the client and the partner instructed only to talk with one another for four minutes. Training consisted of presenting all clients in the group with instructions and rationale, modeling of the targeted components by having the group observe two therapists conversing with one another while exhibiting the behaviors, and breaking the group up so that each client could have an individual practice conversation. Partners for the practice conversations were the therapists; all conversations were videotaped and feedback was provided in the session during which the girls and the therapists observed their performance on tape. Throughout the study, clients were also required to engage in unstructured conversations with unknown adults. For these interactions, the therapist offered clients 10 cents each time they exhibited a targeted component, such as asking the novel partner a question. Thus, the therapists were incorporating not only praise as a positive reinforcer, but also tangible incentives for a client's use of her newly acquired behaviors in conversation. Social validation of the training outcome was established by having 15 adults observe a series of videotaped conversations from the pretraining and posttraining phases of the intervention. The naive judges rated the clients' overall conversational ability using 8-point scales. In all cases, client posttraining conversations received higher mean evaluations by the entire group of judges.

Similar studies by Kelly, Wildman, Urey, and Thurman (1979) and Kelly, Urey, and Patterson (1980) used skills-training to improve the conversational repertoire of a group of ten retarded adolescents and a group of three formerly hospitalized psychiatric patients. Components receiving treatment attention included asking conversational questions, making self-disclosing statements, and making complimentary or reinforcing comments. Group training sessions in each of these projects were quite similar, with sessions including therapist examples and group discussion about that day's behavioral component, a modeling videotape showing skilled conversationalists exhibiting the components, live-modeling both by the therapist and group members who observed one another's practice verbalization of examples of the component, and feedback or reinforcement from the therapist and other group members. The effectiveness of treatment was further established by periodically utilizing novel conversational partners, conducting follow-up conversations after the intervention concluded, or having naive judges evaluate global conversational competence before and then after training.

Issues from Conversational Skills-Training Research Literature Relevant to Applied Interventions

Although the studies described above vary in several methodological points, they share a number of common features of interest to the applied practitioner who is planning a conversational-skills intervention. With respect to pretreatment assessment, client social competence is always evaluated using sample conversations between the client and some other person (a therapist confederate, another client, or the therapist himself or herself). Assessment interactions are then rated in objective fashion to evaluate the extent to which the client exhibits those behavioral components associated with conversational skill. Training sessions successively target behaviors found to be deficient during pretreatment assessment interactions, and training sessions themselves utilize the learning principles described in Chapter 4.

It is noteworthy that the studies summarized here were conducted in applied settings, such as mental health centers, developmental centers, and residential facilities. All of the interventions required fewer than 16 actual treatment sessions; the longest interventions occurred when treatment was group-administered and when a large number of different components were taught. Although the number of therapists conducting training sessions was not always specified, the majority of studies used either one or two therapists; session length was generally less than one hour, including the time required for clients to engage in a short practice conversation each day.

One important aspect of clinical treatment that has not been emphasized in research on conversational-skills training involves the enhancement of generalization. Although most of the abovementioned studies did use novel practice partners at some point during training, and although follow-up maintenance of skill-performance was assessed, systematic treatment efforts to promote generalization to the natural environment were not described. In an applied intervention, more attention to this critical aspect of training is needed, and the therapist should seek to incorporate specific generalization-enhancement techniques, such as those described in Chapter 4. Clients must not only develop and exhibit new skill behaviors during their practice conversations in the training setting, but they must then use these skills within the natural environment.

Chapter 7

Training for Date-Initiation and Other Heterosocial Skills

A very important goal for most people is establishing an intimate social and sexual relationship with some other person. The development of such intimate relationships requires that an individual first meet, converse with, and arrange for continued contacts with prospective dates. Those social competencies that bring about contact with opposite-sex persons are termed "date-initiation" or "heterosocial" skills. In a narrow sense, date-initiation refers to the actual behavior of asking another person to join in some prearranged social dating activity, while heterosocial skills refer to the more general abilities involved in maintaining conversations with someone of the opposite sex. However, in practice, these competencies are closely related, since the actual initiation or suggestion to go on dates almost invariably occurs within the context of heterosocial conversation between two people. Further, once a date has been arranged, the individuals must then utilize appropriate and effective heterosocial skills while engaged in the dating activity.

As we will see, many of the behavioral competencies needed to initiate dates and relate effectively during interactions with opposite-sex persons are not fundamentally different than those that comprise general conversational skill. In fact, almost all of the specific behaviors that have been proposed as components of date-initiation or heterosocial competence are the same as those that have been postulated to make up conversational competence. The major differences between date-initiation and ordinary conversational behavior appear to include:

1. *The intent or purpose of the social interaction.* Date-initiation behavior is intended specifically to bring about continued or future heterosexual or heterosocial contact with the other individual.

2. *Verbal content aspects within the interaction.* This includes demonstrable affectionate comments, statements expressing a desire to date in the future, comments regarding intimacy, and similar contents that would occur principally in the context of a heterosocial interaction and would be less appropriate during everyday conversation.

152

3. *Affectionate, heterosocial motor behavior.* This might include such actions as touching or holding hands while interacting during a dating situation.

4. *The sexes of the persons involved in the interaction.* Heterosocial skills refer specifically to interactions between opposite-sex persons, especially in the context of the intention to date.

Even these characteristics do not always differentiate date-initiation from general conversational skills. For example, highly affectionate verbal content statements or motor behaviors may be appropriate in an established heterosocial relationship between two persons. The same behaviors might be quite inappropriate during the initial meeting between two people who have not yet actually dated.

Anxiety is frequently associated with date-initiation behavior, even among clients who can effectively handle everyday conversations that are not in the context of dating. This appears to occur for a variety of reasons, which include most individuals' desire to establish heterosocial relationships; the social importance and status associated with dating; the fact that dating is a social skill that emerges relatively late in development and, therefore, is not based on an extensive set of personal learning experiences earlier in life; and the relationship between dating and heterosexual involvement, with the latter also being a potential source of anxiety, especially in adolescence. Difficulty in establishing dating and heterosocial interactions appears to be a relatively frequent problem. Arkowitz, Hinton, Perl, and Himadi (1978) report that 31% of 3,800 randomly selected college undergraduates evaluated themselves as "somewhat" to "very" anxious about dating, and 50% of that population expressed interest in a dating-skills training program.

Four models have been used to account for why clients exhibit anxiety or skill-performance deficits in heterosocial interactions. These include conceptualizations that stress client social-skill deficits, conditioned anxiety, negative cognitive self-evaluations, and personal attractiveness (See Arkowitz, 1977; Arkowitz et al., 1978; Curran, 1977). The social-skills deficit model assumes that an individual lacks the interpersonal behaviors needed to perform effectively during heterosocial interactions, with anxiety developing as a result of past rejection or inadequate social performance. As elaborated by Arkowitz et al. (1978), the conditioned-anxiety model postulates that heterosocial anxiety develops as a result of the classical conditioning of fear or anxiety with date-related situations, in a manner analogous to phobic responses. Cognitive models stress the causal relationship of negative self-evaluations to subsequent heterosocial anxiety; sources of negative self-evaluation might include excessively high performance standards, anxiety-related cognitions, selective recall of unsuccessful past experiences, and so on (Glasgow & Arkowitz, 1975; Arkowitz, 1977). Finally, some researchers have examined the role of personal attractiveness itself and found high attractiveness ratings strongly associated with a higher frequency of dating interactions (Berscheid & Walster, 1973).

As Curran (1977) points out, it is likely that difficulties during heterosocial or dating situations are multidetermined, with all four factors potentially contributing to impaired functioning. Further, while one individual may date infrequently because of inadequate behavioral skills, another client might have an adequate skills repertoire but experience extreme conditioned heterosocial anxiety and therefore avoid dating interactions. Applied interventions, which include treatment elements such as those described in Chapter 4, can address a variety of the problems experienced by low-frequency daters or heterosocially anxious persons. For example, social-skills training itself increases the acquisition and use of appropriate behaviors in heterosocial situations. Because training includes repeated exposure to practice interactions, the intervention may also serve a desensitization or anxiety-reduction function (see Arkowitz et al., 1978; Curran, 1977). Using thought-modification procedures to reduce negative self-evaluations and to increase cognitions that facilitate social performance addresses the cognitively mediated aspects of heterosocial anxiety or dating-inhibition. Finally, assisting clients in planning opportunities to use newly acquired skills in the natural environment and reinforcing their report of skills usage also serve to desensitize them to the in-vivo performance of dating and heterosocial skills.

Client Populations with Whom Date-Initiation or Heterosocial Skills Training Has Been Used

Virtually all applications of date-initiation or heterosocial skills-training reported in the research literature have used college students as clients. Of the studies considered in two major review papers (Arkowitz, 1977; Curran, 1977), only one project concerned date-initiation training with clients other than college students—Marzillier, Lambert, & Kellett, 1976; in this study, socially inadequate psychiatric outpatients were treated. Several conversational-skills training interventions utilizing opposite-sex confederate practice partners have been described (Urey et al., 1979; Kelly, Urey, & Patterson, 1980); however, they were not specifically intended to increase dating behavior and were considered in the previous chapter on conversational skills.

One reason that college students have frequently been selected as a population to receive date-initiation training is that dating concerns often represent a genuine and "real-life" source of difficulty for them; this is in contrast to the use of college students as analogue "patients" in other types of treatment studies. Some investigators have conducted date-initiation training for students seeking assistance from a university counseling center (Martinson & Zerface, 1970), but low-frequency daters have more typically been located using advertisements in campus newspapers or self-report screening measures of infrequent dates and heterosocial anxieties.

At the same time, heterosocial-skills training might logically be used with many client populations other than college students. It would appear that persons of high school or even junior high school age may experience great discomfort or social ineptness in date-related situations and would be appropriate clients for this form of skills-training. Regardless of their age, individuals present in mental health or counseling centers with problems associated with dating or establishing heterosocial relationships should be evaluated to assess their need for training. These clients may include persons who have recently become divorced or who have terminated long-term relationships and seem motivated but unable to establish new relationships. Successful date-initiation can also be severely problematic for some mentally retarded individuals, as well as persons who have previously been institutionalized and now seek to establish relationships with opposite-sex persons. In these latter cases, specific heterosocial deficits may exist within the general context of deficiencies across a variety of other interpersonal skills.

Components of Heterosocial Skill: Behavioral Definitions

As in the previous chapter, we will first define the behavioral components that have been associated with competence in heterosocial interactions. Then procedures will be discussed for rating client sample or practice interactions for these behaviors. Self-report inventories of heterosocial skills will also be considered. Behaviors that have been specifically related to skill in date-initiation or heterosocial interactions include: eye contact; affect, including smiles, voice quality, facial expression, head nods, appropriate laughter; duration of speech; conversational questions; self-disclosing statements; complimentary comments; follow-up or acknowledgment statements; and requesting a date. In addition to these desirable components, investigators have associated a number of behaviors with unskilled or anxious performance in heterosocial interactions. Such unskilled behaviors, if present in pretraining assessment, should be reduced as the intervention proceeds. They include: silences in excess of 5 to 10 seconds (Bander, Steinke, Allen, & Mosher, 1975; Barlow, Abel, Blanchard, Bristow, & Young, 1977; Martinez-Diaz & Edelstein, 1980); negative-opinion statements (Heimberg, Madsen, Montgomery, & McNabb, 1980; Twentyman & McFall, 1975); speech dysfluencies, such as "uh," or "ah" (Heimberg et al., 1980; Twentyman & McFall, 1975); and long or delayed latencies of response before the client begins speaking following the partner's last comment (Martinez-Diaz & Edelstein, 1980; Williams & Ciminero, 1978).

We will now turn our attention to behavioral definitions of those components that comprise effective heterosocial skills and techniques for assessing them in client sample interactions. Components that were discussed in the previous chapter will not be described in great procedural detail here.

Eye contact.   An eye contact rating can be defined as the ratio of time when the client looks at the face of the interaction partner to the time when the client is actively conversing with the partner (client speaking to the partner or partner speaking to the client).

Affect.   Just as for general conversational skill, affect refers to the emotional responsiveness or emotional appropriateness of the client's interaction style. It can be most easily rated when the therapist assigns a numerical score (such as on a 7-point scale) to represent the client's overall affect. Some of the behaviors that contribute to high affective ratings in date-initiation interactions might include appropriate smiles (Bander et al., 1975; Heimberg et al., 1980); head nods (Bander et al., 1975; Greenwald, 1977); voice quality in terms of pitch, loudness, and flow (Barlow et al., 1977); facial expression in accord with the situation and with the partner's expression (Barlow et al., 1977); and laughter (Barlow et al., 1977).

Speech duration.   This component denotes the total length of time that the client spends talking during the simulated interaction; it is usually measured by activating a stopwatch whenever the client is speaking. Either extremely low or excessively great speech-duration could be indicative of social-skill inadequacies. As in the case of general conversational skills, client speech-duration often serves as a corollary measure of social-skill, since it will reflect improvement when the client acquires and exhibits new, appropriate verbal component behaviors.

Conversational questions and self-disclosing statements.   Both of these verbal components are defined in heterosocial interactions just as they are during ordinary conversations. A conversational question refers to any interrogative comment that the client directs to the interaction partner and that results in the partner's conveying information about interests, behavior, activities, or feelings. Several investigators have suggested that clients should particularly include the word "you" when asking questions during heterosocial interactions (e.g., "Where do you go to school?"); by asking "you" questions to an interaction partner, the client will be conveying personal interest and attention to the other person (Kupke, Calhoun, & Hobbs, 1979; Kupke, Hobbs, & Cheney, 1979). Additionally, client comments that are not directly phrased as questions but that nonetheless function as conversational questions can be counted in this category (Minkin et al., 1976). These might include statements such as: "Tell me more about that"; "I'd be interested in hearing more about what you did then"; or "So you went to a show last night."

Self-disclosing statements are comments made by the client that convey information about interests, activities, feelings, and so on to the partner. "I was raised in Ohio"; "My favorite sport is swimming"; or "I went to Florida last winter" are examples of self-disclosing comments. Both questions and self-disclosures can be rated during a client's assessment or practice interaction by counting the total number of times each occurs during the entire interaction.

Complimentary comments. Several investigations of heterosocial skill have taught persons to direct compliments to the confederate with whom they interacted in practice situations (see Curran, 1975; Farrell, Mariotto, Conger, Curran, & Wallender, 1979; Wessberg, Mariotto, Conger, Farrell, & Conger, 1979). Examples of compliments might include "You're a very nice person"; "That's a pretty outfit you are wearing"; or "You really handled that problem well."

Follow-up or acknowledgment statements.   A relatively subtle but potentially important verbal component is use of follow-up statements, which convey acknowledgment of what the other person just said. This component has been identified by Barlow et al. (1977) and is similar to a behavior described by Minkin et al. (1976). A follow-up or acknowledgment statement serves to communicate to the partner that the client has heard, understands, or approves of something the partner said. Follow-up statements can be brief comments ("Yeah," "Oh," "That's really something"), or they can be somewhat longer statements that paraphrase what the partner has just said. Functionally, these verbalizations create the impression that the client is attending to the partner and is interested in the other person, and they follow the partner's remarks. These behaviors can be rated by tallying their total frequency over the course of the sample interaction.

Request for a date.   Obviously, a key element in date-initiation training is the actual behavior of asking the other person for a date. Most investigators have defined a date as a prearranged social contact with a person of the opposite sex; this is in contrast to unplanned heterosocial contacts, which might themselves serve as opportunities to bring about future dates. It is somewhat surprising that within the heterosocial or date-initiation training literature, there has been relatively little attention given to either specifically defining appropriate behaviors that can be used when asking for dates or to teaching this important aspect of heterosocial initiation. However, an appropriate request for a date should include verbal statements indicating: (1) that the client would like to see the other person again: (2) an inquiry as to whether the other person would also like to meet again; (3) some indication of the planned date activity (e.g., getting a pizza, going to a show, studying together); and (4) offering a specific time and place for the date activity (Curran, 1975; Curran et al., 1976).

It is important for a skills-training therapist to recognize that the specific act of asking for a date occurs within the context (and towards the conclusion) of a more extended heterosocial interaction. For example, it would almost certainly be inappropriate for a client to approach opposite-sex persons and immediately ask them for dates, since some period of heterosocial interaction or conversation will ordinarily precede a date request. Further, the social skill exhibited by the client during conversation preceding an actual date request will influence how the other person responds to the request to date. For these reasons, it is useful that during any practice interaction, a client be instructed not to ask for a date until some fixed period of time has elapsed (e.g., 10 minutes of simulated interaction). During the period before the actual date request, the client would use the heterosocial components just summarized; when the predetermined interval has elapsed, the client would then specifically ask for a date. The quality and appropriateness of the actual date-request component behavior are evaluated with respect to whether the client conveys the wish to date, solicits information on the partner's willingness, and proposes a specific activity, time, and place.

Heterosocial-Skill Assessment Procedures

Rating Client's Sample Heterosocial Interactions for Skill-Components

Just as for other types of social skill, one of the preliminary objectives in an intervention focusing on heterosocial skills is assessing the degree to which a client exhibits each component-behavior during a sample interaction that the therapist can observe. Since date-initiation involves an interaction with an opposite-sex person, the conversational partner will need to be someone of the opposite sex from the client's. In general, a semistructured or unstructured interaction format of fixed duration (8 minutes, 10 minutes, etc.) is used. The same interaction format (conversing with an opposite-sex confederate) can be used as a vehicle for skill practice in training sessions throughout the intervention.

A sample form that can be used by the therapist to rate a client's heterosocial or date-initiation skill is presented in Figure 7.1. Two of the behavioral components, eye contact and affect, are assigned an overall rating score based on the client's overall exhibition of them during the entire interaction period. Specific, discrete verbal components (questions, self-disclosures, compliments, etc.) can be most feasibly evaluated by determining the frequency with which each occurs over the sample interaction period. Speech duration is a stopwatch-timed measure, assessed by determining the total cumulative number of seconds that the client was speaking. Deficits found in any component during pretraining assessment interactions provide the therapist with information indicating that the deficient behavior will need to be targeted for later training.

As was the case for rating general conversational skills in Chapter 6, the therapist evaluating a client's heterosocial competence during practice interactions may find that other identifiable aspects of performance will require treatment attention. These might be undesirable behaviors or characteristics such as negative self-disclosures, speech dysfluencies, or long periods of silence. Such behaviors can also be rated from sample interactions to determine their rate of occurrence, thereby allowing the therapist to evaluate improvement over the course of the intervention. Similarly, any other desirable heterosocial components (beyond those listed in Figure 7.1) that the therapist wishes to initially assess and later train can be added to the rating form.

Self-Report Inventories and Heterosocial Skills

There are a number of client self-report inventories that can be used in date-initiation training interventions. As we have stressed earlier, self-report measures cannot provide the therapist with the sufficiently detailed behavioral information that is needed to develop an intervention that identifies and targets a given client's specific heterosocial deficits. However, inventories can be appropriately used: (1) in conjunction with behavioral-skills assessment to more completely conceptualize the nature of a client's pretreatment heterosocial functioning; (2) to indirectly assess the client's pretreatment anxiety, self-appraisals, frequency of heterosocial interactions, or fears related to dating; (3) to serve as a preliminary screening device when many clients are being screened prior to more thorough heterosocial-skills assessment and training; and (4) as one of the measures used to evaluate the effectiveness of a skills-training project, such as when the measure is administered before and after the intervention.

The Situation Questionnaire (Rehm & Marston, 1968) consists of 30 descriptions of situations related to heterosocial functioning and requires that the respondent indicate the amount of discomfort that would be experienced in each by means of a 7-point scale. The content of the scale items is such that the Situation Questionnaire is appropriate only for male clients. Investigations by Curran and his associates (Curran, 1975; Curran & Gilbert, 1975; Curran, Gilbert, & Little, 1976) have demonstrated that client discomfort, as assessed by this inventory, decreases as a function of heterosocial-skills training.

The Survey of Heterosexual Interactions (Twentyman & McFall, 1975) also lists a variety of heterosocial situations and asks the male respondent to rate on a 1 to 7 scale the degree to which he is able to handle each of them. Figure 7.2 presents the 20 items comprising the SHI. Because the poorest skill

FIGURE 7.1. Sample Rating Form for Date-Initiation or Heterosocial Skills

Client Name: _____

Date of Conversation: _____

Type of Interaction: _____ Pretraining Assessment

                            _____ Session Practice (Training
                                    Focused on What Component?
                            _____)

                            _____ Follow-up

Length of Interaction: _____ minutes

COMPONENT BEHAVIORS

1. Eye Contact (Approximate ratio of eye contact to total time
              that client was actively conversing)

   0%   10%   20%   30%   40%   50%   60%   70%   80%   90%   100%
   eye contact   eye contact
   never made   made entire time

2. Affect (Emotional appropriateness/responsiveness)

   1   2   3   4   5   6   7
   extremely   extremely
   inappropriate   appropriate
   or affective   and affec-
   responsiveness   tively res-
   absent during   ponsive during
   interaction   interaction

3. Client Speech Duration (Measured in seconds throughout entire
                          interaction)
                          _____ seconds

4. Conversational Questions (The total number of times that
                            client directed conversational
                            question to partner)
   Tally: _____ Total: _____

5. Self-Disclosing Statements (The total number of times that
                              client made a statement disclosing
                              appropriate information to partner)
   Tally: _____ Total: _____

6. Complimentary Comments (The total number of compliments made
                          by client to partner)
   Tally: _____ Total: _____

7. Follow-up/Acknowledgment Statements (The total number of follow-
                                       up or acknowledgment
                                       comments made by client)
   Tally: _____ Total: _____

8. Date Request (Check to describe client's behavior)

   _____ Specific date request not made by client

   _____ Specific date request made by client; included:

           _____ Request to see partner again

           _____ Inquiry to determine if partner wants to date

           _____ Suggestion of date activity made by client

           _____ Proposal of specific arrangements (time,
                   day, location to meet, etc.)

self-ranking a client can provide is "1" for each situation, the lowest possible (skills-deficient) score on the SHI is 20; the maximum possible (highly skilled) score is 140. Twentyman and McFall (1975) report a scale mean of 88.2 using a large sample of college undergraduate males; the same investigators utilized a maximum SHI score of 70 as part of a screening for inclusion in a heterosocial-

FIGURE 7.2.   Items Comprising the Survey of Heterosexual Interactions[a]

Please circle the appropriate number in the following situations.
Try to respond as if you were in that situation.

    You want to call a girl up for a date. This is the first
time you are calling her up as you only know her slightly. When
you get ready to make the call, your roommate comes into the room,
sits down on his bed, and begins reading a magazine. In this
situation you would:

1	2	3	4	5	6	7

be unable to   be able to   be able to
call in every   call in some   call in
case   cases   every case

    You are at a dance. You see a very attractive girl whom you
do not know. She is standing <u>alone</u> and you would like to dance
with her. You would:

1	2	3	4	5	6	7

be unable to   be able to   be able to
ask her in   ask her in   ask her in
every case   some cases   every case

    You are at a party and you see two girls talking. You do
not know these girls but you would like to know one of them
better. In this situation you would:

1	2	3	4	5	6	7

be unable to   be able to   be able to
initiate a   initiate a   initiate a
conversation   conversation   conversation
                               in some cases   in every case

    You are at a bar where there is also dancing. You see a
couple of girls sitting in a booth. One, whom you don't know, is
talking with a fellow who is standing by the booth. These two go
over to dance leaving the other girl sitting alone. You have
seen this girl around, but do not really know her. You would
like to go over and talk to her (but you wouldn't like to dance).
In this situation you would:

1	2	3	4	5	6	7

be unable to   be able to   be able to
go over and   go over and   go over and
talk to her   talk to her   talk to her
                               in some cases   in every case

(continued)

[a]From Dr. Craig Twentyman, 1975. Reprinted by permission.

skills training intervention. Low scores on this inventory, indicative of low self-reported skill, have been shown to correlate significantly with client reports of anxiety during simulated heterosocial interactions with a female confederate, observer ratings of poor social skill during these simulated interactions, and infrequent dating and heterosocial activity in the natural environment as assessed by the client's self-monitoring entries in his diary (Twentyman & McFall, 1975).

(continued)

On a work break at your job you see a girl who also works there and is about your age. You would like to talk to her, but you do not know her. You would:

1	2	3	4	5	6	7

be unable to
talk to her
in every case

be able to
talk to her
in some cases

be able to
talk to her
in every case

You are on a crowded bus, a girl you know only <u>slightly</u> is sitting in front of you. You would like to talk to her but you notice that the fellow sitting next to her is watching you. You would:

1	2	3	4	5	6	7

be unable to
talk to her
in every case

be able to
talk to her
in some cases

be able to
talk to her
in every case

You are at a dance. You see an attractive girl whom you do not know, standing <u>in a group</u> of four girls. You would like to dance. In this situation you would:

1	2	3	4	5	6	7

be unable to
ask in every
case

be able to
ask in some
cases

be able to
ask in
every case

You are at a drugstore counter eating lunch. A girl whom you do not know sits down beside you. You would like to talk to her. After her meal comes she asks you to pass the sugar. In this situation you would pass the sugar:

1	2	3	4	5	6	7

but be unable
to initiate a
conversation
with her

and in some
cases be able
to initiate a
conversation

and be able
to initiate
a conversa-
tion

A friend of yours is going out with his girlfriend this weekend. He wants you to come along and gives you the name and phone number of a girl he says would be a good date. You are not doing anything this weekend. In this situation you would:

1	2	3	4	5	6	7

be unable to
call in every
case

be able to
call in some
cases

be able to
call in
every case

The Survey of Heterosexual Interactions for Females (Williams & Ciminero, 1978) is a modification of the Twentyman and McFall (1975) inventory, making it suitable for female clients. The 20 situations described in the Survey of Heterosexual Interactions for Females correspond to the situations in the males' inventory, except for alterations in wording. It is scored in a manner similar to the males' version of the Survey of Heterosexual Interactions, with low total scale scores indicative of self-reported inability to effectively handle the surveyed situations; high scores indicate that the respondent has little trouble handling the situations described by inventory items.

You are at the library. You decide to take a break, and as you walk down the hall you see a girl whom you know only casually. She is sitting at a table and appears to be studying. You decide that you would like to ask her to get a coke with you. In this situation you would:

1	2	3	4	5	6	7

be unable to ask her in every case

be able to ask her in some cases

be able to ask her in every case

You want to call a girl up for a date. You find this girl attractive but you do not know her. You would:

1	2	3	4	5	6	7

be unable to call in every case

be able to call in some cases

be able to call in every case

You are taking a class at the university. After one of your classes you see a girl whom you know. You would like to talk to her, however, she is walking with a couple of other girls you do not know. You would:

1	2	3	4	5	6	7

be unable to talk to her in every case

be able to talk to her in some cases

be able to talk to her in every case

You have been working on a committee for the past year. There is a banquet at which you are assigned a particular seat. On one side of you there is a girl you do not know, on the other is a guy you do not know. In this situation you would:

1	2	3	4	5	6	7

be unable to initiate a conversation with the girl and talk only with the guy

be able to initiate a conversation with the girl in some cases but talk mostly to the guy

be able to initiate a conversation in every case and be able to talk equally as freely with the girl as with the guy

(continued)

In addition to the self-report inventories specific to discomfort in heterosocial interactions, the therapist might wish to consider the use of a more generalized measure of social anxiety or discomfort, such as the Social Avoidance and Distress Scale or the Fear of Negative Evaluations Scale (Watson &

(continued)

> You are in the lobby of a large apartment complex waiting for a friend. As you are waiting for him to come down, a girl whom you know well walks by with another girl whom you have never seen before. The girl whom you know says hello and begins to talk to you. Suddenly she remembers that she left something in her room. Just before she leaves you she tells you the other girl's name. In this situation you would:

1	2	3	4	5	6	7

find it very
difficult to
initiate and
continue a
conversation
with the
other girl

find it only
slightly
difficult

find it easy
to initiate
and continue
a conversa-
tion

> You are at a party at a friend's apartment. You see a girl who has come alone. You don't know her, but would like to talk to her. In this situation you would:

1	2	3	4	5	6	7

be unable to
go over and
talk to her

be able to go
over and talk
to her in some
cases

be able to
go over and
talk to her
in every
case

> You are walking to your mailbox in the large apartment complex building where you live. When you get there you notice that two girls are putting their names on the mailbox of the vacant apartment beneath yours. In this situation you would:

1	2	3	4	5	6	7

be unable to
go over and
initiate a
conversation

be able to
initiate a
conversation
in some
cases

be able to
initiate a
conversation
in every
case

> You are at a record store and see a girl that you once were introduced to. That was several months ago and now you have forgotten her name. You would like to talk to her. In this situation you would:

1	2	3	4	5	6	7

be unable to
start a con-
versation with
her in every
case

be able to
start a
conversation
with her in
some cases

be able to
start a
conversation
with her in
every case

Friend, 1969, described in Chapter 6). Although the items comprising each of these inventories do not specifically inquire about clients' date-initiation or heterosocial functioning, SAD and FNE scores have been shown to differentiate between high- and low-frequency daters, to correlate with other measures of heterosocial anxiety, and to change as a result of date-initiation training. (See Arkowitz, 1977, for a summary of this research.)

Representative Date-Initiation Training

As we noted earlier, most research on heterosocial-skills training has been conducted with college students who report difficulties in this area (low-frequency dating, anxiety when interacting with persons of the opposite sex, and so on). Studies that have used social-skills training procedures have often compared this treatment approach to other types of intervention (no-treatment control, systematic desensitization, reflective therapy, sensitivity training, or

```
You are at the student union or local cafeteria where friends
your age eat lunch.  You have gotten your meal and are now looking
for a place to sit down.  Unfortunately, there are no empty tables.
At one table, however, there is a girl sitting alone.  In this
situation you would:

     1         2         3         4         5         6         7

wait until                     ask the girl                  ask the girl
another place                  if you could                  if you could
was empty and                  sit at the                    sit at the
then sit down                  table but not                 table and
                               say anything                  then initiate
                               more to her                   a conversa-
                                                             tion in every
                                                             case


A couple of weeks ago you had a first date with a girl you
now see walking on the street towards you.  For some reason you
haven't seen each other since then.  You would like to talk to
her but aren't sure of what she thinks of you.  In this situation
you would:

     1         2         3         4         5         6         7

walk by                        walk up to                    walk up to
without                        her and say                   her and say
saying                         something                     something in
anything                       in some                       every case
                               cases


Generally, in most social situations involving girls whom I
do not know, I would:

     1         2         3         4         5         6         7

be unable to                   be able to                    be able to
initiate a                     initiate a                    initiate a
conversation                   conversation                  conversation
                               in some                       in every
                               cases                         case
```

others). Since our present objective is to review several representative clinical studies on skills-training, attention will be focused on projects that principally utilized this treatment approach and which have the greatest potential for application in direct-service settings.

Curran and his associates have conducted a series of studies investigating the effectiveness of heterosocial-skills training. One of the earlier projects involved a comparison of group skills-training with systematic desensitization and no treatment (Curran, 1975). Clients in this study were male and female college students, many of whom had a history of minimal dating or no previous dates at all. Before the intervention phase, all clients completed the Situation Questionnaire (Rehm & Marston, 1968) and a social-fear inventory. Each client also engaged in an individual semistructured interaction with an opposite-sex confederate. In this 3-minute interaction, clients were asked to imagine that they were waiting for their order at a pizza parlor during a first date with the confederate. The client was instructed to converse with the partner as though he or she were in that situation; the confederate partner always provided brief, neutral responses and allowed the client to maintain conversational initiative. Observers rated each client's performance in this sample interaction on 7-point scales for interpersonal skill and social anxiety.

Clients in the skills-training group received a total of six 75-minute training sessions spaced over a 3-week period. Two graduate-student therapists led each group session. Some of the component-behaviors targeted for treatment included giving and receiving compliments, listening skills, feeling talk (self-disclosures), assertion, and nonverbal communication. For each component, the therapist provided instruction and presented a modeling videotape showing the correct use of that behavior. Clients then engaged in a behavior-rehearsal interaction to practice the component. Because both male and female clients were in the group, clients served as opposite-sex rehearsal partners with one another. Group and videotape feedback were used following the practice interactions. Homework assignments to practice each skill-component, and attention to increasing physical attractiveness were also included in the intervention.

Clients assigned to the systematic desensitization group received a comparable amount of treatment attention, with the procedure aimed specifically towards reducing heterosocial anxiety. Control-group clients received either no treatment or an attention-placebo treatment of relaxation training not targeted to date-related situations. Curran (1975) found that while clients who had been randomly assigned to the treatment and control groups did not differ on any pretreatment measures, both the skills-training and the desensitization clients were rated as lower in anxiety and higher in social competence when semistructured interactions with confederate partners were repeated at posttreatment. Control-group clients did not show improvement.

Curran and Gilbert (1975) elaborated the Curran (1975) project in several ways. These included intensifying the treatment intervention to 8 weekly sessions, each of 90-minutes' duration; examining changes in actual client dating frequency as a result of training; and obtaining follow-up data 6 months after training to evaluate the intervention's durability. Clients in the skills-training group received training on components similar to those in Curran (1975), with the addition of "asking for a date" and "handling silences." Both males and females were in the group and each 90-minute session focused on one or two components. Curran and Gilbert (1975) report that within each session, instruction and discussion of that day's targeted component by the co-therapists lasted 10–15 minutes. A 10- to 15-minute modeling videotape was shown, followed by a 30- to 40-minute period for each client's behavior rehearsal within the group session. In the rehearsal, clients used the targeted component during short practice interactions with one another, and received feedback plus reinforcement from the therapists and the other group members who observed the practice. Finally, sessions ended with clients presenting specific information about in-vivo heterosocial interactions in which they had used their newly acquired skills during the previous week. This information was obtained by providing recording diary-forms each week and having clients record all relevant situations on a daily basis. Additionally, the clients were asked to bring their recordings to the group sessions, where both the therapists and the other clients reinforced reports of clients using appropriate skills in the natural environment.

Curran and Gilbert (1975) found that clients who received this skills-training intervention and clients who received systematic desensitization for dating situations both demonstrated significantly greater reduction in anxiety by the end of training than control-group clients who received no intervention; this anxiety-reduction effect was shown for both self-report measures and for observer ratings of anxiety exhibited by clients during their semistructured interactions with opposite-sex confederates. During the posttraining interactions, clients receiving skills-training were rated as more skillful than control-group clients; when follow-up practice interactions were repeated 6 months after the intervention, the skills-training group was evaluated by judges as more competent than clients who had received either systematic desensitization or no treatment. Increased dating was found among clients who received heterosocial-skills training and systematic desensitization.

In a similar study, Curran, Gilbert, and Little (1976) compared a heterosocial-skills training intervention with a sensitivity-training procedure of comparable intensity. The skills-training group was handled in the same manner as Curran and Gilbert (1975). However, because most clients were males, female confederates attended the skills-training group sessions to serve as partners during the practice or rehearsal interactions that occurred as a part of each session. This project found that the skills-training intervention was associated with improvement on a number of self-report measures of heterosocial anxiety, improved behavioral ratings of client social skill, decreased anxiety during simulated interactions with an opposite-sex confederate, and frequency of actual dates.

In contrast to the group-training projects of Curran and his associates, Twentyman and McFall (1975) utilized an intervention consisting of individual client treatment. All clients were males who were "shy" and who dated infrequently. Pretreatment assessment included several simulated interactions with a female confederate, including a semistructured 5-minute conversation such as might take place between the client and a woman who sits next to him in class. Observers rated the client's anxiety and interpersonal skill during the conversation. Physiological recordings were made of the client's pulse-rate during the simulated interactions to obtain an additional measure of anxiety independent of client self-report. All clients also completed the Survey of Heterosexual Interactions questionnaire.

Clients were randomly assigned to either individual heterosocial-skills training or no-treatment control condition. Each training session utilized a modeling tape recording to demonstrate effective social skills in heterosocial interactions, instructions and coaching provided by the therapist, and behavior rehearsal with a female confederate. Behavior rehearsal in each session was repeated whenever the client was unhappy with his first rehearsal performance. Twentyman and McFall (1975) focused training on several different date-related interactions. For example, one session particularly stressed the use of effective skills when telephoning someone for a date. Other sessions addressed the exhibition of appropriate skill-components during face-to-face interactions. In-session behavior-rehearsal was tailored to the type of situation receiving attention that day; for example, when telephone skills were taught, rehearsal consisted of role-play phone calls with the female confederate on the other end of the telephone line.

At the conclusion of each client's training, the simulated interactions with confederates used prior to treatment were repeated. Additionally, clients maintained self-monitoring diaries of their interactions with women for one week before, and again one week after, the intervention. Twentyman and McFall (1975) found, when compared to clients who received no treatment, that those in skills-training were: (1) rated as more skilled and less anxious during their posttraining interactions; (2) showed reduced pulse rate after the intervention; (3) had increased heterosocial activity in the natural environment based on their diary entries; and (4) achieved greater improvement in scores on the Survey of Heterosexual Interactions.

Each of the above-mentioned projects has demonstrated that social-skills training, whether conducted with individual clients or group-administered, can improve the heterosocial skills and decrease the heterosocial anxiety of interpersonally deficient clients. In addition to the interventions we have just reviewed, investigations have focused attention on other treatment elements that are relevant to the applied therapist. These include the importance of in-vivo practice of heterosocial skills, enhancing clients' physical attractiveness, and stressing cognitive modification as a part of treatment.

Dating-skills Practice in the Natural Environment

Arkowitz and his associates have conducted a series of projects that demonstrate, simply yet effectively, the importance of behavioral practice in heterosocial-skills training. Christensen and Arkowitz (1974) recruited 14 male and 14 female college students for an intervention designed to increase their frequency, skills, and comfort when dating. Pretraining and posttraining measures included the Social Avoidance and Distress Scale and the Fear of Negative Evaluations Scale (Watson & Friend, 1969). Clients also self-monitored their frequency of dates and nondate heterosocial interactions for 12 days before and 12 days after training. The intervention itself consisted of 6 practice-dates with other clients in the project. Opposite-sex clients were randomly paired with one another for practice-dates by the therapists; the male and female clients who had been matched for a practice-date on a given week were provided with one another's names and phone numbers, and were asked to settle on all date details with one another when the male called the female with whom he was matched. All clients were aware that their dates would be with other clients and that the purpose of the intervention was to simply provide dating practice. No two clients were matched with each other more than once. Following a practice-date, each client completed a feedback form describing aspects of his or her partner's behavior that were desirable or that needed attention. The forms were given to the therapist, who then forwarded them to the appropriate client.

Christensen and Arkowitz (1974) reported improvement from pretraining to posttraining both for self-report measures and for frequency of actual dating with persons other than clients. Clients also reported decreases in their heterosocial anxiety over the course of training. In a second study, Christensen, Arkowitz, and Anderson (1975) included a control group and varied whether or not clients in the practice-dating intervention received weekly feedback from their matched dating partners. The investigators found that clients in the practice interventions, with or without partner feedback, showed greater improvement on a variety of anxiety, dating frequency, and social-skill measures than did the control group clients.

These projects are noteworthy because clients received only in-vivo practice with feedback, rather than formal training in effective heterosocial skills. However, it is important to recognize that clients in these studies were not extremely skills-deficient; in the Christensen and Arkowitz (1974) project, clients who participated in the intervention averaged 1.5 dates during the 12-day assessment before the practice dating took place. We might assume that these individuals had reasonable dating histories but still experienced some degree of heterosocial discomfort. If this was the case, the anxiety-reduction or desensitization aspect of practice-dating alone was probably a sufficient treatment. For more seriously deficient clients, skills-training would have to precede in-vivo practice.

Apart from interventions that use practice-dating as a primary mode of treatment, other social-skills training projects reviewed in this section often made use of self-monitoring diaries or other procedures to measure changes in heterosocial behavior outside the training setting. Although the purpose of this was usually to obtain research information on generalization of skills-training, an applied intervention can make use of client in-vivo self-monitoring information as a part of treatment itself. The therapist in individual-client training, or the therapist and other group members in group-administered training, can review client self-monitoring data to reinforce client reports of date-initiation or increased heterosocial interactions. This was incorporated as a part of training in the Twentyman and McFall (1975) project.

In regard to dating practice, it may be necessary for the therapist to work with the client on increasing exposure to situations in the natural environment where there will be an opportunity to meet opposite-sex persons. One heterosocially unskilled college student seen by the author reported that he simply did not know where to meet other people. He characteristically would spend evenings sitting alone on campus, hoping that a woman might also sit down and initiate an interaction. With this client, and with other individuals who have very limited exposure to situations where they can meet potential dates, it may be necessary to do some practical planning to increase opportunities for heterosocial-skill use. This might include encouraging the client to attend social gatherings, dances, become involved in interest groups related to the client's hobbies, do volunteer work in settings where one can meet opposite sex persons, or so on. Again, it is important that the client first acquire an adequate skills repertoire to successfully handle these situations.

Physical Attractiveness in Relation to Dating

In addition to a substantial research base suggesting that attractive physical appearance is quite strongly related to all types of successful interpersonal functioning (see Berscheid & Walster, 1973), Glasgow and Arkowitz (1975) have specifically reported differences in physical attractiveness between high- and low-frequency daters. Several skills-training interventions included attention to improving one's physical appearance (Curran & Gilbert, 1975; Curran et al., 1976), and Arkowitz (1977) has pointed out the need to strengthen physical-appearance training within date-initiation interventions. Although some aspects of a client's physical appearance may be unmodifiable, it is likely that many other contributors to attractiveness can be altered. These include changes in hair style, dress, complexion, weight, or posture. If it appears that unattractive physical attributes of a client are contributing to dating or heterosocial problems, the therapist may find it useful to provide attention to enhancing the individual's appearance as well as his or her social skills. Arkowitz (1977), for example, has even suggested using special appearance consultants to instruct clients in ways to improve their dress, hairstyle, or grooming, if this is indicated.

Cognitive Modification Aspects of Training

In Chapter 4, it was suggested that cognitive-modification procedures be included in skills-training interventions in order to decrease anxiety-related thoughts and increase socially facilitative cognitions as clients approach and interact in previously troublesome situations. A study by Glass, Gottman, and Shmurak (1976) actually compared a heterosocial training-procedure without cognitive training, a procedure using only cognitive modification, and a technique combining behavioral-skills training with cognitive modification. The cognitive aspect of treatment taught clients to recognize their negative thoughts related to heterosocial situations and then generate positive, alternative cognitions in their place (see Meichenbaum, 1972). Results of this project indicated that the skills-training-alone group and the combined-skills-training-with-cognitive-modification group performed more skillfully than the cognitive-modification-alone group on social-interaction tests that had been the specific target of training. However, the cognitive-modification treatment was related to enhanced performance in novel social-interaction tasks, suggesting that this form of treatment may provide enhanced generalization to new interactions other than those specifically trained. In his review paper on heterosocial-skills training, Curran (1975) points out that the Glass et al. (1976) results seem to indicate that clients' initial level of heterosocial competence differentially affected their response to treatment. It appears that clients who were most skills-deficient achieved the greatest benefit from the combined skills-training with cognitive-modification treatment, while more frequent daters improved with cognitive modification alone. Presumably, clients who are extremely deficient in heterosocial functioning lack both the behavioral skills and the positive cognitions needed to handle such interactions. For them, skills-training combined with thought-modification techniques appear quite promising. As outlined in Chapter 4, one practical way to combine these approaches in an intervention is to first focus on skills-training and, later in training, utilize cognitive-modification techniques and therapy procedures to increase client use of the new skills in the natural environment.

Chapter 8

Assertiveness-Training

Assertion-training is undoubtedly the form of social-skills treatment that has received the greatest attention in both the applied research literature and in clinical practice. Indeed, until somewhat recently, the terms "assertion-training" and "social-skills training" were often used in an interchangeable fashion; it was not recognized that assertiveness represents one specific kind of interpersonal competency. Although a large number of definitions have been proposed, assertiveness has been generally construed as the ability of an individual to effectively, and without discomfort, convey personal positions, opinions, beliefs, or feelings to another person. As we noted in Chapter 1, assertive responses may occur in the context of a disagreement or dispute between individuals, as when someone unreasonably attempts to block the goal-directed behavior of a person. The form of assertiveness that is an appropriate response to such a situation is termed refusal assertion, because the individual is refusing the unacceptable act or statement of the antagonist and attempting to bring about more acceptable behavior in the future. Commendatory assertion refers to an individual's ability to express warm, complimentary feelings or opinions to others when their positive behavior warrants it. While investigators and clinicians have noted the importance of using each kind of assertiveness in daily living (see Lazarus, 1971; Wolpe, 1969), refusal assertion has received the greatest attention in the social-skills training literature.

An important distinction should be made between refusal assertion and aggressiveness when confronted with unreasonable behavior from another person. Both *do* differ from passivity or compliance in the sense that the individual is not accepting an antagonist's unacceptable behavior. However, the intent of an assertive response is to effectively communicate one's own position and provide the antagonist with specific feedback concerning how he or she should behave in the future. While an assertive response is made in a firm, clear, and convincing manner, it is not hostile in tone, style, or verbal content. The purpose of refusal assertion is to calmly communicate one's feelings and "invite" the antagonist to change his or her behavior, not to unleash belligerent comments on the other individual. Several recent studies have utilized naive observers or social-interaction participants to evaluate the behavior of persons who acted in either a passive, an assertive, or an aggressive manner when confronted by an antagonist (Hull & Schroeder, 1979; Mullinix & Galassi, 1978; Woolfolk & Dever, 1979). For the most part, assertive skills were evaluated in favorable terms, while both passive and aggressive response styles were evaluated more negatively by the person observing them. One possible exception to this pattern involves the sex of the individual who is seen behaving assertively; some investigators have found that males handling troublesome situations in an assertive manner are evaluated by naive observers in more positive terms than females who behave assertively in identical situations (Kelly, Kern, Kirkley, Patterson, & Keane, 1980). We will later consider the importance of using cognitive-modification procedures to help clients become less fearful of the possibility that other people may not respond well to their newly developing assertive skills.

Refusal assertiveness differs from the other forms of social competency that we have considered to this point because it does not primarily bring about the establishment of new social relationships such as friendships, conversations, or dates. Instead, refusal-assertion skills prevent the loss of reinforcement to clients when people might otherwise take advantage of them. For example, individuals are occasionally confronted with situations in which someone else attempts to impose demands, take advantage, or otherwise unreasonably attempt to control them. If that individual persistently capitulates to the unwarranted demands of others when he or she would prefer to behave otherwise, it is likely that feelings of helplessness, loss of control, diminished self-worth, or depression will result. However, when a client learns to behave more assertively in conflict situations, several desirable consequences can occur. One of the foremost is that the client can effectively bring about change in the antagonist's behavior. When an overly passive client fails to convey his own position or feelings to others and fails to communicate a reasonable behavior-change request to another person, it is unlikely that the client will effect any behavior change from the other party. On the other hand, a demonstrative and clear statement of one's own position is much more likely to serve functional purposes for the client by bringing about behavior change or, at least, further discussion to resolve any conflict. A second positive consequence of effective refusal-assertion skills is that, regardless of whether or not a client successfully does change an antagonist's unreasonable behavior, the client will be aware that he or she acted appropriately, rather than passively complying with someone else's unreasonableness. Presumably, development of a skills-repertoire to deal with conflict situations will lead to increased perceptions of self-efficacy rather than those of helplessness or frustration.

Commendatory assertion, as we noted in an earlier chapter, serves to make a client a more effective "dispenser" of verbal reinforcement to others. Almost everyone enjoys receiving genuine positive recognition or compliments from others. Children generally like praise from their teachers, and teachers appreciate praise from their principals; clients generally respond well to commendation from their therapists, while therapists like to hear they have done a good job from their own bosses. Interstingly, in the child behavior-therapy literature, one of the most basic techniques to increase a child's appropriate actions is providing specific praise from a parent or teacher whenever the child engages in the desired behavior. In essence, the parent is systematically using commendatory assertion to change the behavior of the child and bring about a more positive relationship with him. In somewhat analogous fashion, training in commendatory social skills teaches a client to be a more reinforcing agent to others in the environment. Because complimentary social behavior can exert a strong and positive influence on the conduct of other people, developing the ability to warmly and sincerely commend positive actions of others can be a powerful interpersonal skill. Many clients who report that others do not like them or who report that they are unable to influence the actions of others seem to be deficient in their use of commendatory assertiveness.

I was once asked to consult to a manufacturing company that was experiencing problems in supervisor-employee relations, including excessive absenteeism, tardiness, reduced production, and high employee turnover. An area of conflict appeared to involve the day-to-day interactions of supervisors and the "on-line" employees under their direction. To assess this, a series of role-play situations were constructed to approximate some everyday interactions that a supervisor might have with a subordinate. Some role-plays were of situations in which the subordinate behaved unreasonably, persistently coming to work late, performing poor-quality and careless work, and so on. Supervisors were asked to role-play how they would handle these situations which require effective refusal-assertion skills. Other role-play scenes required the supervisor to interact with a role-play partner in situations where the partner, playing the subordinate, did something unusually well, such as offering to stay late to finish an important project, completing a job ahead of schedule, or always coming to work a few minutes early. The latter scenes represent situations where effective commendatory skills would be desirable. Upon examining the role-play performance of company supervisors, it was evident that while most were quite skilled in handling the unacceptable behavior of the partner in the refusal-assertion scenes, very few were able to demonstrate effective commendatory skills for handling employees' good behavior in the role-play situations. It was not possible to conclusively attribute employee-relation difficulties at the company to the apparent inability of its supervisors to use commendatory skills effectively. However, one might suspect that skills-training to increase the supervisors' capacity to recognize and commend desirable behavior among employees would result in a better working relationship and employment environment at the company.

The use of commendatory assertiveness is certainly not limited to interactions occurring in the work setting. Commendatory skills are appropriate whenever a client feels positively about some aspect of another person's behavior and wishes to express it. At least two beneficial outcomes can be derived from the use of effective commendatory assertion. First, a client will be in a position to actually modify the behavior of others by actively and directly reinforcing their positive behavior. Since many clients do not perceive themselves as having the capability to influence other people in this way, training can add an important skill to the individual's behavioral repertoire. Second, because most people appreciate receiving genuine expressions of positive recognition from others, it is likely that the client's own reinforcement value to them will be increased by virture of this response capability.

Client Populations for
Refusal-Assertion

Many early reports of refusal-assertion training described the treatment of socially passive college students. However, this form of skills-training has been extended to an extremely wide range of clinical populations as well. Although it would be virtually impossible to catalogue the many client groups for whom refusal-assertion training has been used, they include students seeking assistance from university counseling centers, chronic psychiatric inpatients of various diagnoses, formerly institutionalized schizophrenics, mental health center outpatients, unassertive adolescents, specialized women's groups, and so on. In addition to these types of client populations, refusal-assertion training procedures have also been adapted for much more specialized problems. Examples include teaching former alcoholics to refuse offers of drinks made by other people, teaching predelinquent adolescents to assert themselves when they are interacting with peers and might otherwise become involved in further antisocial acts, and assisting retarded persons to handle situations where they could be abused or exploited. While the selection criteria used to determine whether clients need refusal-assertion training vary enormously across treatment studies, they have generally included: a client's own reports of passivity in situations where the client wishes to be more assertive and forceful; staff observations that indicated that the client behaves unassertively in a hospital, clinic, or school setting; or inferences made by a therapist from interview data that a client's current mood or interpersonal distress was a consequence of that person's failure to handle situations assertively.

An interesting exception to the pattern of using refusal-assertion training for clients who are extremely passive is the application of this treatment for highly explosive or aggressive individuals (see Foy, Eisler, & Pinkston, 1975; Frederiksen, Jenkins, Foy, & Eisler, 1976; Frederiksen & Kelly, 1977). It appears that some clients handle troublesome situations or frustrations in an explosive manner because they do not have the skills to deal with interpersonal conflict in a more appropriately assertive fashion. Indeed, some clients who "explode" in violent rage characteristically appear to be quite passive and unexpressive, except for their occasional episodes of extreme anger. It is possible that if such individuals can be taught the assertive skills needed to appropriately handle and resolve everyday conflicts, their extremes of social passivity and periodic explosiveness could be moderated.

Another client group that has received a good deal of recent attention in the refusal-assertion training literature is women. Historically, sex-role stereotypes have associated assertiveness, the expression of opinions, leadership, and decision-making competencies with masculinity. Traditional feminine roles have stressed submissiveness, self-subordination, emotionality, and nurturant characteristics. Early-life socialization experiences and later sex-role expectations have probably restricted many females' opportunities to learn and exhibit appropriate refusal-assertion skills, since assertiveness is not a quality that has been highly reinforced among women; investigators have generally found females to be less assertive than males (see Bloom, Coburn, & Pearlman, 1975; Hollandsworth & Wall, 1977). However, as a result of new social developments—which include issues raised by the feminist social-political movement; less rigid sex-stereotyping in educational, training, and employment practices; and increased opportunities and expectations for women to occupy roles that require more forceful social skills—there has been increased attention focused on assertion-training for females.

In summary, refusal-assertiveness training has been successfully used with an extremely wide range of client groups. These include inpatient, residential, and outpatient populations. Clients who are relatively low-functioning, such as chronic psychiatric patients, and clients who are relatively high-functioning but experience difficulty asserting themselves in certain situations can derive benefit from this form of skills-intervention. Regardless of the population, a key element of refusal-assertion training is making certain that the intervention identifies and targets situations known to be relevant for a particular client or group of clients.

Client Populations for
Commendatory-Assertion Training

A number of clinicians have pointed out the importance of commendatory assertive behavior and have distinguished it from refusal assertion (Eisler et al., 1975; Hersen, Eisler, & Miller, 1973; Lazarus, 1971; Wolpe, 1969). However, there has been relatively less use of specific commendatory-assertion training reported in the applied literature and it appears that most assertiveness training has focused upon either refusal skills alone or refusal and commendatory skills together. One project described the treatment of a highly anxious patient who was very unreinforcing during interactions with his family and with co-workers at work (Kelly at al., 1978). Bellack, Hersen, and Turner (1976) also taught hospitalized psychiatric patients both refusal and commendatory skills in an effort to increase each variety of their expressive social behavior.

In spite of the relative paucity of populations for whom commendatory training has actually been used, this technique would appear applicable for many client groups. The main criteria for training include a client's inability to respond to positive behavior from others, as well as difficulties in interpersonal relationships that can be attributed to the person's failure to initiate or com-municate warm, affectionate responses. For clients who appear deficient in both refusal and commendatory-assertion skills, a single intervention might consolidate training for both of these competencies.

Assertion-Skills Assessment

In contrast to behavioral assessment of conversational or heterosocial skills, which evaluates client performance during extended semistructured or unstruc-tured sample interactions, assessment of assertiveness generally involves the rating of client skill during more structured role-plays. Because the format for staging assessment role-plays was discussed in Chapter 3, it will not be repeated in detail here. However, the scenes used in any client role-play assessment should represent approximations or samples of situations that the client has actually found troublesome in the past or will need to handle effectively in the future. As we noted in Chapter 3, role-play scenes consist of three parts: (1) a narrated "background" description of the situation that the client will be role-playing; (2) comments or prompts made by the role-play partner to the client; and (3) the client's assertive responses made directly back to the partner. In refusal-assertion role-plays, the scene narration describes a specific situation in which the client is faced with unreasonable behavior from someone else; the partner's comment to the client is that which the antagonist would make. For commendatory-assertion role-plays, the narration describes a situation in which another person does something positive and the partner directs a positive remark to the client. In order to make role-play scenes more realistic, a scene might include several different partner comments, each of which requires the client's response. For example, a refusal-assertion role-play might consist of two or three partner comments that escalate in unreasonable-ness, better testing the client's assertion repertoire to deal with interpersonal conflict. Finally, assessment of client assertiveness before training, as well as in practice during the course of treatment sessions, should be based on a number of different role-play scenes, rather than just a single, brief role-play interaction.

Behavioral Definitions of Components of Assertion

In the behavioral evaluation of conversational and heterosocial skills, the interval during which the therapist observes the client's skill is the entire semistructured or unstructured assessment interaction. For assertive role-plays, each response made by the client to a partner's comment is studied by the therapist to determine the adequacy of behavioral skill-components. The components described below should therefore be present whenever the client makes an assertive response to the role-play partner.

Refusal-assertion components are as follows: eye contact; affect; speech loudness; gestures; understanding statement or statement of problem; verbal noncompliance; request for new behavior or solution proposal; and speech duration.

Commendatory assertion components are as follows: eye contact; affect; speech loudness; praise/appreciation statement; personal feeling statement; reciprocal positive behavior; speech duration.

Let us now turn our attention to behavioral definitions for these components of skilled assertive responses, so that the therapist both can assess their presence during pretraining client role-plays and later teach them to the skills-deficient individual.

Refusal-Assertion Components

Eye contact, affect, and speech loudness.   As was the case for conversational and date-initiation competence, eye contact, appropriate affect, and sufficient speech loudness are also necessary components of refusal assertion. Eye contact represents the proportion of time that a client looks at the partner while speaking; if the client's response to the partner's comment is of approximately 10 seconds' duration, but eye contact was made for only about 2 seconds, the eye contact rating would be 20% and quite deficient. Firm affect is also a requisite of effective refusal assertion and can be rated for each client reponse using a 7-point scale. To be highly rated, the client's emotional tone should be firm, convincing, and appropriate to the conflict situation; extreme passivity and the lack of emotional firmness or, at the opposite pole, hostility and belligerence are examples of inappropriate affect. Finally, a speech loudness judgment can be made by the therapist also using a 7-point scale, with the ideal response spoken in a highly audible, clear manner.

Gestures.   Gestures, particularly those involving movement of the hand and arm while the client speaks, have also been proposed as a component of refusal assertion by many investigators. Gesturing is a nonverbal behavior that adds emphasis to the client's assertive responses and conveys the appearance of greater ease while interacting. The therapist rating a client's role-play response might define a gesture as hand or arm motion of at least six inches while the individual is speaking. Gestures can be counted as either present or absent in each role-play response made by the client to the partner.

Understanding statement or statement of problem.   In addition to nonverbal-content components, what are the verbal statements that should be present in a client's refusal-assertion response? Several specific types of content components have been widely proposed as contributors to effective assertion. The first is a statement by the client that indicates the existence and nature of a conflict situation, or that conveys client recognition of the antagonist's viewpoint. This can be termed an "understanding statement" or a "statement of the problem." When a client begins an assertive response with a statement that communicates the nature of the conflict issue or the client's awareness of the other person's point of view, it can moderate the response so that it will not be perceived as aggressive and also convey empathic understanding to the antagonist (Mullinix & Galassi, 1978; Romano & Bellack, 1980; Woolfolk & Dever, 1979). It is important to note that an understanding statement of this type is not an apology, a self-deprecating comment, or an excuse for the antagonist's behavior. Instead, it is a way to introduce the assertive response in a nonhostile fashion and ensure that the other person knows why the client is objecting.

To illustrate an example of this component, we might consider a role-play of a situation at the job in which a co-worker consistently leaves work early. The client is then left to complete the co-worker's responsibilities, and it is irritating to the client. An illustration of an understanding-statement component in the client's role-play response would be if the client said to the partner, "It's almost quitting time and I know we both want to leave work for the day. However . . ." Similarly, a statement of the problem component would be included if the client said to the partner, "I think we have a difficulty here because you're always in a hurry to leave work and I have to cover your responsibilities. . . ." Any role-play response that includes such a comment made by the client can be rated by the therapist as demonstrating the presence of making an understanding statement.

Noncompliance.   It is also important that a refusal-assertion response include a statement expressing clear noncompliance or disagreement with the antagonist's unreasonable behavior. A noncompliance statement is any verbalization that the other person's behavior is unacceptable, unsatisfactory, or will not be tolerated by the client. Examples of verbal noncompliance include: "This is not acceptable to me"; "I am not willing to do that"; "I will not continue to handle things for you that you should be doing yourself"; "You must stop that"; and so on. Whenever a client makes an explicit statement indicating noncompliance or resistance to unreasonable actions from the role-play partner, this component is considered to be present in the response. Noncompliance is absent whenever the client capitulates to the unreasonable partner behavior or whenever the client fails to include a direct statement indicating noncompliance or resistance in a role-play response.

Request for new behavior or solution proposal. If a client only states the existence of a problem, conveys awareness of the antagonist's position, and specifically indicates noncompliance with the other person's actions, it still does not communicate what the client would like the partner to do differently in the future. Since one ultimate aim of a refusal-assertion response is to effect behavior change from an antagonist, it is also necessary for a client to suggest a more acceptable course of action for the antagonist to follow in the future. A request for new behavior or conflict-solution proposal can be distinguished from noncompliance in the sense that noncompliance only indicates that the actions of the other person are unacceptable, while the behavior-change request goes beyond this by communicating an acceptable alternative to the person.

To better illustrate these verbal components of refusal assertion, let's consider again the role-play of the situation where a client's co-worker leaves work early, creating a situation where the client must cover his co-worker's responsibilities. In a role-play of this situation, the scene might describe the antagonist about to leave the office a half-hour early. The role-play partner initiates:

Partner: Good night, Charlie. I've got a busy evening planned and am going to leave a little early today.

Client: We have a problem, Jack, because whenever you leave early, I have to cover things that come up in your absence *[statement of the problem]*. I know you would like to leave so you can get a head start on your plans for the night *[understanding statement]*. However, it isn't reasonable for you to expect me to do your job for you and I am not willing to do this *[noncompliance]*. I'd like you to stay until all of our work is done, rather than leave early. That way, we can both finish faster *[request for new behavior/solution proposal]*.

If these comments had been observed in a client's role-play, the therapist would score, as present in the response, each of the verbal behaviors constituting effective refusal-assertion. If this role-play response also includes good eye contact, reasonably loud speaking voice, and appropriately firm affect, the observer rating it will probably judge this to be an appropriately assertive response with respect to all component behaviors. As we have noted, any role-play scene can be extended by having the interaction partner direct several prompts or comments to the client, with the client responding to each of them. The therapist then rates each different response made by the client to assess the presence of skill-components.

Speech duration. Duration of speaking has been widely identified as a component of refusal assertion, just as it was for the other types of social skill we have already considered. Speech duration may initally be too short, especially in skills-deficient individuals who do not know what to say in an assertive response. As new verbal skills are acquired over the course of treatment, increasing duration of replies should also be found. If the therapist wishes to objectively assess whether or not this occurs, a client's role-play responses can be timed in pretreatment assessment and then later in the intervention to determine change in this behavior. It is also possible that some clients will initially provide overly long, but nonetheless ineffective, assertive responses during role-plays. This could occur when the client talks excessively, circuitously, but without including the appropriate verbal components described above in a role-play response. In those cases, one would expect speech duration to decrease with training as the individual learns to make more succinct, clear, and direct remarks.

Rating Client Refusal-Assertion Role-Plays for Skill-Components

During the behavioral assessment of a client's refusal-assertion skills, which precedes the training intervention, the therapist will construct a set of role-play scenes approximating troublesome situations that the client has encountered or will be encountering in the natural environment. In the pretreatment assessment phase, the client can be asked to role-play responses to each of the scenes with a confederate partner or, less desirably, the therapist playing the antagonist and delivering the prompt comments to the client. The therapist who observes the role-plays rates every client response for each of the behavioral components we have discussed. A sample rating-form, which can be used to evaluate the adequacy of refusal-assertion responses, was presented in Chapter 3. When the therapist has observed the client's handling of the sample role-plays and has identified deficient verbal and nonverbal components, those behaviors can be targeted for particular attention in the assertive-training intervention itself. During treatment sessions, when the individual begins incorporating appropriate behaviors in his or her rehearsal/practice role-plays, the therapist can use the same rating procedure to objectively analyze whether previously deficient components are now present in the practice role-play responses.

Rating Client Commendatory-Assertion Components

Eye contact, affect, and speech loudness. Just as these three nonverbal behaviors are rated in refusal-assertion role-plays, they are also components of commendatory skill and should be evaluated when clients role-play scenes calling for commendatory assertion. Eye contact and speech loudness are rated in a fashion identical to refusal assertiveness. Affect in commendatory role-plays can again be judged by the therapist on a 7-point scale for each client response. "Ideal" commendatory affect should consist of a warm, friendly emotional tone; emotional responsiveness appropriate to the situation described in the role-play scene; the presence of smiles; and so on. Deficient client affect is characterized by the absence of these behaviors.

Praise/appreciation statement.   This verbal component is scored as present in a role-play response if the client specifically praises the partner's positive behavior and/or expresses appreciation to the partner for having engaged in some desirable behavior. Examples of praise/appreciation statements include any of the following kinds of comments in the role-play response: "It was very nice of you to stay late and help me with this"; "I really appreciate you telling me that"; "That's very nice of you"; "You did a fine job"; and so on. In each of these comments, the client is verbally reinforcing the partner for having done something nice.

Personal feeling statement.   A second verbal component of a socially skilled commendatory response is conveying to the other person information about one's own positive personal feeling that followed his or her desired action. This behavior is present if the client makes a statement to the other person such as: "It made me feel very good when you did that"; "I have enjoyed knowing you and working with you for the past year"; "I'm very proud of your accomplishment"; or "I feel very comfortable talking to you." This category of statement differs from a praise statement because it conveys information on one's own internal feelings, rather than complimenting the behavior of the other individual.

Reciprocal positive behavior.   Within a client's response, there can also be an offer to reciprocate the positive behavior shown by the other person at some time in the future. This can take the form of returning the other person's favor, offering to assist the partner is some future task or activity, or doing something the other party is likely to appreciate. Examples of some reciprocal positive behavior statements that can occur in a commendatory situation: "If I can ever do anything to help *you* out, let me know"; "I'd be glad to show you how I made this"; "Because you've been such a good employee, I want to put a merit citation in your file"; or "I'd like to return your favor by taking you out to lunch."

Speech duration.   The length of a client's reply to the role-play partner's positive comment has also been postulated as a component of effective commendatory skill. Just as in the case of refusal assertion, speech duration in commendatory assertion will ordinarily increase as a skills-deficient client learns to use the verbal content behaviors we have just reviewed.

To illustrate how these verbal components can each occur and be rated in a client's role-play performance, we might consider a scene in which a person has just returned from a week's vacation. The weather was dry, and a neighbor had taken it upon himself to water the client's newly planted garden. The role-play partner plays the neighbor and says to the client:

Partner: It didn't rain while you were gone, so I watered your plants for you.

Client: It was really nice of you to water the garden for me *[praise statement]*. I worked pretty hard to plant it and it makes me feel good to have a neighbor as thoughtful as you *[personal feeling statement]*. Whenever you get ready to go on your vacation, let me know and I'll be glad to look after your place too *[reciprocal positive behavior]*.

In this sample client response, each verbal component of commendatory assertion was present. Thus, it constitutes a demonstrative and warm reaction to the other person's positive action. To the extent that these verbal behaviors are missing, or the nonverbal components of adequate eye contact, loudness, and affect are absent in pretreatment role-plays, the therapist would identify them as deficiencies requiring training. During the behavior rehearsal or practice role-playing that occurs in later treatment sessions, the therapist can continue to evaluate client role-plays to determine whether the behaviors are exhibited. Figure 8.1 presents a sample form for rating commendatory assertion role-plays.

Self-Report Measures of Assertiveness

In conjunction with behavioral role-play assessment of a client's assertion skills, a therapist may wish to utilize a self-report measure of assertiveness. This can be done as a part of the client's pretraining skills-assessment, as well as later in the intervention to determine changes in the individual's self-perceptions of assertive functioning. As we have noted previously, it is important that a self-report inventory never take the place of more specific interview-based and behavioral assessment of social competency, since even well-constructed assertiveness inventories do not provide the therapist with detailed information on the specific situations that are troublesome for a given client or on the client's actual behavior within those situations. However, self-report scales do tap an important assessment domain, e.g., the client's generalized self-description of assertiveness competencies, and can be a useful adjunct source of data on behavior-change following an intervention.

Because assertion-training has received a great deal of attention, there have been a correspondingly large number of self-report inventories discussed in the literature. The items on most scales are intended to tap refusal-assertion abilities, although some inventories also include questions about the respondent's commendatory expressiveness. The following is a discussion of the three inventories most often used in recent assertion-training projects.

Assertion Inventory

Gambrill and Richey (1975) constructed an inventory of client assertiveness that consists of 40 brief situational descriptions and asks the client to indicate both degree of discomfort and likelihood of engaging in that situation. The authors suggest that this distinction may be of importance in treatment, with "high-discomfort" responders receiving particular training to increase their

FIGURE 8.1. Sample Rating-Form for Commendatory Assertion Role-Plays

Client Name:_____

Date of This Interaction:_____

Type of Interaction: _____ Pretraining Assessment

                            _____ Session Practice (Training
                                   Focused on What Component?

                            _____)

                            _____ Follow-up

Description of This Role Play Scene:_____

COMPONENT BEHAVIORS

1. <u>Eye Contact</u> (Approximate ratio of eye contact to total speaking
            time in this response)

   0%   10%   20%   30%   40%   50%   60%   70%   80%   90%   100%

   eye contact   eye contact
   almost never   made entire
   made   time

2. <u>Affect</u> (Emotional appropriateness/responsiveness)

      1   2   3   4   5   6   7

   Extremely   extremely warm,
   inappropriate,   friendly,
   absent or cold   appropriate to
                                                    situation

3. <u>Speech Loudness</u>

      1   2   3   4   5   6   7

   extremely   appropriate
   soft-spoken   loudness and
   so as to be   clarity
   inaudible

ease of expression and with "assertive-avoidant" persons perhaps requiring more work in basic-skills acquisition. Although these assumptions have not been specifically tested, the scale's distinction between a client's reported comfort and reported behavior in situations requiring assertiveness seems useful.

As Figure 8.2 indicates, items in the Gambrill and Richey (1975) inventory concern both refusal and commendatory skill. Presumably, a therapist could examine responses to items of each type, depending upon whether an intervention was concerned with training refusal assertion, commendatory assertion, or a consolidation of the two. The client completing this scale uses a 1 to 5 rating to describe himself or herself. Low scores on the "degree of discomfort" ratings indicate that the client is comfortable in situations in which he is required to be assertive. Low scores on the "response probability" ratings indicate a high likelihood of responding assertively. A client's total scale score can range from 40 (extremely comfortable, extremely assertive) to 200 (extremely uncomfortable, extremely unassertive). Normative data from large samples of college undergraduates provided inventory means of 90 to 96 on the discomfort measure and 102 to 111 on the response-probability measure (Gambrill & Richey, 1975). While males and females in the normative sample gave comparable scores on the discomfort index, males in the normative sample described

4. Praise/Appreciation Statement (Was this verbal content
                                  explicitly present in the
                                  response?)

                    _____ Absent

                    _____ Present

5. Personal Feeling Statement (Was this verbal content explicitly
                               present in the response?)

                    _____ Absent

                    _____ Present

6. Reciprocal Positive Behavior (Was this verbal content explicitly
                                 present in the response?)

                    _____ Absent

                    _____ Present

7. Speech Duration (Length of client's role-play response, in
                    seconds)

                    _____ seconds

8. Other Components Being Rated (or any undesirable, inappropriate
                                 behavior being examined)

    Definition/Description of Behavior: Frequency Count or
                                             Rating:

FIGURE 8.2. Directions and Items Comprising the Assertion Inventory[a]

Many people experience difficulty in handling interpersonal situations requiring them to assert themselves in some way, for example, turning down a request, asking a favor, giving someone a compliment, expressing disapproval or approval, etc. Please indicate your degree of discomfort or anxiety in the space provided before each situation listed below. Utilize the following scale to indicate a degree of discomfort.

1 = none
2 = a little
3 = a fair amount
4 = much
5 = very much

Then, go over the list a second time and indicate after each item the probability or likelihood of your displaying the behavior if actually presented with the situation. For example, if you rarely apologize when you are at fault, you would mark a "4" after that item. Utilize the following scale to indicate response probability.

1 = always do it
2 = usually do it
3 = do it about half the time
4 = rarely do it
5 = never do it

*Note. It is important to cover your discomfort ratings (located in front of the items) while indicating response probability. Otherwise, one rating may contaminate the other and a realistic assessment of your behavior is unlikely. To correct for this, place a piece of paper over your discomfort ratings while responding to the situations a second time for response probability.

Degree of Discomfort		Situation	Response Probability
_____	1.	Turn down a request to borrow your car.	_____
_____	2.	Compliment a friend.	_____
_____	3.	Ask a favor of someone.	_____
_____	4.	Resist sales pressure.	_____
_____	5.	Apologize when you are at fault.	_____
_____	6.	Turn down a request for a meeting or date.	_____

[a]From Gambrill, E. D. & Richey, C. A. "An assertion inventory for use in assessment and research," *Behavior Therapy*, 1975, 6, 552–553. Reprinted by permission.

186

themselves as somewhat more likely to behave assertively than did females. Limited reliability and validity data have been presented by the inventory authors, including the finding that scale scores change in the expected directions—less discomfort and more assertive-response probabilities following an assertion-training intervention (Gambrill & Richey, 1975). Because this measure taps a variety of situations and assesses both client anxiety and self-reported behavior, it appears to be an unusually comprehensive inventory of assertiveness.

_____	7. Admit fear and request consideration.	_____
_____	8. Tell a person you are intimately involved with when he/she says or does something that bothers you.	_____
_____	9. Ask for a raise.	
_____	10. Admit ignorance in some area.	_____
_____	11. Turn down a request to borrow money.	_____
_____	12. Ask personal questions.	_____
_____	13. Turn off a talkative friend.	_____
_____	14. Ask for constructive criticism.	_____
_____	15. Initiate a conversation with a stranger.	_____
_____	16. Compliment a person you are romantically involved with or interested in.	_____
_____	17. Request a meeting or a date with a person.	_____
_____	18. Your initial request for a meeting is turned down and you ask the person again at a later time.	_____
_____	19. Admit confusion about a point under discussion and ask for clarification.	_____
_____	20. Apply for a job.	_____
_____	21. Ask whether you have offended someone.	_____
_____	22. Tell someone that you like them.	_____
_____	23. Request expected service when such is not forthcoming, e.g., in a resturant.	_____
_____	24. Discuss openly with the person his/ her criticism of your behavior.	_____
_____	25. Return defective items, e.g., store or resturant.	_____
_____	26. Express an opinion that differs from that of the person you are talking to.	_____

(continued)

Rathus Assertiveness Schedule

Rathus (1973) developed a 30-item self-report measure of client refusal-assertion. Because it largely does not tap situations where commendatory skills are needed, this inventory would not be relevant to that form of skills-training. When completing the Rathus Schedule, the client indicates the degree to which each statement item is descriptive of his or her own behavior using a code of +3 ("very characteristic of me") to –3 ("very uncharacteristic of me"). Several sample items from the inventory are: "I have avoided asking questions for fear of sounding stupid"; "I often have a hard time saying no"; and "Anyone attempting to push ahead of me in a line is in for a good battle." While the Rathus Assertiveness Schedule has a number of positive construction features, including item-keying to control for acquiescence and acceptable reliability, some investigators have suggested that its item-content reflects social aggression rather than appropriate assertiveness (see Galassi & Galassi, 1978; Twentyman & Zimering, 1979).

(continued)

_____ 27. Resist sexual overtures when you are not interested. _____

_____ 28. Tell the person when you feel he/she has done something that is unfair to you. _____

_____ 29. Accept a date. _____

_____ 30. Tell someone good news about yourself. _____

_____ 31. Resist pressure to drink. _____

_____ 32. Resist a significant person's unfair demand. _____

_____ 33. Quit a job. _____

_____ 34. Resist pressure to "turn on." _____

_____ 35. Discuss openly with the person his/her criticism of your work. _____

_____ 36. Request the return of borrowed items. _____

_____ 37. Receive compliments. _____

_____ 38. Continue to converse with someone who disagrees with you. _____

_____ 39. Tell a friend or someone with whom you work when he/she says or does something that bothers you. _____

_____ 40. Ask a person who is annoying you in a public situation to stop. _____

College Self-Expression Scale (CSES)

Galassi, Deleo, Galassi, and Bastien (1974) have also developed a self-report inventory of client assertiveness termed the College Self-Expression Scale. Composed of 50 items, the CSES taps refusal assertion, commendatory assertion, and what its authors term "self-denial" (overapologizing, excessive anxiety, exaggerated concern for how others feel, etc.). CSES items are phrased as questions: "Would you exchange a purchase you discover to be faulty?"; "Is it difficult for you to compliment and praise others?"; "Are you overly careful to avoid hurting other people's feelings?" The client marks each with a number to signify his or her response, from $0 = always$ to $4 = never$. The responses to all 50 items are summed to yield an overall assertiveness score, with some items reverse-keyed to control for acquiescence. Galassi et al. (1974) have provided data on the reliability and validity of the CSES, including correlations between assertiveness scores and scales of pen-and-pencil personality measures. However, for a sample of student teachers, there were only very modest correlations between CSES scores and observer (supervisor) ratings of the students' assertiveness. As elaborated in Chapter 5, this may be due to the fact that any assertion inventory samples a client's general self-perceptions; these self-perceptions may not be highly consistent with the person's actual behavior when it is more objectively, externally measured.

Representative Assertion-Training Research

Let us now turn our attention to several assertion-training projects, both with individually treated clients and groups. As in previous chapters, we will focus primarily on procedures used for client assessment and skills-training sessions that are relevant for applied practitioners.

Assertion-Training with Individual Clients

A study by Hersen and Bellack (1976) illustrates very clearly how assertive-training can be conducted with individually treated clients. In this project, two patients were enrolled in a partial hospital program and had been diagnosed as schizophrenic. Staff observations indicated that each was interpersonally withdrawn, nonsocial, and minimally responsive during traditional treatment activities such as group therapy or other scheduled activities. Because they appeared highly unassertive, the clients were selected for training in both refusal and commendatory assertion.

Initial pretreatment assessment consisted of having each client role-play eight scenes with a confederate partner. Some of the scenes required refusal-assertion skills, while others required commendatory behavior while interacting with the partner. Both male and female partners were used. Assessment role-plays were repeated on several occasions to establish a clear baseline before treatment began. Role-play performance was always evaluated by observers who noted the presence and adequacy of behavioral skill-components in the client's responses. One client, for example, was found to be deficient in eye contact, and also in noncompliance with the partner's unreasonable behavior, in requests for new behavior from the partner, and in adequate speech duration. The component deficits observed in each client's pretreatment assessment role-plays were identified as those behaviors that would receive training attention.

For each client, treatment sessions were held daily. One client's daily sessions lasted 20 to 40 minutes for a period of about 4 weeks; the second client, described by Hersen and Bellack (1976) as more "chronic," required slightly longer daily sessions for 5 weeks. In all sessions, the client was seated next to a role-play partner with whom he would be interacting. The therapist served as the trainer and also observed the client's role-play practice with the partner. Sessions included: (1) instruction from the therapist on the behavioral component (eye contact, noncompliance, etc.) that would receive training attention that day; (2) observation of an individual live-modeling an effective assertive response, which included that component behavior; (3) a practice role-play, with the therapist narrating the scene description, the partner providing a prompt comment, and the client responding to it; and (4) feedback and corrective information provided by the therapist who observed the role-play. Whenever the client failed to correctly exhibit the targeted component in a role-play scene, the scene was repeated until improvement was evident and the next scene was then rehearsed. In every session, all 8 role-play scenes were always practiced, with feedback and instruction following each scene.

For both clients reported in the Hersen and Bellack (1976) study, social-skill components received attention sequentially and cumulatively over the course of the intervention. For example, the first three treatment sessions after initial assessment focused upon increasing the client's eye contact during role-plays. Later, other components also received attention (noncompliance, requests for new behavior, and speech duration for refusal scenes; affect, smiles, and so on for commendatory scenes). Approximately three sessions were devoted to each component. Throughout the intervention, the role-play practice scenes in each session were always rated to determine whether the client was effectively exhibiting the behavior that was being trained in that session. Because clients increased their use of a given component-behavior only when it was specifically targeted for training, the multiple baseline methodology demonstrated that treatment was responsible for improved skills during the practice role-plays. By the end of the intervention, and to a large degree at 2-month follow-up, clients were exhibiting all behavioral components in each role-play scene. Also, global ratings were made of the clients' overall assertiveness; these global judgments were substantially higher by the end of training.

Foy, Massey, Duer, Ross, and Wooten (1979) used a similar assertive-training procedure with three male clients in a short-term residential alcohol-treatment program. Each of the clients had experienced interpersonal difficulties at his job, and the nature of the difficulties suggested that the clients were unable to assert themselves appropriately when confronted with unreasonable behavior from others. A number of role-play scenes were developed to simulate work situations that required refusal assertiveness; clients were asked to role-play how they would normally handle each scene. One therapist served as the role-play partner; an observer rated each role-play performance for the behavioral components of refusal assertion. Therapist observation of these assessment role-plays revealed deficits on a number of refusal-assertion components including noncompliance, requests for new behavior from the antagonist, eye contact, and speech duration. Global, subjective judgements of overall assertiveness, made on a 1-to-5 scale, indicated that clients were also seen as unassertive in their overall impact during the role-plays.

Individual training sessions in this project were quite brief, lasting 10 to 15 minutes, and any client's entire intervention consisted of 9 to 12 sessions following the pretreatment assessment-phase. Components were introduced sequentially, with several training sessions devoted to each specific behavior. The Foy et al. (1979) study varied somewhat the way that each training session was conducted. In early sessions, the client was asked to simply observe a videotape that showed an assertive model handling the situations that the client would role-play in that session's practice. However, no specific therapist instructions were given either before or after the film, and the client merely role-played a scene immediately after the modeling film of it was shown. When these client practice role-plays were rated, very little improvement was evident. Then, the therapists "added" instruction to the treatment session format, by directing the client to note how and when the model exhibited specific components of assertion. Additionally, the therapist described the target behaviors in detail and provided a rationale for each. When sessions included these elements of treatment, client practice role-plays improved considerably, both in terms of the presence of specific skill behaviors and in overall, subjective ratings of the client's assertiveness. Role-plays repeated 6 months after training showed that clients maintained their skill improvement.

Other investigators have also examined variations in the type of assertive-training given to indivdually trained clients. Edelstein and Eisler (1976), in a study similar to Foy et al. (1979), confirmed that watching a videotaped assertive model alone had little effect on a client's performance in practice role-plays. However, the addition of detailed therapist instruction on how to exhibit each target behavior, and the provision of feedback following role-play practice did result in improved performance. Hersen, Eisler, Miller, Johnson, and Pinkston (1973) also found that the combination of modeling with instruction from the therapist was a more effective procedure than either modeling alone or instruction alone.

These projects, representative of the large number of individual-client assertive-training interventions reported in the literature, suggest that an optimal format for assertive-training sessions includes instruction on a behavioral component, modeling exposure of some type, role-play rehearsal of a scene requiring assertiveness, feedback, therapist reinforcement, and corrective instruction if it is needed. Since a role-play scene is fairly brief even when it consists of multiple partner-prompts and client responses, a number of different scenes can be practiced within a single session. It would appear desirable for therapist instructions and feedback to be used for each role-play scene that a client practices in the session. When the client has successfully mastered one component behavior and exhibits it correctly during all role-play scenes, the next skill component can then be targeted for training in the intervention. Finally, while most projects teaching assertiveness to individual clients have focused on refusal assertion, the same training procedures have been used successfully for commendatory skills (Hersen & Bellack, 1976; Kelly, Frederiksen, Fitts, & Phillips, 1978; Turner & Adams, 1977). Here, role-play scenes simulate situations in which the client has the opportunity to respond to the positive behavior of the partner, and the behaviors trained in the intervention are components of commendatory skill.

Generalization of Assertiveness to the Natural Environment

Unfortunately, most research on assertive-training with individual clients, including the studies just reviewed, has given little attention to enhancing the generalization of skill-improvement to troublesome situations within the natural environment. All too often, studies have not even examined evidence of client behavior-change beyond the doors of the training clinic. As we discussed in Chapter 4, an intervention can be considered clinically successful only when clients are able to utilize their newly acquired skills within the context of naturally occurring social relationships outside the training setting. In that earlier chapter, a number of techniques for increasing the generalization of skills-training interventions were discussed. Let us consider how they can be incorporated specifically in assertive-training.

Selecting relevant role-play scenes.   Carefully selecting role-play scenes for assessment, and later for session practice, that are known to be relevant for a particular client is crucial. Research on assertion-training has often relied on a standardized "inventory" of role-play scenes, which is used for the training of any skills-deficient client. Although such standardization is useful for research consistency, an applied intervention should always tailor role-play situations to the needs and problems of a particular client. If the situations used in training and practice closely approximate real problem-situations that the client will encounter, better generalization can be expected. Also, the role-play partner should behave, as much as possible, as the other person would if the situation occurred within the natural environment.

Teaching general principles. Training should focus on teaching the client general principles rather than memorized or "parroted" verbalizations. Providing rationales for skill-components and encouraging a client to generate personalized and novel examples of a skill-behavior are desirable, provided the client's behavior captures the general principle being taught. Novel role-play scenes and partners should be used whenever possible to ensure that a client is not merely responding to highly specific cues associated with practice.

Use of client self-monitoring. Client self-monitoring or diary data should be used in training. As discussed previously, the client can learn to be an observer of his or her own behavior in the natural environment between training sessions. In refusal-assertion training, clients can maintain recordings of daily situations in which they wanted to behave more assertively, had the opportunity for self-assertion, or actually did handle an interaction assertively. A portion of each skills-training session can be spent reviewing such self-monitoring data brought in by the client. In commendatory training, similar information can be kept on situations involving the positive behavior of others. Situations that the individual did not handle well can be incorporated in role-play practice during the session. The therapist should strongly reinforce instances when the client attempted to use the assertion skill.

Use of homework assignments. "Homework" assignments can be incorporated in treatment, especially later in training, when the client has learned more effective self-assertion skills than he initially had. Particularly if self-monitoring data do not reveal frequent in-vivo use of assertion skills, clients should be instructed to seek out situations where they can behave assertively. This could involve instruction to compliment other people's positive behavior at work or in social situations, to offer one's own opinion to someone else during any discussion or meeting, and so on. Although it is often not feasible to "assign" clients who have received refusal-assertion training to situations where others will infringe upon their rights, it is possible to ask clients to remain in or enter into situations that they might have previously avoided and to then use their assertive skills. Assertion homework of this kind should always include the task of recording, in self-monitoring fashion, the details of such situations and discussing them with the therapist in the next session.

Use of cognitive modification. Cognitive modification techniques should be included in the intervention. Cognitive restructuring is an important element in any form of skills-training; it seems especially salient for assertive-training because clients may have fears that others will not like their new assertiveness. As long as cognitive inhibitions and anxieties are strong, the likelihood that a client will actually use assertive behavior is reduced. Several studies have directly compared social-skills training and cognitive restructuring interventions. Linehan, Goldfried, and Goldfried (1979) found that treatment combining behavioral skills-training with a cognitive modification approach was generally more effective than either approach used alone. The cognitive restructuring used by these investigators involved teaching clients to identify their self-defeating or anxiety-maintaining thoughts, relabel or re-evaluate situations in a less threatening manner, generate positive self-statements about assertion, and so on.

These techniques and others reviewed in Chapter 4 should be used in treatment sessions. Additionally, clients can be instructed to practice cognitive change techniques in the natural environment, just as they are instructed to practice their newly acquired skill behaviors in the in-vivo situations.

Assertion-Training in Groups

A number of investigators have conducted group assertion-training projects and we will consider several of the more comprehensive interventions in detail.

Galassi, Galassi, and Litz (1974) treated unassertive male and female college students using a group-administered assertion-training procedure. In addition, they compared clients who received the group assertiveness-training with control groups consisting of students who received no treatment. Assertive-training groups were composed of 8 students (4 males and 4 females) and sessions were held twice weekly over 4 weeks; each session lasted about 90 minutes.

Before the initiation of training, each client completed the College Self-Expression Scale (Galassi et al., 1974) and role-played a variety of scenes that required refusal and commendatory assertiveness. A confederate partner played the other person in the scene; role-play scenes with multiple partner-prompts, requiring responses by the client to each prompt, were used. Each client's assessment role-plays were rated for the presence of behavioral components comprising effective refusal and commendatory assertion. Clients were also asked to evaluate on a 0 to 100 scale how much discomfort they felt during these role-plays.

Each assertion-training session throughout the intervention was broken down into three 30-minute segments. During the first segment, group members discussed the rationale for self-assertion, discriminating assertion from unassertive or aggressive behavior, and they discussed in-vivo situations in which they had behaved assertively. The therapist assigned "homework" to each group member (assignments to practice their skills outside the training setting); these results were also discussed at the beginning of each session. In the next session segment, clients viewed and discussed modeling videotapes showing appropriately assertive interactions. Finally, the group broke down into dyads, with one member of each dyad playing the partner in role-plays requiring assertiveness and the other member practicing assertive responses. Feedback during this practice was provided by the client playing the partner in the dyad, as well as by the therapist, who observed each dyad's rehearsals. Some client pairs were videotaped while role-playing, and they then viewed the videotape replay of their practice interaction. Feedback comments were directed toward specific components of assertion, as well as the client's anxiety and ease of interaction. The authors note that relatively easy scenes were used for practice in early training sessions, with progressively more difficult role-play scenes used later in the intervention.

After the intervention's conclusion, additional role-plays were presented and formally rated for the presence of targeted assertion-components. The CSES and perceived anxiety measures were also re-administered. Galassi et al. (1974) found that students in the assertive-training groups improved on almost all measures compared to their pretraining levels; clients in assertion-training also improved relative to those persons who were in the control group conditions.

This project illustrates how assertion-training procedures can be incorporated within a group-treatment format. The use of client dyads for skill practice in each session permitted all individuals to intensively rehearse the behaviors they had just discussed in the group and seen in the videotape models. Also, the use of session time to review each client's use of assertive skills in the natural environment was a very desirable aspect of training. Finally, feedback on practice came from a variety of sources, including the client's practice partner, the therapist, and via self-observation on videotape. The study's participants were unassertive college students; however, a similar-format intervention could prove useful for many other client groups.

Ollendick and Hersen (1979) conducted assertiveness-training with a group of male juvenile delinquents whose mean age was 14 years, within a residential training center. The assertive-training group had 9 members and was compared to a more traditional discussion-only therapy group and to clients who received no treatment. All clients were assessed before the intervention phase using self-report inventories and a set of role-play scenes that called for both refusal and commendatory skills. The situations depicted in the assessment role-plays were interactions that could occur within the residential training-school environment, and the assessment role-plays were different than those used in training. Client performance in refusal scenes was rated for components of effective refusal-assertiveness; commendatory scene role-plays were evaluated for the presence of commendatory skill behaviors.

The assertive-training group, led by two male co-therapists, met weekly for ten 75-minute sessions. In each group, training focused on teaching all participants to exhibit skill components during role-plays of troublesome interactions. Instructions in skill use were provided by the therapists, with group discussion of alternative ways to handle interactions that require assertiveness. Role-plays used in the training groups were of situations that the adolescents actually reported as troublesome; the therapists specifically asked that members bring to the group information on interpersonal problems they were having with other clients and staff. These problem situations were then made into role-plays for behavior rehearsal. Live-modeling in the sessions was provided when the therapists role-played appropriately assertive behaviors, and the adolescents themselves then role-played each scene with one another. Feedback and reinforcement were provided by the therapists and by the clients, who observed one another's in-group behavior-rehearsal. Finally, clients were given instructions to practice appropriate refusal and commendatory skills in the school during the upcoming week. Part of each group-training session was devoted to the review, discussion, and reinforcement of each client's reports of skill-usage in the natural (school) environment.

During the 10-week period when the clients were receiving assertion-training, adolescents in the discussion group were meeting weekly for more traditional, discussion-based therapy. Also led by co-therapists, this discussion-only group focused on interpersonal problem situations and alternative ways to handle them. However, behavioral skills-training techniques were not used. Two weeks after the intervention phase, adolescents in the skills-training, discussion, and no-treatment control groups repeated the set of role-plays and inventories that had been administered before the intervention. Ratings of the pretreatment and posttreatment measures indicated that adolescents in the assertive-training group were superior to the discussion-group and control-group clients in exhibiting many components of affective assertion during their role-plays. Further, self-report measures indicated that decreased anxiety and improved self-evaluation were associated with skills-training. A general improvement in client day-to-day social conduct within the facility, shown by improved performance in a token-economy/behavioral-contracting program, was demonstrated only by the adolescents in the assertive-training group.

The Ollendick and Hersen (1979) project illustrates several useful points for conducting group assertiveness training. One of the most practical is the therapists' requirement that clients themselves bring information to the group each week on real interpersonal problems they experienced, and the construction of behavior-rehearsal role-play scenes in training sessions to approximate those situations. This procedure ensures that clients receive training on better handling interactions known to be troublesome to them. Combined with "homework" assignments and group time devoted to reinforcing the clients' reports of skill-usage in the natural environment, this may have been responsible for improvement in the adolescents' day-to-day performance on the token/behavioral-contracting system at the facility.

Given that it is possible to conduct assertive-training with either one individual or with a group of clients, is one mode of training perferable to another? A study by Linehan, Walker, Bronheim, Haynes, and Yevzeroff (1979) compared individual and group-training interventions in a sample of unassertive women. The training group consisted of 8 clients and was led by two cotherapists. The same therapists each saw four additional clients in individual assertive-training sessions. Eight 1 ½-hour group sessions or eight 1-hour individual sessions constituted the respective interventions. In both individual and group training, clients were taught to exhibit components of refusal assertion during extended role-play interactions. Treatment consisted of therapist instruction, modeling, behavior rehearsal, feedback, cognitive modification, and in-vivo practice assignments between sessions. For individual training, the therapist served as the role-play practice partner, while in group training, clients role-played their practice scenes with other clients for behavior rehearsal.

After the interventions, clients who had received individual training were compared with those who had been in the assertive-training group on both assertive role-play scenes and the Rathus Assertiveness Schedule (Rathus, 1973). There were no significant differences between the group-treated or individually treated clients on any measure. Although more detailed and larger scale data are needed, it appears that group and individual assertive-training both can yield positive clinical results.

Chapter 9

Job-Interview Skills-Training

Very few brief social interactions can influence a person's future more profoundly than the job interview. Most employment interviews are brief; one survey of experienced campus personnel interviewers indicates that the great majority make their evaluation of prospective graduating college-student job candiates in less than 30 minutes (Drake, Kaplan, & Stone, 1972). For lower educational level jobs, the interview may be considerably shorter. However, in spite of the brevity of the social interaction between an interviewer and an employment applicant, it has been demonstrated that employers attribute a great deal of importance to the behavior of an applicant in this situation. The social impression created by the applicant is often more important than such "objective" work background characteristics as school grades or work experience (Drake et al., 1972; Lumsden & Sharf, 1974; Tschirgi, 1973). This, of course, is fortunate, since while most job-seekers cannot change their past experience or grades, they can learn the social competencies needed to handle interviews effectively.

Job interviews are a source of anxiety for a number of reasons, some of which were discussed earlier. First, the interview is a social interaction for which few people have an extensive learning history. Because most people do not engage in employment interviews frequently, they may have little knowledge of how to behave that is based on their own past personal experience in these situations. Since interviews are private interactions, people also rarely have the opportunity to observe how skilled models handle their job interviews. Second, candidates seeking employment do not usually receive specific feedback on their performance following the interview interaction. While an individual does get a very global form of feedback ("hired" versus "not hired"), it is not "tied" to specific aspects of the person's behavior. Consequently, the applicant who performs badly in an interview probably will not learn what aspects of his or her behavior were deficient and will no be in a position to change them. The vocationally competent client reported by Hollandsworth et

198

al. (1978), who went on 60 different unsuccessful job interviews before seeking treatment, provides an example, albeit extreme, of the manner in which inadequate performance-feedback in natural-setting interviews can contribute to repeated social-skill failure. Finally, because employment interviews are important but short interactions, in which the individual knows his or her social behavior is closely scrutinized by someone else, many persons experience anticipatory social-evaluative anxiety in that situation. To the degree that excessive anxiety is present, the candidate's objective skill-performance will be impaired.

Although we might speak of the job interview as a fairly specific, clear-cut kind of social interaction, it is apparent that there are many different types of interviews; relatively different social behaviors may be required in each. For example, the exact questions that an applicant will be asked depend upon the habits, interests, and style of the interviewer; the sophistication and level of job for which the candidate is applying; whether the applicant is attempting to get a "first" job or is in the midst of a career change; and statements made by the candidate earlier in the interview, which can influence the kinds of questions that will be asked by the interviewer later in the interaction. Additionally, effective skill requires that the candidate do more than simply answer the interviewer's questions; the ability to ask relevant questions, initiate topics of conversation, comment spontaneously on past experiences, and so on are also requisite aspects of skill. However, while there is considerable variability in the exact method in which a given interview is conducted, most interviewers appear to look for similar characteristics in an applicant: evidence of ambition, motivation, social competence and ease, leadership or independence qualities, and evidence of good performance in previous work-related areas (cf. Cohen & Etheridge, 1975; Drake et al., 1972; Lumsden & Sharf, 1974). The purpose of job-interview skills-training is to assist clients in learning those social behaviors that will create a positive interviewer-impression along these dimensions. Regardless of the quality of the individual's background, preparedness, or employment potential, unless the individual also develops the social skills to convey vocational or social competence in the interview setting, it is unlikely that the person will actually be hired.

Client Populations for Job-Interview Training

Job-interview training interventions have focused on several distinct client populations, which include students who are completing their education or training and are about to enter employment, chronically unemployed persons, and clients who have had some form of past social or emotional incapacitation but are now entering or re-entering the employment market. The work of Hollandsworth and his associates has focused primarily on interview training for job-seeking students, with clients receiving individual treatment (Holland-sworth et al., 1978) and group-administered interventions (Hollandsworth et al., 1977; Hollandsworth & Sandifer, 1979). Although these efforts have been with graduating college and vocational-technical students, a related population for whom interview-skills training might be conducted is high school students who will be entering the labor market upon graduation. Each of these groups is likely to include many persons with little experience and skill in the job-interview social interaction.

Chronically unemployed, disadvantaged clients have also been the recipients of job-interview training in several interventions (Barbee & Keil, 1973; Keil & Barbee, 1973). As these investigators note, culturally disadvantaged indi-viduals may perform poorly in employment interview due to passive self-presentation, lack of verbal facility, poor self-confidence, and a history of sufficient past unemployment that it becomes difficult to convey their current vocational competence. Without specific training in job-interview skills, many chronically unemployed persons are unlikely to leave favorable impressions on the employment interviewers with whom they interact.

Job-interview skills-training procedures have also been successfully used with more specialized, clinical populations of clients discharged from residen-tial facilites. These include predelinquent adolescents who would later be seeking jobs (Braukmann, Fixsen, Phillips, Wolf, & Maloney, 1974); former drug abusers (Stevens & Tornatzky, 1976); and mildly retarded individuals who were considered to have employment potential but lacked the social skills needed to present themselves favorably in interviews (Kelly, Wildman, & Berler, 1980). In a series of studies, we have conducted job-interview training with formerly hospitalized psychiatric patients, many of whom completed vocational rehabilitation but still had been unable to obtain standard (nonshel-tered) employment in the community (Furman et al., 1979; Kelly, Laughlin, Claiborne, & Patterson, 1979; Kelly, Urey, & Patterson, in press). For each of these client populations, job interviews may be difficult, not only because the clients often exhibit relatively pervasive social-skill impairment, but also because the individual may be asked to account for periods in the past when he or she was not working and the client does not want to reveal detailed information about the extended hospitalization.

In summary, job-interview training might be considered for inexperienced job-seekers, including students who will be seeking work. It can also usefully be included in social-rehabilitation-type programs in which clients will be attempting to gain employment. Finally, job-interview training is appropriate for individual clients of any kind who appear potentially employable but seem unable to portray themselves favorably within the interview situation, which might be inferred from a history of multiple unsuccessful interviews for positions that the client was qualified to obtain, or excessive client anxiety associated with the prospect of interviewing.

Job-Interview Skills-Assessment

Because the format for conducting a behavioral assessment of client job-interview skills differs somewhat from the other interaction sample-procedures we have considered to this point, we will first review it. Then components of effective interview-skill will be discussed.

The Job-Interview Role-Play

In the assertion-training role-plays that were considered in the last chapter, a role-play scene consisted of a narrated situation description followed by one or more prompt-comments delivered by the interaction partner, to which the client responds. And a number of different role-play scenes are presented, both for pretraining assessment and for behavior-rehearsal during training sessions.

In the case of job-interview role-plays, client performance in only one situation—the simulated interview—is being assessed or practiced. However, the interaction partner delivers an entire series of questions or comments to the client over the course of this single role-play interaction. In most reports of job-interview training interventions, the comments of the partner who plays the interviewer follows a "script," so that a set of predetermined questions or comments are always made. For example, in an assessment interview, the client might be seated across a desk form the "interviewer" and comments such as the following could be directed to the client:

> I don't like to read application forms, Mr./Ms. _____ . Can you tell me something about yourself?
>
> What sort of experience do you have for this position?
>
> Tell me about school and your educational background.
>
> What qualities do you think are your best?
>
> Tell me about your last job and why you aren't there now.
>
> What are your hobbies?
>
> Why should I hire you instead of someone else?
>
> What do you hope to be doing in five years?
>
> Do you have any questions for me?

In order for a role-play of this kind to be a useful assessment device and, later, a useful practice device, the questions directed to the client should approximate the questions that the client will actually encounter on a genuine interview. Somewhat different interview role-play scripts might be developed for individual clients, since the interview encountered by a college engineering graduate will probably consist of different questions and content than an interview encountered by, say, a high-school student seeking an entry-level labor job. A therapist might even wish to informally survey some local personnel interviewers to determine what sorts of questions they routinely ask applicants whose backgrounds or position-goals are similar to those of the therapist's own client. A role-play interview is also apt to be most salient when both the client and the partner play their parts with a specific position in mind. If a client is really seeking work as a bank teller, for example, the interviewer might behave as a bank's personnel officer would, and both the client and partner would make comments in the role-play accordingly.

When the interviewer directs a comment to the client and the client has role-played a response to it, the interviewer might then pause for a brief interval of time (perhaps five seconds) before proceeding to the next question in the script. This will allow the client time to fully elaborate any response and, in later role-plays, will permit the client time to incorporate new skill-behaviors in responses without being "clipped" as a new question is asked by the interviewer. To avoid an unnaturally stilted role-play, the interviewer might make additional comments to the client that are not on the script; these include ad-libbed answers to questions asked by the client, occasionally summarizing the client's responses, and so on.

Behavioral Definitions of
Components of Job-Interview Skills

In assertion-training role-plays, the therapist observing the client evaluates each *separate* response following a partner comment to determine whether all behavioral components are included in that response. In contrast, the entire role-played job interview is typically the unit that is evaluated by the therapist, and the frequency or presence of skill-behaviors occurring throughout the interview is rated. Behaviors that have been shown to contribute to interview effectiveness include: eye contact; appropriate affect; speech loudness, clarity, and fluency; positive self-statements about past experience; positive self-statements about personal hobbies, interests, and pursuits; questions directed to the interviewer; and statements conveying job interest and enthusiasm. We will examine these in detail

Eye contact, appropriate affect, and speech loudness, clarity, and fluency are defined in the same manner as they were for skills that we considered in the preceding chapters. Eye contact represents the percentage of active speaking and listening time throughout the interaction during which the client maintains visual contact with the role-play interviewer; it can range form 0% to 100% of the time. Appropriate affect refers to the client's appropriateness of emotional tone during the role-play and is often rated on a scale of *1=extremely poor* to *7=extremely good*. Extremely poor affect might be characterized by an absence of lively voice intonation, an absence of smiles, a

bored or disinterested demeanor, little emotional responsiveness to the interviewer, and so on. Appropriate affect includes lively modulation or tone of
voice, facial expression conveying interest in and responsivity to the interviewer, smiling at appropriate times, etc. The third nonverbal component is speech
loudness, clarity, and fluency. It, too, can be most easily rated by the therapist
using a 1-to-7 scale. The deficient end of the range is characterized by inaudible
speech, frequent verbal disruptions such as "ah," "umm," "well," and the lack
of speech clarity.

Positive self-statements about past experience, training, or education   are
any verbalizations made by the client that convey desirable information to the
interviewer concerning job-relevant experiences in the past. These might be
facts about what the client did in previous jobs, responsibilties that one had,
statements conveying that the client enjoyed or performed well in past jobs, or
special vocational competencies acquired by the person. For clients who have
had little actual job experience, this component category could also include
information statements about educational background, vocational training,
volunteer work, or related skills. Statements about experience should be
positive in tone, and should consist of information that is both relevant to
employment and likely to be perceived favorably by an interviewer. Some
examples of positive statements about experience include: "I operated a die
press machine"; "I worked at Acme Manufacturing Company for 6 years"; "My
sales in 1979 were the largest in our department"; "I can type 50 words per
minute"; "My favorite subject in high school was home economics"; and "I
missed only 2 days of work in three years." In some cases, clients may link
several statements about experience together in one sentence, such as "In
college, I majored in chemistry and also worked part-time to pay for my
tuition." Here, the individual is actually conveying two different pieces of
information ("majored in chemistry" and "worked part-time"), and each might
be rated as an instance of the self-statement component.

The therapist observing a role-play interview can tally the total number of
positive statements about experience made by a client over the course of the
entire interview. The rationale for assessing and training this behavior is that
many skills-deficient clients fail to convey sufficient positive, specific information about their background and experience during job interviews.

Positive self-statements about personal hobbies, interests, and pursuits
can serve to help an interviewer learn more about the candidate as a person, an
area of interest to many personnel interviewers (see Drake et al., 1972;
Lumsden & Sharf, 1974). Examples of this verbal component include client
statements such as: "I play golf in my free time on weekends"; "I jog 4 miles a
day"; "My husband and I like to water ski"; and "I played basketball all

through high school." Because interviewers value candidate characteristics indicative of motivation, ambition, activity, and a "well-rounded" personality, it is preferable for clients to talk about those activities or interests that reflect such characteristics. Just as positive statements about experience are rated by tallying each one that occurs throughout the role-play interview, positive comments about personal pursuits can also be rated with a frequency-count system.

Questions directed to the interviewer occur when the client seeks information by asking a question relevant to the prospective position. Asking questions in a job interview serves at least two purposes: First, it demonstrates to the interviewer that the client is interested in the job, and signals inquisitiveness and attentiveness on the part of the client. Second, the client is able to obtain information that will be important in making a decision about whether the position is one in which he or she is actually interested. Examples of appropriate questions include: "Can you tell me about the responsibilities of this position?"; "To whom will I be accountable?"; "What opportunities will there be for advancement?"; "Are uniforms furnished by the company?"; and "When do you expect to reach a hiring decision?"

Statements conveying job interest and enthusiasm are comments that explicitly communicate to the interviewer that the client is interested in the position or that the client will do a good job if hired. Some examples of this component are: "This sounds like a very interesting job"; "From what you have said, I think I would feel very good about working at your company"; "I learn quickly and will work hard"; and "You will be pleased if you decide to hire me." In contrast to the positive statements about previous experience, these verbal statements describe the client's current feelings or future performance in positive terms. The purpose of these behaviors is to convey confidence and interest about the work. They, too, can be rated on a frequency-count basis as they occur throughout the entire role-play interview.

Rating Client Role-Play Interviews for the Presence of Skill-Component Behaviors

As the therapist observes a client's role-play job-interview, and as the client responds to the questions asked by the interviewer partner, the therapist tallies the occurrence of any verbal component-behaviors on the rating-form. A sample form for rating a client's job-interview skill is presented in Figure 9.1. Some verbal components are likely to "cluster" at certain points in the interaction. For example, when the interviewer asks a question about past work history, the client may respond with several positive self-statements

FIGURE 9.1.   Sample Rating-Form for Client's Job Interview Role-Play

Client Name:_____

Date of This Interaction:_____

Type of Interaction: _____ Pretraining Assessment

                       _____ Session Practice (Training Focused

                               on What Component?_____)

                       _____ Follow-up

COMPONENTS

1. Eye Contact (Approximate ratio of client speaking/listening
                 time when eye contact was maintained with the
                 interviewer)

   0% 10%   20%   30%   40%   50%   60%   70%   80%   90%   100%

       eye contact   eye contact
       never made   made entire
                                                time

2. Affect

        1   2   3   4   5   6   7

    Extremely dull,   Extremely
    emotionally   good affect,
    unresponsive,   emotionally
    disinterested   responsive,
                                                 lively,
                                                 interested

3. Speech Loudness, Clarity, Fluency

        1   2   3   4   5   6   7

    Extremely   Extremely
    inaudible   clear spoken,
    unclear speech,   appropriate
    nonfluent   loudness

4. Positive Self-Statements About Past Experience, Training,
    Education

    Tally:_____ Total:_____

5. Positive Self-Statements About Personal Hobbies, Interests,
    Pursuits

    Tally:_____ Total:_____

6. Questions Directed by Client to Interviewer

    Tally:_____ Total:_____

7. Statements Conveying Job Interest and Enthusiasm

    Tally:_____ Total:_____

8. Other Components Being Rated (or any undesirable, inappropriate
                                  behaviors being examined)

    Definition/Description of Behavior: Frequency Count or Rating:

about experience. However, this and other components can be appropriately exhibited at different interview times as well, and should be tallied whenever they occur.

The therapist can attend to the nonverbal behaviors of eye contact, affect, and speech quality during the role-play and, upon the interaction's conclusion, assign ratings to each of these components. Finally, in an assessment role-play, other behaviors exhibited by the client might also be evaluated. In several studies, formerly hospitalized psychiatric patients were found to spontaneously self-disclose inappropriate information to the role-play interviewer, making references to past "nerve trouble," psychiatric hospitalization, and so on (Kelly, Laughlin, Claiborne, & Patterson, 1979). Instances of these inappropriate behaviors were rated during pretreatment assessment role-plays and again later in treatment to determine if they ceased to occur following training in appropriate verbal skills.

When one or more assessment role-plays have been conducted and systematically rated, the therapist can analyze the rating-form data to pinpoint inadequacies in the client's job-interview performance—those components will require later treatment attention. Certainly, if the behaviors discussed in this section are absent or occur at very low rates, they can be identified as deficient. However, there has been virtually no empirical data on the ideal frequency of occurrence for any component of job-interview competence. This is a potentially problematic issue, since we wish to have clients fully elaborate their relevant experience, but not talk excessively; a client who never expresses interest or enthusiasm in a position is likely to be perceived unfavorably, but so is the client who overstates enthusiasm to the point of appearing arrogant and pushy. Thus, a therapist may be forced to rely somewhat on his or her own subjective determination of whether a client's performance in assessment role-plays is at a deficient level on a given component.

Representative Research on Job-Interview Training

Let us examine several studies that illustrate how job-interview training has been used in applied settings, first considering interview training with individually treated clients and then group-training interventions.

Interview Training with Individual Clients

Keil and Barbee (1973) conducted skills-training with disadvantaged clients enrolled in a federal government vocational-technical skills program. All clients were either minority-group members or had limited education prior to their vocational program participation; clients' mean age was 27. Each of the clients had successfully completed vocational training and would be graduating from the program within 60 days. However, while the clients were "job-ready," the investigators noted that many clients would be likely to experience difficulties in actually attaining employment due to their inadequately developed job-interview skills repertoire. For this reason, social-skills training was conducted. The intervention itself was brief and consisted of only a single training session.

Prior to treatment, each client participated in a videotaped assessment interview. The simulated interviews were conducted by a genuine personnel interviewer, who participated in the project. Although the interactions were somewhat structured, they were not based on a role-play interview script. Instead, the experienced interviewer asked whatever questions he felt appropriate during the pretest interview. When role-plays were repeated at the conclusion of the intervention, the interviewer was given a list of the questions and content areas that he had covered in pretraining interactions with each client, so that a given individual would be assessed with a comparable interview both pretreatment and posttreatment.

During training sessions, each client was paired with a counselor. First, the client and counselor together viewed the videotape of the client's assessment role-play interview, and developed a list of those specific behaviors that the client exhibited well and those where improvement was needed. Next, the counselor (playing an interviewer) and client (playing an applicant) rehearsed interview questions and responses in areas in which deficits had been noted in the film. The trainer verbally reinforced improvement in the client's responses, provided feedback, and made specific suggestions on ways to exhibit the target behaviors more effectively. Occasionally in the session, the client played the interviewer and the counselor played the applicant, so that the counselor could live-model examples of appropriate skill-components. Finally, the counselor and client discussed other aspects of interview skill and the importance of using new skill-behaviors during genuine interviews.

Following treatment sessions, each client had a second complete simulated interview with the same person who had conducted the pretreatment interview. A control group, consisting of clients who had received no training, also underwent the same simulated interviews. Videotapes of all clients' pretraining and posttraining interviews were shown to a panel of judges, all of whom were professional personnel managers. The judges rated each interview on 19 different aspects of client skill and summed up their own reaction to the client (e.g., "ability to explain and sell present job skills"; "ability to follow directions"; "would you hire this applicant if a suitable position existed in your company?") using 7-point rating scales. On a number of these judges' ratings, Keil and Barbee (1973) found improvement to be associated with having received the skills-training intervention. However, on some indices, including the crucial question, "Would you hire this applicant?" no improvement was found. This may well have been due to the brevity of the single-session treatment and the clients' own skill-deficits, which probably required a more intensive intervention.

Furman et al. (1979) reported on a more lengthy intervention. In this project, the clients were three formerly hospitalized but potentially employable psychiatric patients. Sessions were conducted at a mental health center after-care program, where each client was receiving treatment. Before training, each client was assessed with role-play job interviews on three different occasions. The assessment interviews followed a structured-script format, with a staff-person playing the interviewer and directing a set of 8 standard questions to the client in the manner described earlier in this chapter. Assessment role-plays were videotaped and component deficits were identified for each client. These included statements about past experience, verbal statements of job interest and enthusiasm, gesturing, and job-relevant questions directed to the interviewer. Component ratings were made by the therapists using a form similar to that included in this chapter. Also before treatment, each client engaged in one simulated interview with an experienced personnel interviewer. These interactions were not structured in any way and the interviewer was asked to conduct the session just as he ordinarily would.

Clients received skills-training that consisted of between 8 and 19 sessions; each lasted approximately 30 minutes. The number of sessions that a particular client received was determined by the extent of that client's initial deficiency (i.e., the number of skill-components on which deficits were observed during pretreatment assessment role-plays) and how quickly the client was able to exhibit new behaviors during session practice. Training sessions were always devoted to a single component of effective interview skill; when the client had mastered that component, a new behavior was introduced for training in the next session, until all of a client's previously deficient behaviors had been successively targeted in the intervention.

Training sessions in the Furman et al. (1979) project consisted of instruction; coaching; examples, the rationale for the component targeted in that day's session; informal practice responses to typical interview questions, with the therapist playing the interviewer and the client incorporating the behavior in his or her responses; a full role-play practice interview, identical to that used in the pretreatment assessment phase, with one of the therapists serving as the role-play partner; and observation of a videotape of the just-completed practice role-play, with the therapist and client together critiquing the client's performance in the interview. The therapists always rated the session-practice role-plays to objectively determine how frequently the client actually exhibited the skill-components that were receiving attention.

At the conclusion of the entire intervention, when the client had mastered all component behaviors and exhibited them consistently during the in-session practice role-plays, an unstructured role-play interview with a genuine personnel manager was repeated. This was to determine whether the clients could generalize use of their new skills to a novel interviewer who asked interview questions different than those comprising the structured practice role-plays. In all cases, client interview performance in the posttraining generalization interviews was much more effective than performance before treatment. Not only did clients exhibit the component-behaviors more frequently, but videotapes of the interviews were evaluated more favorably by naive personnel managers who observed the tapes on global, subjective criteria of social effectiveness. Two of the three clients began working shortly after the intervention, whereas all had been unemployed for at least two years previously.

In contrast to Keil and Barbee's (1973) project, the Furman et al. (1979) study was a more intensive intervention, consisting of multiple treatment sessions and directing attention to various verbal and nonverbal skill-components over the course of training. Although each study incorporated similar procedures into training sessions (including coaching, behavior rehearsal with the therapist, feedback, and so on), the fact that Furman et al. (1979) concentrated attention on only a single component within any given session and devoted several sessions to a component may have been responsible for the apparently greater generalization and durability of treatment effects.

In Chapter 2, the job-interview training procedure used by Hollandsworth et al. (1978) to treat an anxious and socially deficient graduating college student was described. The format of each training session was generally similar to the projects we have just reviewed. The therapist provided instructions and examples of the component receiving attention that day, the rationale for the behavior was discussed, a videotape modeling-film of a skilled interviewee was shown, and a role-play practice job-interview was conducted. Self-observation-based feedback was provided when a videotape of this practice interview was replayed at the end of the training session. However, the Hollandsworth et al. (1978) project included an additional element in its treatment sessions. Pretraining assessment role-plays suggested that the client had difficulty formulating direct, focused, and informative responses to the role-play interviewer's questions. Instead, his responses appeared to verbally ramble and were quite disorganized. In order to treat this aspect of the client's interview-skill deficiency, the investigators incorporated a "Pause-Think-Speak" approach to training. Whenever the interviewer would ask a question in role-play practice during sessions, the client was advised to break eye contact with the interviewer, think momentarily about key elements to include in his response, and only then respond to the question directly and clearly. In essence, the "Pause-Think-Speak" sequence reduced the likelihood that the client would deliver rapid but disorganized rambling responses, by allowing him to pause for a few seconds to cognitively plan more coherent, succinct statements. This aspect of training proved successful, because when it was incorporated in treatment sessions, ratings of the client's role-play interviews revealed improvement in the "focused" quality of his responses. The Hollandsworth et al. (1978) project is one of relatively few job-interview training studies that directly and explicitly trained style of self-presentation, in addition to behavioral components of interview-effectiveness.

Group Job-Interview Training

Group training in job-interview skills has been reported in projects with formerly hospitalized psychiatric patients (Kelly, Laughlin, Claiborne, & Patterson, 1979); mental health center clients (Kelly, Urey, & Patterson, in press), and mentally retarded adolescents (Kelly, Wildman, & Berler, 1980). Each of these studies utilized relatively similar procedures; we will focus here only on the skills-training group-intervention with retarded adolescents, since its procedures are representative of the others.

Clients in this project were four youths, age 15 to 17, who would soon be leaving a short-term residential program for the mentally retarded. Each client was mildly retarded; all seemed potentially employable for standard (nonsheltered) work positions in the community. Before the group intervention began, each client's pretraining skills were assessed with individual role-play job interviews. College student practicum students were used as role-play interviewers and followed a standard interview script, as outlined earlier in this chapter. Ten questions were always included in the role-play interaction, although the interviewers occasionally made other comments and answered client job-related questions in an ad-lib manner during the role-plays. Because the investigators sought to establish a clear baseline of client skill before training began, four separate assessment role-plays were conducted. Interviews were always audiotape-recorded and rated to determine the frequency of verbal components such as positive statements about experience, positive statements about hobbies or interests, job-related questions directed to the role-play interviewer, and statements conveying interest/enthusiasm in working. All occurred at very low levels during the assessment role-plays.

A total of 16 group sessions were conducted, with several sessions devoted to each component. Co-therapists led each group. Sessions began with instructions, examples, and group discussion concerning the particular component that would receive training that day. A modeling job-interview videotape was shown to the group, with the therapists pointing out examples of the targeted component whenever the adolescent model in the film exhibited it. Behavior rehearsal within the group was then conducted. On some occasions, one of the therapists would ask several interview questions to a group member, and the client would practice incorporating the component in his responses. Other clients would observe their peer and afterward offer feedback, suggestions, and praise. At other times, two clients would be paired together for in-group rehearsal, with one playing an interviewer and the other an interviewee. Rehearsal techniques were varied in order to add variety to the group session. However, in every session, each client had an opportunity to rehearse responses to interview questions and to receive feedback and comments from both the other clients and the therapists. At the conclusion of the group session, each adolescent was escorted to a separate office for a complete role-played interview, with the college practicum student acting as interviewer and following the script that had been used in assessment role-plays. These interviews were also audiotaped and rated to determine whether the clients exhibited skill-components in them. If increased used of a component coincided with the time when that behavior received attention in the training group, multiple-baseline control could be established.

Kelly, Wildman, and Berler (1980) found that the adolescents did exhibit increased interview skill-components during their role-play interviews, and improvement was evident only when the group worked on a given component. To assess generalization of treatment, the investigators enlisted the assistance of a local fast-food restaurant, which hired many teenage employees. Before the intervention, and again after training was completed, each client was interviewed by the store's manager at the restaurant itself. These in-vivo interviews were unstructured and the manager was asked to conduct the interview as he ordinarily would. When tape recordings of the in-vivo pretraining and posttraining generalization were evaluated, the investigators found that clients increased their rates of positive statements about experience and hobbies or interests. In addition, posttraining taped interviews were evaluated more favorably than pretraining interviews on a number of global measures of skill effectiveness by other personnel interviewers who were asked to listen to them.

This project demonstrates that group training, using procedures similar to those of individual training, can enhance clients' job-interview skills repertoires. The major differences between group-administered and individually administered treatment in the studies we have reviewed so far include for group training: (1) discussion in the sesson among clients of the rationale or importance of various skill-behaviors; (2) clients engaging in behavioral practice with other clients, instead of practice taking place exclusively with the therapist or a therapist confederate; (3) client in-group practice serving as a vicarious learning experience for other clients watching it; and (4) clients, along with the therapist, providing feedback and comments to one another following their in-session rehearsal. While the 16-session intervention in the Kelly, Wildman, and Berler (1980) project was relatively long, it is important to note that the clients were mildly retarded and may have required more repetition to acquire new skills than would other types of clients.

A study by Speas (1979) sought to delineate some aspects of treatment that are responsible for client skill-improvement in group job-interview training. From a population of soon-to-be released prisoners, Speas randomly assigned clients to training groups that consisted of modeling-exposure only, role-playing only, modeling-exposure plus role-playing, or modeling-exposure plus role-playing and videotape feedback. Printed self-help materials on job-interviewing were given to all clients, regardless of training condition. Other clients were placed in a no-treatment control group. Clients who received training met for six 1½-hour sessions, except for the modeling-only group, which received somewhat less session time; sessions were always led by two co-therapists. Before, and again after, the intervention, each client participated in a simulated individual job-interview. The pretraining and posttraining interviews were rated on a variety of measures related to social skill, and the results were analyzed to compare the performance of clients who had received each type of training. Speas (1979) found that, in general, the group that had received the full combination of treatment procedures (modeling, role-playing, plus feedback) was superior in interview performance to most other groups at the end of treatment and, even more impressively, at follow-up several weeks after training was completed. Interestingly, the group who spent session-time observing skilled videotape models, but not actually practicing job-interview skills, did not perform better in the posttraining simulated interviews than clients who had received no training at all. It appears that although learning-theory-based techniques such as modeling and role-playing were relatively ineffective when used alone, the combination of these procedures in sessions was maximally effective in building, and then maintaining, job-interview skills.

Other Issues in Applied Job-Interview Training

Before concluding our discussion of social-skills training for the job-interview interaction, there are several other treatment-related issues that merit attention. These are: (1) the importance of clients' generalizing their skills-improvement to in-vivo, genuine interviews and (2) stylistic aspects of self-presentation in employment interviews.

Enhancing the Generalization of Job-Interview Skills-Training

Just as for the other forms of social skill considered to this point, it is crucial that clients exhibit new job-interview skill behavior not only in practice role-plays, but also in genuine employment interviews they will actually encounter. What steps can be taken to promote this generalization?

As we noted earlier, the interview questions asked of clients during their assessment and practice role-plays should approximate the kinds of questions they will actually encounter on real job interviews. Thus, the interview role-play script might be tailored not only to the level of employment that the client seeks, but also the exact position sought by the individual. However, no matter how carefully the therapist constructs practice interview questions, one cannot entirely predict the exact questions and interviewer style that a client will encounter on a given real job-interview. Thus, the client will need to generalize skill-usage to situations different than those of the training role-play interview. If a client learns only to respond to the exact interviewer questions that he or she practices during simulated interviews, the individual may fail to perform well when slightly different questions are asked, or may fail to spontaneously offer important, job-relevant information if the real-life interviewer fails to ask a question that had elicited that information in practice role-plays.

These potential problems may be dealt with in several ways. First, although a standard role-play script can be used for practice job-interviews during training sessions, at some point the client should encounter variations of the standard questions. This might occur near the end of the intervention, when the basic role-play has already been well-mastered. In some of these more "difficult" role-plays, the interviewer might intentionally *fail* to ask about applicant experience, training, education, or fail to inquire whether the applicant has any questions; the client will then need to more spontaneously offer appropriate comments on these topics during the practice interview. Also, interviewer characteristics could be varied. If practice role-plays have ordinarily been with a male partner, a female partner can be used; the role-play interviewer might also adopt different styles (warm, rushed, many questions, few questions) to determine that the client can perform well under all of these conditions. Whenever deficits are noted in the client's performance, further training can be conducted.

As with other forms of skill-training, it is important that contact be maintained as the client attempts to use new skills in the natural environment. Clients can be asked to keep notes on actual job interviews they encounter, any difficult questions they were asked, whether they used the skills that had been previously trained, and so on. The therapists's role at this point includes reinforcing client reports of skill-usage and providing additional training when it appears necessary.

Stylistic Aspects of Self-Presentation in Job Interviews

Although job-interview training teaches clients to incorporate various verbal and nonverbal components in their handling of an interview, the therapist observing a client's practice role-plays should remain cognizant of the style of the client's behavior as well. The "Pause-Think-Speak" training approach described by Hollandsworth et al. (1978) can be used throughout training on individual verbal components to assist clients in briefly and covertly organizing their responses to an interviewer's questions before they begin to respond. Similarly, clients should be encouraged not to simply memorize answers to particular interview questions, but to grasp certain response "rules." These rules might include: when asked about one's work experience, to talk about one's major past jobs and, for each job, to be certain to include such information as the name of the employer, one's job title, several specific responsibilities or accomplishments, and something positive that one enjoyed in that position.

Several research studies on job-interview training have had experienced personnel managers listen to clients' pretreatment and posttreatment role-plays and evaluate them on global, subjective criteria of effectiveness (see Barbee & Keil, 1973; Furman et al., 1979; Kelly, Wildman, & Berler, 1980). In research studies, utilizing such external judgments can serve to establish the social validity of behavioral change. However, this is also a potentially useful prcedure for clinical and applied interventions. A therapist, with the client's permission, might enlist the assistance of an individual who has actual experience interviewing job-applicants and ask that person to listen to a tape recording of the client's practice role-play from late in the training intervention. The personnel interviewer's comments and reactions to the role-play interview can be obtained and, if it is evident that areas of deficiency remain, additional training can be conducted.

Finally, there may be certain difficult or "critical" interview questions that some clients will encounter and that will require particular attention in training. This might include questions about work experience (if a client has none), why one left his or her last job (if the client was fired), why one hasn't worked recently (if the client has been chronically unemployed, insitutionalized, or incarcerated), and so on. Each of these interviewer questions has the potential of eliciting extremely detrimental responses from the client who handles it poorly or has failed to practice skilled responses to such difficult questions. Some training-session time can be devoted to handling such questions, depending upon whether the client's background makes it likely that he or she will encounter them. In general, it would seem best that clients learn to never spontaneously provide information to an interviewer that will be potentially damaging to their chances of being hired. Thus, clients should not offer information about past work problems, terminations, emotional problems, and the like. On the other hand, if specifically asked by an interviewer (or under circumstances where the interviewer will obviously know about such events), a client can respond honestly by very briefly summarizing the past problem, and then always elaborating accurate reasons why the client is now responsible, ambitious, able to work, an asset to the potential employer, and so on. Therapist instruction, modeling, rehearsal, and feedback can be used to teach responses to critical questions, just as these principles are used throughout job-interview training.

Chapter 10

Social-Skills Training with Children

It is only in the comparatively recent past that the treatment of social-skill deficits in children has received systematic clinical and research attention (Michelson & Wood, 1980). Perhaps one reason for this is that children who are skills-deficient often remain unnoticed and in the background within their classrooms, daycare programs, or neighborhood playgrounds. While disruptive, aggressive, and "hyperactive" behavior readily draws the attention of parents, teachers and, ultimately, therapists, the isolated child with few peer relationships may go quietly unnoticed and unreferred for treatment. A second likely reason for the paucity of past attention to children's social-skill deficits is that many therapists simply did not know how to deal effectively with the socially isolated child. As we will see, many of the behaviors that contribute to socially skilled behavior in childhood (such as prosocial play) are qualitatively different than elements of interpersonal competence exhibited in adult interactions. Until peer-valued social competencies in childhood could be clearly identified, and procedures for teaching them those skills investigated, the development of effective training techniques was correspondingly hindered.

Remediating social-skill inadequacies during childhood is important for a variety of reasons. Certainly one of the foremost is to increase the happiness, self-esteem, and peer-adjustment of the child as a child. However, as we noted in Chapter 2, it appears likely that socially skilled behavior during childhood is also a prerequisite for the development and elaboration of an individual's later interpersonal repertoire. If a child lacks peer-valued play and interaction skills in early life, he or she will have less close interpersonal contact with others as time goes on. By virtue of reduced peer-contact, opportunities will also be weaker to naturalistically observe, practice, and be reinforced for the acquisition of new and more complex social skills. Early-life skill-deficits might then perpetuate circumstances of continued social isolation, which precludes the learning of additional skills. A number of investigators have found, through longitudinal study, that poor peer acceptance in childhood is associated with a wide variety of serious later-life difficulties, including: adjudication for delinquent acts (Roff, Sells, & Golden, 1972); dropping out of school (Ullman, 1957); receiving conduct discharges from military service (Roff, 1961); and utilizing the services of community mental health centers in adulthood (Cowen, Pederson, Babigian, Izzo, & Trost, 1973).

While we have termed this chapter "Social-Skills Training with Children," it is important to bear in mind that socially skilled behavior among children is not a unitary, generalized trait; there are undoubtedly different forms of interpersonal competency in childhood, just as there are in adulthood. Further, skill behavior is also likely to be situationally determined, and may depend upon such factors as the age and sex of the child; the age, sex, and familiarity of the other peers in an interaction; where the interaction occurs (at home, during structured classroom activities, on a playground, etc.); and the nature of the social interaction itself (playing an outside recess game, initiating play with others, talking with a friend, working collaboratively on a school project, handling a disagreement, and so on). Somewhat different types of skill-behaviors may be needed under each of these circumstances. Some investigators have targeted for intervention relatively specific types of social skill, which parallel corresponding skill in adults, including refusal assertiveness when others attempt to take advantage of the child (Bornstein, Bellack, & Hersen, 1977) and effectively praising the positive behavior of peers (Warren, Baer, & Rogers-Warren, 1979). More typically, the aim of skills-training interventions has been to increase the general frequency of peer interaction of formerly isolated children, or to increase their popularity based on sociometric (peer nominations of popularity) indices (Foster & Ritchey, 1979). This is usually accomplished by teaching interpersonally deficient children the competencies deemed important for initiating and then maintaining peer interactions in cooperative play and play-plus-conversation, and in unstructured interactions. It is this aspect of childhood social skills that will be the focus of attention of this chapter.

Child Populations for Social-Skills Training

As we might expect, the children that have received greatest attention in the skills-training literature are those who appear to have low rates of peer interaction, based on behavioral observation in the natural setting or on peer sociometric measures. Interventions have most frequently targeted isolated preschoolers, in some cases including children as young as three years old (Evers & Schwarz, 1973) and those from disadvantaged backgrounds (Kirschenbaum, 1979; Geller & Scheirer, 1978). Other successful projects have been reported with isolated children in various elementrary-school grades (See Weinrott, Corson, & Wilchesky, 1979; LaGreca & Santogrossi, 1980; Gottman, Gonso, & Schuler, 1976; Berler, Kelly, & Romanczyk, 1980).

Although social isolation and lack of interaction with peers have been client-selection criteria for many skills-training projects with children, other studies have taught interpersonal skills to children who were highly disruptive, aggressive, and uncooperative during their peer interactions (see Bornstein, Bellack, & Hersen, 1980; Durlak & Mannarino, 1977; Filipczak, Archer, & Friedman, 1980; Zahavi & Asher, 1978). The rationale for skills-training here is that aggressive children, in addition to social isolates, often seem to lack the prosocial repertoire of appropriate behaviors needed to establish cooperative peer relationships. Other interventions with children have focused on the developmentally handicapped (McDaniel, 1970; Strain, Shores, & Timm, 1977; Strain & Timm, 1974), since retarded and language-delayed children are likely to experience particular difficulty establishing appropriate social relationships with peers. It has been suggested that developmentally handicapped children who are "mainstreamed" into integrated classrooms often lack the peer-valued interpersonal skills necessary to develop friendships with their nonretarded peers and, as a result, remain socially isolated (Kelly, Furman, Phillips, Hathorn, & Wilson, 1979). Skills-training with this population may prove quite useful. In a similar vein, children with learning disabilities and concurrent interpersonal skill-deficits have received attention in the social-skills training literature (Cooke & Apolloni, 1976; LaGreca & Mesibov, 1979).

From a clinical perspective, training in social skills is indicated in those cases where a child lacks the abilities to enter into and maintain participation during positive interactions with peers. This might be manifested in any of several ways, including: (1) simple noninvolvement with peers, lack of participation in other children's activities, and the absence of friends; (2) being actively rebuffed or rejected by others when social initiations are attempted; or (3) an aggressive, belligerent interaction style, when this is due to inadequacies in the child's prosocial-skills repertoire. After reviewing the behavioral makeup of socially skilled interactions in children, we will direct our attention to procedures for the clinical assessment of these social-skill deficits in more detail.

Components of Social Skill Among Children

A number of different verbal and motor behaviors have been identified as components necessary to initiate and maintain cooperative social relationships in childhood. However, the manner in which these behaviors have been identified varies considerably. Some investigators have administered sociometric measures to an entire group of children (such as a class) and asked each child to select his or her best friends, so that popular and unpopular individuals within the group could be identified. Then, the popular and unpopular children are observed during social and play interactions to determine those specific verbal and nonverbal behaviors that distinguish between the two groups (see Hartup, Glazer, & Charlesworth, 1967; Gottman, Gonso, &

Rasmussen, 1975). In other cases, the process is essentially reversed. Here, children are first taught to exhibit behaviors that a therapist intuitively feels comprise social competence, and the effect of the intervention, and presumably the effect of the new behaviors being exhibited by the child, are evaluated in terms of improved sociometric standing or more frequent rates of interaction with peers (see Gottman et al., 1976; LaGreca & Santogrossi, 1980).

Even when such empirical procedures are used to identify components of social skill among children, certain problems remain. As Foster and Ritchey (1979) have pointed out, some investigators have defined social competence in terms of sociometrically measured popularity, while others have used criteria such as the extent or overall quality of observed social interactions with peers. The behaviors that comprise one definition of social skill may not be equally related to another. Also, because differing skill-behaviors are needed for different types of peer interactions, those skill-behaviors used in one situation (meeting a new schoolmate) are not necessarily the same as those used in another (playing a group game at recess). The age of a child is also related to behaviors that will be judged as socially competent; in early childhood, the skills needed to initiate and maintain play-behavior are very important, whereas in later childhood, conversational verbal content becomes increasingly salient. Although such issues involve assessment research, they also bear on clinical treatment, since it is important to ensure that we teach children those skill-component behaviors that will actually increase their peer-adjustment (Foster & Ritchey, 1979). With these qualifications in mind, specific components that have been related to social skill in childhood include: greetings; social in-itiations; asking questions and answering questions; praise; proximity and orientation; task participation or playing; cooperation or sharing; and affective responsiveness. Let us now examine these components in more detail.

Greetings are verbal statements that precede an interaction and acknow-ledge, in a positive manner, the peer whom the child sees. Verbal greetings need not be long or elaborate ("Hi, John"; "How are you, Sue"; "Hey—it's the Champ!") and simply serve as positive signals that the child recognizes the presence of the peer.

Social initiations are verbal behaviors, often accompanied by movement toward peers, which a child uses to begin interacting with others. Social initiations may include inviting others to join in one's own activity, or joining into the activities of other children. In either case, they serve to initiate the child's involvement with peers and increase the opportunities for social parti-cipation. Examples of appropriate social initiations include verbal statements like "Hi, John. Do you want to play cards with me?"; "Can I play on your team?"; "Let's go swimming!"; "I'd like to be in your group"; "Why don't you get on the swing and I'll push you?" Although some of these statements are phrased as questions, they primarily serve to communicate the child's interest

in beginning some mutual activity with another child. They are often accompanied by motor behaviors such as walking toward another child, holding out a
toy, or so on.

Asking and answering questions   are conversational behaviors that facilitate the development of peer relationships in the same manner that they
contribute to conversational competence in adults. Gottman et al. (1975), for
example, found that the frequency of eliciting information from peers (asking
questions) and providing information about oneself to them (answering questions) differentiated popular and unpopular children. It would appear that ideal
conversational questions are those that are open-ended and do not yield simple
"yes-no" answers ("What's your favorite T.V. show?"; "What did you do on
vacation this summer?"; "What does your big brother do?"). Similarly, answers
to questions from other children should be fully elaborated and convey information about one's own hobbies, activities, and so on (Gottman et al., 1975;
LaGreca & Mesibov, 1979).

Praise   consists of compliments directed to a peer when the other child has
done something well. In essence, the child who develops the ability of praising
his or her peers will be an effective dispenser of reinforcement to them
(LaGreca & Mesibov, 1979); this role has been associated with increased
popularity in several studies (Gottman et al., 1975; Hartup, 1970). Examples of
this verbal behavior might include: "That's a neat model you made"; "I like
your shirt"; "You're a good basketball player"; or "Terrific!"

Proximity and orientation   refer to the physical location of the target child
in relation to other children with whom he or she might interact. Clearly, if a
child is physically distanced from others, almost any form of social interaction
will be impossible. Proximity to peers, then, represents a necessary but in itself
insufficient prerequisite for socially skilled behavior to occur. In addition to the
child's nearness to peers, orientation toward them (looking, attending, and so
on) is a basic requirement for skilled behavior. Proximity in a playroom setting
would be considered present if the child were sitting with others, and was
oriented toward their activity; it would be deficient if the child was standing ten
feet away from the location of other children and was not attending to their
activities.

Task participation or playing   denotes a child's active interaction with
peers in the context of some shared activity or task. Many behavioral definitions of play have been proposed, but we will be concerned here only with what
has been termed "associative" or "cooperative" play. In cooperative play, two
or more children are engaged in a mutual task that involves the reciprocation of
motor behavior or talk and, consequently, interaction with one another. The

play task itself can vary greatly; playing tag, checkers, cleaning a fish tank, working on a collaborative art project, looking through a book, or singing can each be examples of cooperative play, provided the children are mutually interacting during it. Associative or cooperative play can be distinguished from "solitary play," where one child alone engages in a task alone (e.g., bouncing a ball or working alone on a project); it can also be distinguished from what has been termed "parallel play," where children are playing in close physical proximity, but without actually interacting with one another in the process.

Cooperation or sharing behavior   can occur in the context of task-play or conversation among children. This component refers specifically to a child taking turns, offering assistance, sharing a play-object with another child, following game rules, and similar acts (see LaGreca & Mesibov, 1979). When observing children at work on an arts-and-crafts project, one might see a child offer a crayon to a peer or say "Let me help you." Each of these is an example of the cooperation or sharing component of social skill.

Affective responsiveness   refers to the child's emotional demeanor while interacting with others. Smiling, laughter, and affectionate touching at appropriate times are elements of affective responsiveness. If a child meets and is playing with peers but shows no visible signs of emotional enjoyment, one would evaluate affective responsiveness as being deficient.

Just as for other types of social skills in adults, we can define interpersonal skill among children in terms of the presence of these component-behaviors. To the extent that they are exhibited during the course of interactions with peers, we can consider a child to be skillful; to the extent that these behaviors are not exhibited, the child is likely to experience difficulties in interactions with others.

Assessment of Children's Social Skills
Preceding the Training Intervention

Clinical assessment of a child's social skills begins by carefully interviewing persons in a position to comment on the child's peer-interaction behavior, based on their own direct observation of him or her. Ordinarily, these individuals will be the child's parents, teachers, daycare center staff, and so on. The purpose of this initial interview assessment is the same as the preliminary interview of an adult client: to obtain information on specific situations in which the child experiences difficulties in peer interaction, and to obtain information about how the child currently behaves in those situations. The training intervention will be focused on those identified interactions.

It is important for the therapist to gain descriptions of particular peer-interaction situations, rather than generalized traits ascribed to the child. For example, the teacher of an elementary-school-age child might tell the therapist that a child is "shy" or "introverted," and rarely joins in peer activities. However, this description alone is insufficient information for treatment-planning. We would then need to determine those specific situations in which the teacher has observed the child to act shyly with classmates, exactly where the teacher has observed the child to act shyly with classmates, and exactly what the teacher means when she describes the child's behavior in this way. Similarly global descriptions such as "poor social relationships," "bossy," "isolated," and so on are generalized labels that must be translated into more specific descriptions of actual interactions in which the child has experienced difficulty and of how the child behaves with others in them. Because parents, teachers, and other informants may be unable to provide sufficiently detailed information in a single interview, between contacts with the therapist they can be encouraged to keep brief notes of any situation in which they observe peer-interaction difficulties. These notes should always include information about the setting where peer difficulties were observed (in the backyard, on the playground at recess, during a group game at school, working on an arts and crafts project, etc.), what the child did in that situation, who the other peers were, and how the peers responded to the child.

The child can also be interviewed; the quality and amount of information obtained from the interview will depend upon the age and verbal level of the child. Areas that can be pursued in this discussion might include: peer activities that the child enjoys or does not enjoy; whether the child has "best friends" and, if so, who they are, what they do together, and why the child considers them to be best friends; how the child prefers to spend free time; whether the child feels liked, "picked-on," or ignored by others; and so on. The therapist should also note any appearance, dress, or mannerism factors that may adversely affect the child's social relationships and that can receive attention during the intervention. Although they are not social skills per se, such things as extreme obesity, unattractive or unstylish dress, thick glasses, or obvious speech impediments may impact negatively on peer acceptance and are potentially modifiable.

When the therapist has carefully interviewed informants in the child's environment and determined those situations that appear problematic, it is desirable to objectively observe the child's social behavior.

Behavioral Assessment of Child Social Competency

There are three methods through which a therapist can directly observe a child's social skills. These are by constructing role-plays of troublesome interactions, observing the child's interaction with peers during a contrived social task in the clinic setting, or observing the child's behavior with peers in the natural environment. While the purpose of pretreatment behavioral assessment is the same for each of these procedures, and is to identify skill components in which the child is deficient, the three assessment methods differ in terms of the time they require and the quantity of treatment-related information they can yield.

Assessment Role-Plays

Here, the therapist analyzes the interview-data collected from parents, teachers, or other informants and constructs approximations of identified troublesome situations so that they can be role-played with the child in the clinic setting. This behavioral assessment procedure is quite similar to that used in adult social-skills assessment, and the interaction partner is either an adult confederate or the therapist. In some cases, the assessment can take the form of structured role-plays. Bornstein et al. (1977), to assess children's assertive skills, required them to interact with an adult who played the part of a child antagonist in each of the scenes. Geller et al. (1980) also used a role-play format for assessing the skill of a retarded young adolescent to respond to the positive and antagonistic advances of peers; an adult partner played the part of the adolescent peer in the role-play scenes.

Play interactions can be assessed similarly. For example, an adult confederate or the therapist could play a game or work on a project with the child to evaluate the client's social skills in that type of interaction. The particular game or task should correspond to a peer interaction with which the child is reported to experience difficulties, and the task should be one that requires skill-component behaviors to be handled effectively. The adult partner plays the role of a peer in that situation, and the child client's behavior during the interaction is rated to assess the presence of social-skill components.

Unfortunately, there are a number of methodological and validity problems associated with in-clinic role-play forms of behavioral assessment with children. While the therapist can construct assessment situations that parallel genuinely troublesome interactions in the child's natural environment, it is often difficult to realistically duplicate many aspects of the in-vivo environment (the presence of other peers, a classroomlike environment, and so on). Perhaps more importantly, a child's social behavior towards peers is frequently not correlated with that child's social behavior towards adults (Hartup, 1970; Hartup, 1976; Masters & Furman, 1977). Therefore, when a child role-plays assessment conversations, games, or joining an interaction with an adult partner, the observed behavior may not be at all representative of that child's performance in comparable interactions with other children. It can also be quite difficult for adults to realistically behave as a child would during assessment interactions, further limiting the validity of information derived from interactions with adult partners. For these reasons, a much more desirable skills-format is to utilize other children in assessment interactions.

Contrived Interactions with Peers

In this skills-assessment procedure, the therapist constructs tasks that provide the opportunity for the child client to interact with other children. For example, to examine a child's peer-interaction skills during a cooperative play task, the therapist might bring two or more children (at least one whom is a client child) into a playroom and ask them to work together on a puzzle, play "house" together, work with one another on an arts and crafts project, and so on. The play task should be similar to an interaction in which the client child appears to lack appropriate social skills, and it should be a task that provides the opportunity for all of the previously identified component-behaviors to occur. As the interaction between the children takes place, the therapist unobtrusively observes and rates the behavior of the client child for skill component-behaviors. Depending on the length of the play task, several tasks can be presented in a single assessment session, and the child's behavior can be rated in each.

Who might serve as peers in the play interaction? One possibility is that other children who are also skills-deficient can interact with one another. If group-skills training is planned, several of the client children can be placed together in the playroom and the behavior of each can be observed. As we will see, having skills-deficient children interact with one another is not only a useful procedure for the pretraining behavioral assessment of each child, but also can serve as an effective vehicle for the practice or rehearsal of skills that will occur in subsequent training-sessions. When assessment interactions with other skills-deficient children are used, the therapist should be aware that the observed social behavior may not correspond with the behavior that a given child exhibits during interactions with more skilled peers. In spite of this limitation, the procedure may prove quite useful, especially when group training is anticipated.

It is also possible to observe a child's play interactions with socially skilled peers. This, of course, requires access to other children who can serve as interactors. If an assessment interaction is conducted at a school, daycare center, or similar facility, this should prove to be little problem. One can place the child client and one or two other children in a location somewhat removed from everyone else, present them with play tasks, and closely observe the behavior of the client child during the interaction. The validity of this assessment format would seem especially high if the other peers in the interaction are genuine classmates of the client child, perhaps even peers with whom the child has difficulty playing cooperatively and actively. The client child's own right to confidentiality need not be jeopardized, since the other children do not have to be aware that the purpose of the play is specifically to assess the client child's social skills.

Assessment Observations in the Natural Environment

A final procedure for behavioral assessment of children's social skills is observing them in the natural environment itself. The setting for observation would be the school classroom, playground, daycare center, or other environment in which peer difficulties appear to occur, based upon information collected in earlier interviews. When in-vivo assessments are made, the therapist can either observe the child client as he or she interacts with peers as a part of the normal activities of the setting or, alternatively, the therapist can arrange for some planned activity (a game, task, cooperative project) to take place so the child can be observed in it. The advantage of the latter approach is that the therapist, who will be observing for only a relatively short period, seeks to assess the child's behavior in situations where social skills with peers are actually required. If one simply visited a school or daycare center at some random, unplanned time, it is quite possible that the observations would take place at a "noncritical" point, when children are engaged in individual assignments and are not actively interacting, during nap-time, and so on. Consequently, almost no useful information would be obtained. A much more desirable approach is for the therapist to pinpoint, based on information obtained through interviews, those situations when the child's peer-interaction problems are most likely to be evident. The therapist could either arrange to observe those particular activities as they occur naturally in the setting (e.g., observing the child at recess time, during free-play periods, and so on), or could ask that a similar peer task be planned for when the therapist arrives.

Because it takes place in the natural environment, in-vivo client-assessment can be very useful; the child client's interactions with real-life peers can be directly observed in the setting where problems genuinely occur. The major limitation is one of time, since it requires that the therapist actually travel to the setting. However, the quantity and quality of treatment-related information that can be obtained in this manner are sufficient to justify in-vivo observations in many cases.

Rating Observed Interactions for the Presence of Skill-Components

The task of the therapist observing a child's peer interactions is to evaluate whether, and how adequately, the child exhibits those behaviors that contribute to social skill. Figure 10.1 presents a sample form that the therapist can use to rate the presence of the skill-components we reviewed earlier.

We will assume that the therapist is observing a child client who is in a situation in which he or she can play or talk with others, and that the interaction is continuing over some period of time (5 minutes, 10 minutes, and so on). The most basic assessment rating-procedure is for the therapist to simply tally whenever one of the identified skill-behaviors is exhibited by the child under observation. This will yield frequency counts for the discrete components of social initiations, sharing, asking or answering questions, making praise statements, and so on. However, several important component-behaviors, such as proximity and task participation or playing, are not discrete behaviors that can be tallied so easily. If a child received a tally-mark for playing, but did so for only 3 seconds, it would signify something quite different than a tally-mark for playing that continued over 2 minutes. The therapist has several options for

FIGURE 10.1   Sample Rating-Form for Child's Social Interactions

Child Name:_____

Date of This Interaction:_____

Description of Setting Where Observation Was Made: _____

_____

Length of Interaction Rated Here:_____

Type of Interaction: _____ Pretraining Assessment

                        _____ Session Practice (Training Focused on

                                What Component?_____)

                        _____ Follow-up

COMPONENT BEHAVIORS

1. Greeting Made to Peers at Start of Interaction

                        _____ Present

                        _____ Absent

2. Social Initiations Made by Child (Tally of total number of
                                     times this behavior observed)

    Tally:_____ Total:_____

3. Asking Questions and Answering Questions (Tally of total number
                                              of times that child
                                              asked or answered a
                                              question)

    Tally:_____ Total:_____

4. Praise Statements Directed to Peers (Tally of total number of
                                         times child made a praise
                                         statement)

    Frequency Count:_____ Total:_____

5. Cooperation/Sharing (Tally of total number of incidents of
                         cooperative or sharing behavior observed)

    Frequency Count:_____ Total:_____

(continued)

rating behaviors such as proximity and task participation or playing. The easiest, albeit least precise, is estimating the percentage of time when the child engaged in play interactions or was in close proximity to at least one peer after the observation period was completed. This is similar to the method used to estimate an adult client's average eye-contact over the course of some role-play interaction.

If the therapist wishes to measure more precisely the amount of time when a child was interacting with peers in play, a cumulative stopwatch can be activated whenever an episode of play begins and it can be stopped whenever play terminates. Similarly, proximity can be more accurately assessed by timing the periods when the child client is within some fixed distance (perhaps three feet) of any other child. Whether this finer-grained assessment is needed depends principally upon the behavioral precision sought by the therapist.

The components included in the sample rating-form (Figure 10.1) should not be considered a comprehensive list of all child social behaviors that can be rated, and the therapist observing a child's interaction may wish to make note of other behaviors that occur in the session. For example, a given child might fail to make eye contact when talking to peers; if this were casually observed, the therapist could add a more formalized eye-contact component category to the list of behaviors. Children may also exhibit socially undesirable behaviors during peer interactions, such as hitting, grabbing objects from others, making "bossy" comments, responding to peer rejection during play by crying, and so on. Any potentially relevant aspects of a child's social behavior should be rated by the therapist who observes the interaction, so that they can also be given later treatment attention.

(continued)

6. Affective Responsiveness (Rated on a 1 to 7 scale for the
                                entire interaction)

        1   2   3   4   5   6   7

    extremely aloof,   extremely
    unemotional,   friendly, warm,
    lacking warmth,   attentive to
    disinterested   peers, sociable

7. Proximity (Percentage of time when child was located physically
                near to at least one peer and oriented to other
                children)

    0%   10%   20%   30%   40%   50%   60%   70%   80%   90%   100%

8. Task Participation/Play (Percentage of time when child was
                            actively engaged in play or otherwise
                            participating with at least one peer)

    0%   10%   20%   30%   40%   50%   60%   70%   80%   90%   100%

9. OTHER COMPONENTS BEING RATED (or any undesirable, inappropriate
                                behaviors being examined)

    Definition/Description of Behavior: Frequency Count or Rating:

Assessment When Child Clients Interact with One Another

When as assessment interaction takes place among several children, all of whom are clients, the behavior of each can be evaluated in the same interaction task. This can be accomplished most easily by using a single rating-form and simply tallying every instance of a component behavior with the letter of the child's name who exhibited it. For example, if Susan directed a question to a peer, it would be tallied "S"; if Mary asked a question, it could be recorded in the same category with an "M." At the end of the assessment observation period, separate frequencies or ratings for each child on each component could be easily derived.

Behavior of the Therapist while Observing
Children's Social Interactions

Whether children's social behavior is being observed with peers in the natural environment setting or using peer-play tasks in a clinic, it is important that the therapist observing them not disrupt the interaction through his or her presence. If the therapist can watch the interaction surreptitiously, such as through a one-way mirror, this is ideal. Often, especially during the in-vivo observations that take place in classrooms, daycare centers' playrooms, or playgrounds, entirely surreptitious assessment is impossible. The task of the therapist is to remain far enough from the children to avoid eliciting reactions to the observer, yet close enough to reliably evaluate the child client's behavior. It is useful for the therapist to act somewhat detached from the children who are being observed, avoiding direct eye contact, talk, or even smiles. Observation should be as unobtrusive as possible; the interaction between the therapist and child client will occur later, as a part of training.

It is extremely desirable for child-assessment observations to be repeated on several different occasions. This provides a more stable initial baseline of the child's social skills and can give the therapist a better subjective "feel" of the child's social skills on different occasions, perhaps during different interaction or play tasks, and perhaps with different peers. By the end of pretreatment assessment, the therapist will then be in a position to evaluate the behavioral ratings made of the child's interactions and identify those skill-components that will require particular attention in training.

Skills-Training Procedures with Children

The treatment principles of a social-skills training intervention for children are virtually identical to those incorporated in training for adults. A number of analogue research studies have demonstrated that even relatively brief, one-session exposure of socially deficient children to a single element of treatment, such as a modeling videotape, can exert a positive influence on their social-skills behavior with peers (see O'Connor, 1969; 1972); however, it appears more desirable to consolidate various learning-theory procedures within training sessions, to conduct treatment over multiple sessions, and to focus on deficient skill-components in sequential and cumulative fashion over the course of the intervention. Specifically, modeling, coaching/instructions, behavioral practice, and the provision of feedback and reinforcement following practice are all elements of treatment to improve children's interpersonal skills. As was the case with adult training, therapist attention must then be focused on bringing about use of new skills in the natural environment. Let us now turn our attention to how sessions can be conducted, first when only a single child is treated and then for group social-skills training of children.

Social-Skills Training with One Child

Treatment sessions for a child can begin with a short period of information-provision and discussion by the therapist about the behavioral component that will be receiving attention in that session. The purpose of this is to introduce the session's purpose and to direct the child's attention to a particular aspect of social skill. When the therapist discusses any skill-component behavior, it is always important that information be presented in a style and language appropriate to the child's own age and level of verbal sophistication. For example, if one session's targeted behavior is cooperation and sharing, the therapist might first inquire about the child's activities in school that day and then provide specific illustrations of how cooperative acts and sharing with peers could occur in those activities. The child might be asked to identify occasions when he or she did share things with others, occasions when other children shared or cooperatively played with the child client, and why it is good to share.

Exposure to a model who exhibits the skill-behavior is a second important aspect of the training session. As we noted in earlier chapters, this exposure can be either live (with the therapist modeling the desired behavior) or portrayed in a videotape presentation.

Videotape Skills-Models

The therapist who anticipates conducting frequent social-skills training interventions with children may wish to construct a modeling videotape for use in sessions. A typical film that could be used for various child clients might show child models engaged in different play and conversational activities, and exhibiting all components of skill during these interactions. For one example, one vignette might show two children playing a table game with each other while a third child (to whom the client's attention will be directed) initially watches from a distance. The onlooker, after watching the others briefly, then approaches the two peers who are playing (illustrating proximity). After greeting each peer by name (greeting), the former onlooker might ask if he or she can join in their game (social initiation) and begin playing with them. Various other skill-behaviors can then be demonstrated by the three models, including ongoing cooperative play, talking, answering, and asking conversational questions, sharing, laughing, and so on. This entire modeled interaction might last for five or ten minutes. Because the models exhibit all skill-components, the film could be used not only for each treatment session of a given child client, but for other skills-deficient children as well.

Videotape modeling-films have been used successfully in many skills-training projects with children (see Geller & Scheirer, 1978; Gottman, 1977; Gottman et al., 1976; O'Connor, 1969, 1972). The advantages of using modeling videotapes include: (1) the fairly high reinforcement value to most children of watching a "televisionlike" film; (2) the presentation of skill-models who are also children and may have greater salience than would an adult model to the child observing them; (3) the presentation of realistic interaction scenes, such as children at play in a classroom setting; and (4) greater procedural ease, with the therapist able to pause a modeling film at any point, discuss the model's behavior as it occurs, and so on. Models used in the film should exhibit characteristics that are related to greater imitative learning (same age as the child client, same sex, positive outcome achieved by the model, etc.). When the same film will be used for several clients, models of different sexes, races, and ages might be represented in the tape's portrayed interactions.

Construction of a modeling film does require that the therapist have access to videotape-recording apparatus, children who can serve as actors in the tape, and a certain willingness to be a part-time film director. One's own children, the children of colleagues, or a friendly teacher at a nearby school or church can be good sources of modeling-film actors. Children's modeling films need not be elaborately produced and they often represent a very reasonable investment in time, especially when other children will later be receiving similar social-skills training.

Live-Modeling by the Therapist

The adult therapist can also serve as a skills model for the socially deficient child. Informally, this includes providing examples of the targeted verbal components in the session. If two therapists are present, they can role-play a live-modeled interaction with one another and with the children observing them in an episode of conversation or "play." When only one therapist is present in the session, the therapist and the child could interact together, with the trainer playing the part of a socially skilled child and demonstrating the correct use of skill-behaviors as he or she interacts with the child. Thus, if the therapist model and the child play a game with one another, the child's attention is specifically focused on the manner in which the therapist greets the child at the interaction's start, walks over and verbally initiates a request to play, asks or answers questions while playing, shares play objects, and so on.

Following modeling-exposure, the child is verbally directed or "coached" to use the behavior receiving attention in the session. In this coaching phase, the therapist can variously provide more examples of the target behavior, suggest times in a social interaction when its use would be appropriate, or ask the child to generate specific examples of the behavior (see Asher, Oden, & Gottman, 1977; Gottman et al., 1976; Kelly, Furman, Phillips, Hathorn, & Wilson, 1979; LaGreca & Mesibov, 1979; LaGreca & Santogrossi, 1980). The aim of directive coaching is to ensure that the child now understands the behavioral concept under attention and seems able to exhibit it.

At this point in the session, behavior rehearsal can occur. Procedures for skills-rehearsal with children correspond to the format used in an adult's training. Specifically, a child's in-session practice should approximate the kinds of situations in which that child actually experiences peer difficulties; rehearsal also requires the presence of one or more partners, with whom the child client can interact. Ideally, a child's practice partners will be other children; less desirably, but certainly better than having no practice, the child can interact with an adult (the therapist or a therapist confederate), who plays the part of a peer in the rehearsal period.

Peers as Interaction Practice-Partners

A number of social-skills training projects with children have had the skills-deficient child interact with peers, both to serve as a vehicle for session practice and to allow the therapist to objectively evaluate whether the child exhibits the targeted component during peer interactions (see Berler et al., 1980; LaGreca & Mesibov, 1979; Strain & Timm, 1974; Strain et al., 1977). In general, those tasks used for skills-practice with peers have involved relatively unstructured play activities, such as games, art projects, and so on. As an example, a young child who is receiving social-skills training can be brought into a playroom area following the phase of the training session that included instructions, modeling, and coaching on some social behavior. One or two other children might also be in the playroom setting, and the child client is instructed to play with them and practice using the newly acquired skills during the play period. A therapist observing the interaction can rate the client child's play behavior with the other children for a set period of time (such as 5 minutes or 10 minutes). Immediately after the practice interaction, the therapist can meet with the child and discuss whether the behavioral components were exhibited, providing feedback and praise to the child for their use.

Utilizing other children as practice-play partners requires that peers be available to serve in this role. When training is conducted within a setting where other children are present, such as at a school or daycare center, this can be accomplished quite readily. Children who will interact with the client child can be either naive interactors or can function more as therapist confederates in play. If they are naive interactors, the peers might simply be told that they will be playing a game with other children (one of whom is the client child). On the other hand, they might be told that they will be playing with another child and part of their "job" is to help the other child feel comfortable with them, allow the child to join them, ask and answer questions with him, and so on. The latter approach helps to ensure that the child's practice-interaction will be positive and that skill-usage will actually be reinforced by peers in the practice-interaction. As we will see when we consider group social-skills training, children can easily serve as practice-play partners with one another. This obviates the need for locating additional peers and permits each child in a play interaction to rehearse the skill-behaviors that are receiving training attention.

The Therapist or Therapist Confederate as an Interaction Practice-Partner

Here, skills-rehearsal does not occur during play or conversation with peers, but rather with the adult therapist or a confederate of the therapist. Depending upon the situation being rehearsed, the child and adult partner might have a conversation (with the partner playing the part of a child at school), work on a puzzle or game together, practice interactions in which the child client asks the partner to join him in games or activities, and so on. The interactions used in practice should correspond to situations that the child needs to handle more effectively in the natural environment and that permit the exhibition of the specific skill-components that are receiving attention in that session.

A variation of this rehearsal technique that has been used by me with younger children entails role-playing with hand puppets. In it, the child wears a hand puppet that represents himself or herself, while the therapist wears one or two puppets who represent other children. In most cases, the other children represented by the therapist's puppets are actually named for peers in the child's environment (classmates, children in the daycare center, siblings, or neighbor children) and the situations being rehearsed are actual situations that the child client does not handle skillfully. Following instructions, modeling, and coaching in the session, puppet rehearsal permits the child to practice handling those interactions. For example, one 5-year-old boy had difficulty joining in game activities with two other boys who sat at his table at school. To rehearse ways of initiating play activities with them, the therapist instructed the client to imagine that the two named peers were working on a game at the desk they all shared at school; the puppets were those peers. Then, the child client's puppet practiced social initiations by moving the puppet toward the other two and speaking as he would in that situation (greeting the others, asking to join them, cooperatively playing, and so on). Since the therapist controls the peer puppets and vocalizes for them, it is possible to ensure that positive "peer" consequences are achieved in the situations that are practiced. Feedback, suggestions, and praise can be provided by the therapist following each situation rehearsed in this way.

While the rehearsal techniques considered here do involve interaction between the therapist and child in conversation or play, they do not represent unstructured "play therapy" as the term is traditionally used. First, rehearsal procedures are approximations of very specific types of social interactions that prove troublesome for the child in the natural environment. Second, the rehearsal is handled in a directive manner, with the child explicitly taught to exhibit behavioral skill-components during the practice. Rehearsal is followed by specific feedback, praise, and additional instruction with further practice if that is needed. Finally, when skill-behaviors are exhibited during session-practice, the therapist establishes a behavioral plan to facilitate their generalization to peer interactions occurring in the in-vivo environment.

Generalization of Skills-Training Effects

In social-skills training with adult clients, procedures to foster the use of new skill behaviors in the natural environment involve cognitive modification, self-monitoring of specific situations where skills could be used (or were exhibited), and so on. Some of the generalization techniques appropriate for adults are also useful with older children. However, it is important (and usually possible) to arrange more specific and direct positive contingencies for socially skilled behavior among children. Let us consider several ways that this skills-generalization can be encouraged.

Establishment of In-Vivo Situations That Permit Skill Usage

We have already noted that the social-skills training intervention should be focused on those kinds of situations where a given child experiences peer-interaction problems. Thus, the child who is observed to have difficulty playing cooperatively with peers will receive training (and will practice interactions) addressing that type of social situation. However, it is necessary to ensure not only that treatment focuses on a child's real interaction problems, but also that ample opportunities be created in the natural environment for skill-usage to occur once training takes place. This is important because a formerly isolated or socially unskilled child may be excluded by peers and have fewer naturally occurring opportunities to apply his newly acquired skills.

One of the best ways to ensure that the child has opportunities to use new skills is through close, frequent collaboration between the therapist and the child's teachers or parents. As an example, a child with deficits in the skills needed for cooperative play may have a training session in which more effective play-behaviors are discussed, modeled, coached, and practiced. However, unless there are also opportunities to use those behaviors with real peers at school or at home, it is unlikely the new skills will be established in the child's in-vivo repertoire. Therefore, the therapist might contact the child's teacher to apprise the teacher of what occurred in that day's training session and ask that the teacher attempt to "set up" opportunities for cooperative play at school. This might include assigning the child client to tasks or class projects with peers, designating the child to be captain of some team game at recess, making certain the child sits at a table with peers, and otherwise ensuring that the child will have planned opportunities to use the new skills. Similarly, the child's parents can be instructed to arrange special play-activities between their child and peers or siblings. This might include inviting other children to their house, arranging for games between the child client and friends or siblings, and so on. As much as possible, it is desirable that when teachers or parents "stage" such interaction opportunities, they place the child with peers who are likely to be accepting of the child, rather than a class "bully," who might punish the client child's early attempts at skill-usage.

Planned Reinforcement of the Child's Skilled Behavior in the Natural Environment

As a child exhibits new social skills, we expect that he or she will gradually experience greater peer acceptance, receive reciprocal positive behaviors from others, be involved in more rewarding activities, and so on. However, the natural peer-reinforcement contingencies may be insufficient to fully establish new skill-behaviors, especially for the child who has been socially deficient. Therefore, it is desirable to make certain that the child will be more consistently reinforced in the natural environment when he attempts to use the skill-behaviors that have been acquired in training. Since the therapist is not usually in a position to observe the child's daily in-vivo social interactions, and because reinforcement is most effective when it immediately follows the desired behavior, the assistance of teachers and parents must be enlisted. It is useful for the therapist to maintain regular contact with those adults in the child's environment who can observe and reinforce the child for exhibiting skill-component behaviors. This might take the form of weekly phone calls to a teacher, or discussions with the parents describing the specific behaviors that the child is learning. The adults can be asked to remain unobtrusively observant of the child's peer-interactions at home or school, and alert to occasions when the child exhibits any behavior that has been trained. Praise should be provided whenever the child is observed to exhibit a socially skilled behavior. The child can be praised immediately after the behavior occurs, such as when a teacher praises the child client who has just approached and initiated play with others. However, the results of several studies suggest that adult praise of a child in the midst of an intensive peer-interaction may actually disrupt that interaction (see Evers & Schwarz, 1973). Therefore, praise should be provided in such a fashion that it does not disrupt the child's interaction or attract negative attention from the other children. Whenever feasible, the teacher or adult can be asked to keep brief behavioral monitoring records, which indicate how frequently the child exhibited socially skilled behaviors with peers. This can provide the therapist with objective data on the child's behavior change in the natural environment.

Finally, it is possible to implement a more structured behavior-reinforcement program, utilizing not only praise but also other rewards contingent on skill-use. As an example, the child who typically remains alone on a playground while her peers play might be reinforced for each 5-minute interval that she spends in close proximity to peers, or playing with them. Reinforcers used in such a system could include teacher praise plus special activities that the child enjoys, tangible rewards, and so on. Before such a structured program is implemented, it is of course important that the child first have learned the skills needed to interact with peers and thereby earn the reinforcers.

Training Variations for Group Treatment

As we noted earlier, it is often more feasible to conduct children's social-skills training in small groups than with one individual child. A major advantage of group-administered training is that children can engage in practice play-interactions with one another during the sessions, eliminating the need for an adult therapist to play the part of a child in skills-practice, or the requirement that the therapist locate and arrange for peers to serve as play-partners during behavior rehearsal. In general, the format of each group training session parallels that of individual child sessions, incorporating the procedures of instruction, modeling, coaching, practice, and feedback/reinforcement to teach components of peer-interaction skill. During the rehearsal period, the group can be broken down into smaller groups of two or three for practice play such as working on a game, doing an art project, or conversing. Each child is instructed to exhibit the trained behaviors with his or her play-partners, and the therapist observing the practice-play can offer specific prompts, feedback, and praise to each child as the trained behaviors are exhibited.

Several recent studies very nicely illustrate some procedures suitable for children's group social-skills training (Cooke & Apolloni, 1976; LaGreca & Mesibov, 1979; LaGreca & Santogrossi, 1980). Because they are representative of the others, we will examine the procedures used by LaGreca and Santogrossi (1980). The purpose of the project was to evaluate the effectiveness of a skills-training intervention and to compare it against no-treatment and minimal-treatment control groups. Children in this project were students in the third, fourth, and fifth grades of an elementary school who, based on sociometric measures, were not well accepted nor liked by their peers. Social-skills training groups consisted of 5 same-sex children, and each was led by 2 co-therapists. The groups met weekly over 4 weeks; sessions lasted for 90 minutes and were conducted at the elementary school after regular school hours.

The investigators targeted eight behaviors for training attention (smiling/ laughing, greeting others, joining others, extending social invitations, conversational skills, sharing/cooperation, verbal complimenting, and physical appearance/grooming). Two components received attention in each training session. Sessions began with all children in the group watching a modeling videotape that showed peer models engaged in skillful social interactions and exhibiting the component-behaviors. In the tapes, the peer models were seen joining into activities with others, working on a group task assignment, and so on. Several different films were used and each lasted about four minutes.

After modeling exposure, the co-therapists led a group discussion about the content of the tapes by asking the children to identify how the model used the targeted components, and how they themselves could use these skills in their own everyday interactions. The next phase of the treatment session involved coaching and behavior-rehearsal. The interactions used for session practice were based on actual situations that the children reported encountering at school. Examples included joining others in games at recess, cooperating with others in gym class activities, and so on. The therapists arranged for group members to simulate these play and social situations with each other and coached them to exhibit the component skill during their in-session practice. Feedback, reinforcement, and suggestions were provided after each practice-episode. Additionally, the practice-interactions were videotaped and children observed replays of their just-completed practice. This videotape self-observation was accompanied by therapist feedback; the children were also encouraged to critique positive aspects of one another's practice, as well as areas still needing attention. Finally, children were given homework assignments that stressed utilizing the trained behaviors with peers (e.g., "Greet a classmate at least once each day for the next week"). Time in the next session was devoted to a review of each child client's reported success with his or her homework assignments.

LaGreca and Santogrossi (1980) were able to demonstrate that children who received skills-training improved significantly more than control-group children in their own knowledge of appropriate social skills, measured by using a test developed by the investigators. Skills-trained children also more frequently exhibited the trained-component behaviors during role-play interactions that simulated making friends with a new child at school, and their role-play performance was evaluated more favorably by adult observers on a global and subjective rating of social skill. Finally, the investigators had college students unobtrusively observe the children at times when they had the opportunity to engage in peer interactions at school, such as at recess, in gym class, and during club meetings. These in-vivo generalization ratings demonstrated that the children who had received skills-training initiated peer-interactions in these school settings more frequently after treatment than did the control group children.

The well-conducted study by LaGreca and Santogrossi (1980) not only illustrates how behavioral skills-training principles can be applied to the group treatment of socially unpopular children, but also provides impressive evidence on the short-term effectiveness of the intervention. Treatment in this project was relatively brief, consisting of four 90-minute training sessions, and applied interventions may require an intervention of longer duration, especially for highly skills-deficient children. Nonetheless, the training procedures used here, perhaps in combination with a program to directly reinforce children's skill use in the natural environment, can be incorporated in applied training-interventions.

References

Adler, A. *What life should mean to you*. Boston: Little, Brown, 1931.

American Association on Mental Deficiency. *Manual on terminology and classification in mental retardation*, 1977.

Arbes, B. H., & Hubbell, R. N. Packaged impact: A structured communication skills workshop. *Journal of Counseling Psychology*, 1973, *20*, 332–337.

Argyle, M., Trower, P., & Bryant, B. Explorations in the treatment of personality disorders and neuroses by social skills training. *British Journal of Medical Psychology*, 1974, *47*, 63–72.

Arkowitz, H. Measurement and modification of minimal dating behavior. In M. Hersen, R. Eisler, & P. Miller (Eds.), *Progress in behavior modification* (Vol. 5). New York: Academic Press, 1977.

Arkowitz, H., Hinton, R., Perl, J., & Himadi, W. Treatment strategies for dating anxiety in college men based on real-life practice. *Counseling Psychologist*, 1978, *7*, 41–46.

Asher, S. R., Oden, S. L., & Gottman, J. M. Children's friendships in school settings. In L. G. Katz (Ed.), *Current topics in early childhood education* (Vol. 1). Norwood, N. J.: Ablex, 1977.

Association for the Advancement of Behavior Therapy. 1980 Convention Announcement. *The Behavior Therapist*, 1980, *3*, 32.

Baer, D. M., Wolf, M. M., & Risley, T. R. Some current dimensions of applied behavior analysis. *Journal of Applied Behavior Analysis*, 1968, *1*, 91–97.

Bander, K. W., Steinke, G. V., Allen, G. J., & Mosher, D. L. Evaluation of three dating-specific treatment approaches for heterosexual dating anxiety. *Journal of Consulting and Clinical Psychology*, 1975, *43*, 259–265.

Bandura, A. Influence of model's reinforcement contingencies on the acquisition of imitative responses. *Journal of Personality and Social Psychology*, 1965, *1*, 589-595.

Bandura, A. *Principles of behavior modification*. New York: Holt, Rinehart, and Winston, 1969.

Bandura, A., & Huston, A. C. Identification as a process of incidental learning. *Journal of Abnormal and Social Psychology*, 1961, *63*, 311–318.

Bandura, A., & Kupers, C. J. Transmission of patterns of self-reinforcement through modeling. *Journal of Abnormal and Social Psychology*, 1964, *69*, 1–9.

Bandura, A., Ross, D., & Ross, S. A. Imitation of film-mediated aggressive models. *Journal of Abnormal and Social Psychology*, 1963, *66*, 3–11.

Bandura, A., & Walters, R. H. *Social learning and personality development*. New York: Holt, Rinehart, and Winston, 1963.

Barbee, J. R., & Keil, E. C. Experimental techniques of job interview training for the disadvantaged: Videotape feedback, behavior modification, and microcounseling. *Journal of Applied Psychology*, 1973, *58*, 209–213.

Barlow, D. H., Abel, G. G., Blanchard, E. B, Bristow, A. R., & Young, L. D. A heterosocial skills behavior checklist for males. *Behavior Therapy*, 1977, *8*, 229–239.

Barlow, D., & Hersen, M. Single case experimental designs: Uses in applied clinical research. *Archives of General Psychiatry*, 1973, *29*, 319–325.

Bellack, A. S., & Hersen, M. Chronic psychiatric patients: Social skills training. In M. Hersen & A. S. Bellack (Eds.), *Behavior therapy in the psychiatric setting*. Baltimore: Williams and Wilkins, 1978.

Bellack, A. S., Hersen, M., & Lamparski, D. Role-play tests for assessing social skills: Are they valid? Are they useful? *Journal of Consulting and Clinical Psychology*, 1979, *47*, 335–342.

Bellack, A. S., Hersen, M., & Turner, S. M. Generalization effects of social skills training in chronic schizophrenics: An experimental analysis. *Behaviour Research and Therapy*, 1976, *14*, 391–398.

Berler, E. S., Kelly, J. A., & Romanczyk, R. G. The assessment of children's social skills. Paper presented at the Association for the Advancement of Behavior Therapy, New York, 1980.

Bernreuter, R. G. *The personality inventory*. Stanford, CA: Stanford University Press, 1931.

Berscheid, E., & Walster, E. Physical attractiveness. In L. Berkowitz (Ed.), *Advances in experimental social psychology* (Vol. 7). New York: Academic Press, 1973.

Birtchnell, J. Birth order and mental illness: A control study. *Social Psychiatry*, 1972, *7*, 167–179.

Bloom, L. Z., Coburn, K., & Pearlman, J. *The new assertive woman*. New York: Dell, 1975.

Bornstein, M. R., Bellack, A. S., & Hersen, M. Social skills training for unassertive children: A multiple baseline analysis. *Journal of Applied Behavior Analysis*, 1977, *10*, 183–195.

Bornstein, M., Bellack, A. S., & Hersen, M. Social skills training for highly aggressive children. *Behavior Modification*, 1980, *4*, 173–186.

Braukmann, C. J., Fixsen, D. L., Phillips, E. L., Wolf, M. M., & Maloney, D. M. An analysis of a selection interview training package for predelinquents at Achievement Place. *Criminal Justice and Behavior*, 1974, *1*, 30–42.

Breger, L., & McGaugh, J. L. Critique and reformulation of "learning theory" approaches to psychotherapy and neuroses. *Psychological Bulletin*, 1965, *63*, 338–358.

Brockway, B. S. Assertive training for professional women. *Social Work,* 1976, *21,* 498–505.

Burkhart, B. R., Green, S. B., & Harrison, W. H. Measurement of assertive behavior: Construct and predictive validity of self-report, role-playing, and in-vivo measures. *Journal of Clinical Psychology,* 1979, *35,* 376–383.

Butler, P. Assertive training: Teaching women not to discriminate against themselves. *Psychotherapy: Theory, Research and Practice,* 1976, *13,* 56–60.

Campbell, D., & Stanley, J. Experimental and quasi-experimental designs for research on teaching. In N. L. Gage (Ed.), *Handbook of research on teaching.* Chicago: Rand-McNally, 1963.

Cattell, R. B., Eber, H. W., & Tatsouka, M. M. *Sixteen personality factor questionnaire.* Champaign, IL: Institute for Personality and Ability Testing, 1967.

Christenson, A., & Arkowitz, H. Preliminary report on practice dating and feedback as treatment for college dating problems. *Journal of Counseling Psychology,* 1974, *21,* 92–95.

Christenson, A., Arkowitz, H., & Anderson, J. Practice dating as treatment for college dating inhibitions. *Behavior Research and Therapy,* 1975, *13,* 321–331.

Cohen, B. M., & Etheridge, J. M. Recruiting's main ingredient. *Journal of College Placement,* 1975, *35,* 75–77.

Cone, J. D., & Hawkins, R. P. *Behavioral assessment.* New York: Brunner/Mazel, 1977.

Cooke, T., & Apolloni, T. Developing positive social-emotional behaviors: A study of training and generalization effects. *Journal of Applied Behavior Analysis,* 1976, *9,* 65–78.

Cowen, E. L., Pederson, A., Babigian, H., Izzo, L. D., & Trost, M. A. Long-term follow-up of early detected vulnerable children. *Journal of Consulting and Clinical Psychology,* 1973, *41,* 438–446.

Curran, J. P. An evaluation of a skills training program and a systematic desensitization program in reducing dating anxiety. *Behaviour Research and Therapy,* 1975, *13,* 65–68.

Curran, J. P. Skills training as an approach to the treatment of heterosexual-social anxiety. *Psychological Bulletin,* 1977, *84,* 140–157.

Curran, J. P., & Gilbert, F. S. A test of the relative effectiveness of a systematic desensitization program and an interpersonal skills training program with date anxious subjects. *Behavior Therapy,* 1975, *6,* 510–521.

Curran, J. P., Gilbert, F. S., & Little, L. M. A comparison between behavioral replication training and sensitivity training approaches to heterosexual dating anxiety. *Journal of Counseling Psychology,* 1976, *23,* 190–196.

Doll, E. A. *Measurement of social competence: A manual for the Vineland Social Maturity Scale.* Circle Pines, MN: American Guidance Service, 1953.

Drake, L. E. A social I. E. Scale for the MMPI. *Journal of Applied Psychology,* 1946, *30,* 51–54.

Drake, L. T., Kaplan, H. R., & Stone, R. A. How do employers value the interview? *Journal of College Placement,* 1972, *32,* 47–51.

Durlak, J. A., & Mannarino, A. P. The social skills development program: Description of a school-based preventive mental health program for high-risk children. *Journal of Clinical Child Psychology*, 1977, *6*, 48–52.

Edelstein, B. A., & Eisler, R. M. Effects of modeling and modeling with instructions and feedback on the behavioral components of social skills. *Behavior Therapy*, 1976, *7*, 382–389.

Eisler, R. M., Hersen, M., Miller, P. M., & Blanchard, E. B. Situational determinants of assertive behaviors. *Journal of Consulting and Clinical Psychology*, 1975, *43*, 330–340.

Eisler, R. M., Miller, P. M., & Hersen, M. Components of assertive behavior. *Journal of Clinical Psychology*, 1973, *29*, 295–299.

Elkins, D. Factors related to the choice status of ninety eighth-grade children in a school society. *Genetic Psychology Monographs*, 1958, *58*, 207–272.

Ellis, A. *Reason and emotion in psychotherapy*. New York: Lyle Stuart, 1962.

Ellis, A., & Grieger, R. *Handbook of rational-emotive therapy*. New York: Springer, 1977.

Engen, T., Lipsett, L. P., & Kaye, H. Olfactory responses and adaptation in the human neonate. *Journal of Comparative Physiological Psychology*, 1963, *56*, 73–77.

Evers, W., & Schwarz, J. Modifying social withdrawal in preschoolers: The effects of filmed modeling and teacher praise. *Journal of Abnormal Child Psychology*, 1973, *1*, 248–256.

Eysenck, H. J. *Dimensions of personality*. London: Routledge, 1947.

Falloon, I. R., Lindley, P., McDonald, R., & Marks, I. M. Social skills training of out-patient groups: A controlled study of rehearsal and homework. *British Journal of Psychiatry*, 1977, *131*, 599-609.

Farrell, A. D., Mariotto, M. J., Conger, A. J., Curran, J. P., & Wallender, J. L. Self-ratings and judges' ratings of heterosexual social anxiety and skill: A generalizability study. *Journal of Consulting and Clinical Psychology*, 1979, *47*, 164–175.

Filipczak, J., Archer, M., & Friedman, R. M. In-school social skills training: Use with disruptive adolescents. *Behavior Modification*, 1980, *4*, 243–263.

Foster, S. L., & Ritchey, W. L. Issues in the assessment of social competence in children. *Journal of Applied Behavior Analysis*, 1979, *12*, 625–638.

Foy, D. W., Eisler, R. M., & Pinkston, S. Modeled assertion in a case of explosive rages. *Journal of Behavior Therapy and Experimental Psychiatry*, 1975, *6*, 135–137.

Foy, D., Massey, F., Duer, J., Ross, J., & Wooten, L. Social skills training to improve alcoholics' vocational interpersonal competency. *Journal of Counseling Psychology*, 1979, *26*, 128–132.

Frederiksen, L., Jenkins, J., Foy, D., & Eisler, R. Social skills training in the modification of abusive verbal outbursts in adults. *Journal of Applied Behavior Analysis*, 1976, *9*, 117–125.

Frederiksen, L. W., & Kelly, J. A. Social skills and explosive outbursts: An assessment package. Paper presented at the Southeastern Psychological Association Annual Meeting, Hollywood, Florida, 1977.

Furman, W., Geller, M. I., Simon, S. J., & Kelly, J. A. Teaching job interviewing skills to adolescent patients through a behavior rehearsal procedure. *Behavior Therapy*, 1979, *10*, 157–167.

Galassi, J. P., Deleo, J. S., Galassi, M. D., & Bastien, S. The college self-expression scale: A measure of assertiveness. *Behavior Therapy*, 1974, *5*, 165–171.

Galassi, M. D., & Galassi, J. P. Assertion: A critical review. *Psychotherapy: Theory, Research and Practice*, 1978, *15*, 16–29.

Galassi, J. P., Galassi, M. D., & Litz, M. D. Assertive training in groups using video feedback. *Journal of Counseling Psychology*, 1974, *21*, 390–394.

Gambrill, E. D., & Richey, C. A. An assertion inventory for use in assessment and research. *Behavior Therapy*, 1975, *6*, 550–561.

Gay, M. L., Hollandsworth, J. G., & Galassi, J. P. An assertiveness inventory for adults. *Journal of Counseling Psychology*, 1975, *22*, 340–344.

Geller, M. I., & Scheirer, C. J. The effect of filmed-modeling on cooperative play in disadvantaged preschoolers. *Journal of Abnormal Child Psychology*, 1978, *6*, 71–87.

Geller, M. I., Wildman, H. E., Kelly, J. A., & Laughlin, C. S. Teaching assertive and commendatory social skills to an interpersonally-deficient retarded adolescent. *Journal of Clinical Child Psychology*, 1980, *9*, 17–21.

Glasgow, R., & Arkowitz, H. The behavioral assessment of male and female social competence in dyadic heterosexual interactions. *Behavior Therapy*, 1975, *6*, 488–498.

Glass, C. R., Gottman, J. M., & Shmurak, S. H. Response acquisition and cognitive self-statement modification approaches to dating skills training. *Journal of Counseling Psychology*, 1976, *23*, 520–526.

Goldsmith, J. G., & McFall, R. M. Development and evaluation of an interpersonal skill training program for psychiatric inpatients. *Journal of Abnormal Psychology*, 1975, *84*, 51–58.

Gottman, J. M. The effects of a modeling film on social isolation in preschool children: A methodological investigation. *Journal of Abnormal Psychology*, 1977, *5*, 69–78.

Gottman, J., Gonso, J., & Rasmussen, B. Social interaction, social competence and friendship in children. *Child Development*, 1975, *46*, 709–718.

Gottman, J., Gonso, J., & Schuler, P. Teaching social skills to isolated children. *Child Development*, 1976, *4*, 179–197.

Gottman, J., McFall, R., & Barnett, J. Design and analysis of research using time series. *Psychological Bulletin*, 1969, *72*, 299–306.

Greenspoon, J. The reinforcing effect of two spoken sounds on the frequency of two responses. *American Journal of Psychology*, 1955, *68*, 409–416.

Greenwald, D. P. The behavioral assessment of differences in social skill and social anxiety in female college students. *Behavior Therapy*, 1977, *8*, 925–937.

Gutride, M. E., Goldstein, A. P., & Hunter, G. F. The use of modeling and role playing to increase social interactions among asocial psychiatric patients. *Journal of Consulting and Clinical Psychology*, 1973, *40*, 408–415.

Hartup, W. Peer interaction and social organization. In P. Mussen (Ed.), *Manual of child psychology* (Vol. 2). New York: Wiley, 1970.

Hartup, W. Peers, play and pathology. Paper presented to the National Institute of Child Health Development, Washington, D. C., 1976.

Hartup, W., Glazer, J., & Charlesworth, R. Peer reinforcement and sociometric status. *Child Development*, 1967, *38*, 1017–1024.

Heimberg, R. G., Madsen, C. H., Montgomery, D., & McNabb, C. E. Behavioral treatments for heterosocial problems: Effects on daily self-monitored and role played interactions. *Behavior Modification*, 1980, *4*, 147–172.

Hersen, M., & Barlow, D. H. *Single-case experimental designs: Strategies for studying behavior change*. New York: Pergamon Press, 1976.

Hersen, M., & Bellack, A. S. Social skills training for chronic psychiatric patients: Rationale, research findings, and future directions. *Comprehensive Psychiatry*, 1976, *17*, 559–580.

Hersen, M., Eisler, R. M., & Miller, P. M. Development of assertive responses: Clinical, measurement and research considerations. *Behaviour Research and Therapy*, 1973, *11*, 505–521.

Hersen, M., Eisler, R., & Miller, P. An experimental analysis of generalization in assertive training. *Behaviour Research and Therapy*, 1974, *12*, 295–310.

Hersen, M., Eisler, R. M., Miller, P. M., Johnson, M. B., & Pinkston, S. G. Effects of practice, instructions, and modeling on components of assertive behavior. *Behaviour Research and Therapy*, 1973, *11*, 443–451.

Hersen, M., Kazdin, A. E., Bellack, A. S., & Turner, S. M. Effects of live modeling, covert modeling and rehearsal on assertiveness in psychiatric patients. *Behaviour Research and Therapy*, 1979, *17*, 369–377.

Hollandsworth, J. G. Personal communication, 1979.

Hollandsworth, J. G., Dressel, M. E., & Stevens, J. Use of behavioral versus traditional procedures for increasing job interview skills. *Journal of Counseling Psychology*, 1977, *24*, 503–509.

Hollandsworth, J. G., Glazeski, R. C., & Dressel, M. E. Use of social skills training in the treatment of extreme anxiety and deficient verbal skills in the job interview setting. *Journal of Applied Behavior Analysis*, 1978, *11*, 259–269.

Hollandsworth, J. G., & Sandifer, B. A. Behavioral training for increasing effective job-interview skills: Follow-up and evaluation. *Journal of Counseling Psychology*, 1979, *26*, 448–450.

Hollandsworth, J. G., & Wall, K. E. Sex differences in assertive behavior: An empirical investigation. *Journal of Counseling Psychology*, 1977, *24*, 217–222.

Horney, K. *Our inner conflicts*. New York: Norton, 1945.

Hull, D. B., & Schroeder, H. E. Some interpersonal effects of assertion, nonassertion, and aggression. *Behavior Therapy*, 1979, *10*, 20–28.

Hymel, S., & Asher, S. R. Assessment and training of isolated children's social skills. Paper presented at the biennial meeting of the Society for Research in Child Development, New Orleans, 1977.

Jaffe, P. G., & Carlson, P. M. Relative efficacy of modeling and instructions in eliciting social behavior from chronic psychiatric patients. *Journal of Consulting and Clinical Psychology*, 1976, *44*, 200–207.

Kazdin, A. Effects of covert modeling and model reinforcement on assertive behavior. *Journal of Abnormal Psychology*, 1974, *83*, 240–252.

Kazdin, A. E. Effects of covert modeling, multiple models and model reinforcement of assertive behavior. *Behavior Therapy*, 1976, 7, 211–222.

Kazdin, A. E. Assessing the clinical or applied importance of behavior change through social validation. *Behavior Modification*, 1977, 1, 427–452.

Keefe, F. J., Kopel, S. A., & Gordon, S. B. *A practical guide to behavioral assessment*. New York: Springer, 1978.

Keil, E. C., & Barbee, J. R. Behavior modification and training the disadvantaged job interviewee. *Vocational Guidance Quarterly*, 1973, 22, 50–56.

Keller, M., & Carlson, P. The use of symbolic modeling to promote social skills in preschool children with low levels of social responsiveness. *Child Development*, 1974, 45, 912–919.

Kelly, J. A. Group training of social skills: Clinical applications and procedures. In D. Upper & S. Ross (Eds.), *Annual review of behavioral group therapy* (Vol. 4). Champaign, IL: Research Press, in press.

Kelly, J. A. The simultaneous replication design: Use of a multiple baseline to establish experimental control in single group social skills treatment studies. *Journal of Behavior Therapy and Experimental Psychiatry*, 1980, 11, 203–207.

Kelly, J. A., & Drabman, R. S. The modification of socially detrimental behavior. *Journal of Behavior Therapy and Experimental Psychiatry*, 1977, 8, 101–104.

Kelly, J. A., Frederiksen, L. W., Fitts, H., & Phillips, J. Training and generalization of commendatory assertiveness: A controlled single subject experiment. *Journal of Behavior Therapy and Experimental Psychiatry*, 1978, 9, 17–21.

Kelly, J. A., Furman, W., Phillips, J., Hathorn, S., & Wilson, T. Teaching conversational skills to retarded adolescents. *Child Behavior Therapy*, 1979, 1, 85–97.

Kelly, J. A., Kern, J., Kirkley, B. G., Patterson, J. N., & Keane, T. Reactions to assertive versus unassertive behavior: Differential effects for males and females and implications for assertive training. *Behavior Therapy*, 1980, 11, 670–682.

Kelly, J. A. Laughlin, C., Claiborne, M., & Patterson, J. Group job interview training for unemployed psychiatric patients. *Behavior Therapy*, 1979, 10, 299–310.

Kelly, J. A., Urey, J. R., & Patterson, J. Improving heterosocial conversational skills of male psychiatric patients through a small group training procedure. *Behavior Therapy*, 1980, 11, 179–188.

Kelly, J. A., Urey, J. R., & Patterson, J. Small group job interview skills training in the mental health center setting. *Behavioral Counseling Quarterly*, in press.

Kelly, J. A., Wildman, B. G., & Berler, E. Small group behavioral training to improve the job interview skills repertoire of retarded adolescents. *Journal of Applied Behavior Analysis*, 1980, 13, 461–471.

Kelly, J. A., Wildman, B. G., Urey, J. R., & Thurman, C. Group skills training to increase the conversational repertoire of retarded adolescents. *Child Behavior Therapy*, 1979, 1, 323–336.

Kirschenbaum, D. S. Social competence intervention and evaluation in the inner city: Cincinnati's social skills development program. *Journal of Consulting and Clinical Psychology*, 1979, 47, 778–780.

Kupke, T. E., Calhoun, K. S., & Hobbs, S. A. Selection of heterosocial skills. II. Experimental validity. *Behavior Therapy*, 1979, 10, 336–346.

Kupke, T. E., Hobbs, S. A., & Cheney, T. H. Selection of heterosocial skills. I. Criterion-related validity. *Behavior Therapy,* 1979, *10,* 327–335.

LaGreca, A. M., & Mesibov, G. B. Social skills intervention with learning disabled children: Selecting skills and implementing training. *Journal of Clinical Child Psychology,* 1979, *8,* 234–241.

LaGreca, A. M., & Santogrossi, D. A. Social skills training with elementary school students: A behavioral group approach. *Journal of Consulting and Clinical Psychology,* 1980, *48,* 220–227.

Lasseigne, M. W. A study of peer and adult influence on moral beliefs of adolescents. *Adolescence,* 1975, *10,* 227–230.

Lazarus, A. *Behavior therapy and beyond.* New York: McGraw-Hill, 1971.

Linehan, M., Goldfried, M., & Goldfried, A. Assertion therapy: Skill training or cognitive restructuring. *Behavior Therapy,* 1979, *10,* 372–388.

Linehan, M. M., Walker, R. O., Bronheim, S., Haynes, K. F., & Yevzeroff, H. Group versus individual assertion training. *Journal of Consulting and Clinical Psychology,* 1979, *47,* 1000–1002.

Lumsden, H. H., & Sharf, J. C. Behavioral dimensions of the job interview. *Journal of College Placement,* 1974, *34,* 63–66.

McDaniel, C. O. Participation in extracurricular activities, social acceptance, and social rejection among educable mentally retarded students. *Education and Training for the Mentally Retarded,* 1970, *5,* 4–14.

McFall, R., & Lillesand, D. Behavioral rehearsal with modeling and coaching in assertive training. *Journal of Abnormal Psychology,* 1971, *77,* 313–323.

McFall, R., & Marston, A. An experimental investigation of behavior rehearsal in assertive training. *Journal of Abnormal Psychology,* 1970, *76,* 295–303.

Madsen, C. H., Becker, W. C., & Thomas, D. R. Rules, praise and ignoring: Elements of elementary classroom control. *Journal of Applied Behavior Analysis,* 1968, *1,* 139–150.

Maloney, D. M., Harper, T. M., Braukmann, C. J., Fixsen, D. L., Phillips, E. L., & Wolf, M. M. Teaching conversation-related skills to predelinquent girls. *Journal of Applied Behavior Analysis,* 1976, *9,* 371.

Martinez-Diaz, J. A., & Edelstein, B. A. Multivariate effects of demand characteristics on the analogue assessment of heterosocial competence. *Journal of Applied Behavior Analysis,* 1979, *12,* 679–689.

Martinez-Diaz, J. A., & Edelstein, B. A. Heterosocial competence: Predictive and construct validity. *Behavior Modification,* 1980, *4,* 115–129.

Martinson, W. D., & Zerface, J. P. Comparison of individual counseling and a social program with nondaters. *Journal of Counseling Psychology,* 1970, *17,* 36–40.

Marzillier, J. S., Lambert, C., & Kellett, J. A. A controlled evaluation of systematic desensitization and social skills training for socially inadequate psychiatric patients. *Behaviour Research and Therapy,* 1976, *14,* 225–238.

Masters, J. C., & Furman, W. The validation of peer reinforcement measures: Affective reactions of recipients. Paper presented to the American Psychological Association, San Francisco, 1977.

Meichenbaum, D. Ways of modifying what clients say to themselves. *Rational Living,* 1972, *7,* 23–27.

Meichenbaum, D. *Cognitive behavior modification*. New York: Plenum, 1977.

Meichenbaum, D., & Cameron, R. The clinical potential of modifying what clients say to themselves. *Psychotherapy: Theory, Research, and Practice*, 1974, *11*, 103–117.

Melnick, J. A comparison of replication techniques in the modification of minimal dating behavior. *Journal of Abnormal Psychology*, 1973, *81*, 51–59.

Michelson, L., & Wood, R. Behavioral assessment and training of children's social skills. In M. Hersen, P. M. Miller, & R. M. Eisler (Eds.), *Progress in behavior modification* (Vol. 9). New York: Academic Press, 1980.

Miller, N., & Maruyama, G. Ordinal position and peer popularity. *Journal of Personality and Social Psychology*, 1976, *33*, 123–131.

Minkin, N., Braukmann, C. J., Minkin, B. L., Timbers, G. D., Timbers, B. J., Fixsen, D. J., Phillips, E. L., & Wolf, M. M. The social validation and training of conversational skills. *Journal of Applied Behavior Analysis*, 1976, *9*, 127–139.

Mischel, W. *Personality and assessment*. New York: Wiley, 1968.

Mischel, W. Cognition in self-imposed delay of gratification. In L. Berkowitz (Ed.), *Advances in social psychology* (Vol. 1). New York: Academic Press, 1973.

Monti, P. M., Curran, J. P., Corriveau, D. P., DeLancy, A. L., & Hagerman, S. M. Effects of social skills training groups and sensitivity training groups with psychiatric patients. *Journal of Consulting and Clinical Psychology*, 1980, *48*, 241–248.

Monti, P. M., Fink, E., Norman, W., Curran, J., Hayes, S., & Caldwell, A. Effects of social skills training groups and social skills bibliotherapy with psychiatric patients. *Journal of Consulting and Clinical Psychology*, 1979, *47*, 189–191.

Muehlenhard, C. L. The use of decision theory in the assessment and training of womens' dating initiation skills. Unpublished masters thesis. University of Wisconsin, 1976.

Muehlenhard, C. L., & McFall, R. M. Dating initiation from a woman's perspective. *Behavior Therapy*, in press.

Mullinix, S. D., & Galassi, J. P. Social impact of interpersonal behavior in a work-conflict situation. Paper presented at the meeting of the American Psychological Association, Toronto, 1978.

Nietzel, M. T., Martorano, R. D., & Melnick, J. The effects of content modeling with and without reply training on the development and generalization of assertive responses. *Behavior Therapy*, 1977, *8*, 183–192.

Ochiltree, J. K. Effects of the instructions, modeling, and practice components of behavior rehearsal on assertive training with college students. *Dissertation Abstracts International*, 1977, *38*, 372–373.

O'Connor, R. D. Modification of social withdrawal through symbolic modeling. *Journal of Applied Behavior Analysis*, 1969, *2*, 15–22.

O'Connor, R. D. Relative efficacy of modeling, shaping, and the combined procedures for modification of social withdrawal. *Journal of Abnormal Psychology*, 1972, *79*, 327–334.

Oden, S., & Asher, S. R. Coaching children in social skills for friendship making. *Child Development*, 1977, *48*, 495–506.

Ollendick, T. H., & Hersen, M. Social skills training for juvenile delinquents. *Behaviour Research and Therapy*, 1979, *17*, 547–554.

O'Neal, P., & Robins, L. N. The relation of childhood behavior problems to adult psychiatric status: A thirty-year follow-up study of 150 subjects. *American Journal of Psychiatry*, 1958, *114*, 961–969.

Pachman, J. S., Foy, D. W., Massey, F., & Eisler, R. M. A factor analysis of assertive behavior. *Journal of Consulting and Clinical Psychology*, 1978, *46*, 347.

Phillips, E. L. Achievement Place: Token reinforcement procedures in a home-style rehabilitation setting for "pre-delinquent" boys. *Journal of Applied Behavior Analysis*, 1968, *1*, 213–223.

Pinto, R. P. An evaluation of job-interview training in the rehabilitation setting. *Journal of Rehabilitation*, 1979, *45*, 71–76.

Portes, A. On the emergence of behavior therapy in modern society. *Journal of Consulting Psychology*, 1971, *36*, 303–313.

Quigley, L. *The blind men and the elephant*. New York: Charles Scribner's Sons, 1959.

Rathus, S. A 30-item schedule for assessing assertive behavior. *Behavior Therapy*, 1973, *4*, 398–406.

Rehm, L. P., & Marston, A. R. Reduction of social anxiety through modification of self-reinforcement: An instigation therapy technique. *Journal of Consulting and Clinical Psychology*, 1968, *32*, 565–574.

Reynolds, W. F. Acquisition and extinction of the conditioned eyelid response following partial and continuous reinforcement. *Journal of Experimental Psychology*, 1958, *55*, 335–341.

Roff, M. Childhood social interactions and young adult bad conduct. *Journal of Abnormal Social Psychology*, 1961, *63*, 333–337.

Roff, M., Sells, B., & Golden, M. *Social adjustment and personality development in children*. Minneapolis: University of Minnesota Press, 1972.

Rogers, C. R., & Skinner, B. F. Some issues concerning the control of human behavior: A symposium. *Science*, 1956, *124*, 1057–1066.

Romano, J. M., & Bellack, A. S. Social validation of a component model of assertive behavior. *Journal of Consulting and Clinical Psychology*, 1980, *4*, 478–490.

Rosekrans, M. A., & Hartup, W. W. Imitative influences of consistent and inconsistent response consequences to a model on aggressive behavior in children. *Journal of Personality and Social Psychology*, 1967, *7*, 429–434.

Rosenberg, S. Interpersonal processes in the perpetuation and reduction of language retardation: Some speculations and some data. Paper presented at the meeting of the American Association on Mental Deficiency, Milwaukee, May 1959.

Rotter, J. B. *Social learning and clinical psychology*. New York: Prentice-Hall, 1954.

Schinke, S. P., Gilchrist, L. D., Smith, T. E., & Wong, S. E. Group interpersonal skills training in a natural setting: An experimental study. *Behaviour Research and Therapy*, 1979, *17*, 149–154.

Schinke, S. P., & Rose, S. D. Interpersonal skill training in groups. *Journal of Counseling Psychology*, 1976, *23*, 442–448.

Shoben, E. J., Jr. The therapeutic object: Men or machines? *Journal of Counseling Psychology*, 1963, *10*, 264–268.

Shrader, W. K., & Leventhal, T. Birth order of children and parental report of problems. *Child Development*, 1968, *39*, 1165–1175.

Skillings, R. E., Hersen, M., Bellack, A. S., & Becker, M. P. Relationship of specific and global measures of assertion in college females. *Journal of Clinical Psychology*, 1978, *34*, 346–353.

Sloat, K. C., Tharp, R. G., & Gallimore, R. The incremental effectiveness of classroom-based teacher training techniques. *Behavior Therapy*, 1977, *8*, 810–818.

Speas, C. M. Job-seeking interview skills training: A comparison of four instructional techniques. *Journal of Counseling Psychology*, 1979, *26*, 405–412.

Stalonas, P. M., & Johnson, W. G. Conversation skills training for obsessive speech using an aversive-cueing procedure. *Journal of Behavior Therapy and Experimental Psychiatry*, 1979, *10*, 61–63.

Stennett, R. G. Emotional handicaps in the elementary years: Phase or disease. *American Journal of Orthopsychiatry*, 1966, *36*, 444–449.

Stevens, W., & Tornatzky, L. The effects of a job-interview skills workshop on drug-abuse clients. *Journal of Employment Counseling*, 1976, *13*, 156–163.

Strain, P., Shores, R., & Kerr, M. An experimental analysis of "spillover" effects on the social interaction of behaviorally handicapped preschool children. *Journal of Applied Behavior Analysis*, 1976, *9*, 31–40.

Strain, P. S., Shores, R. E., & Timm, M. A. Effects of peer social initiations on the behavior of withdrawn preschool children. *Journal of Applied Behavior Analysis*, 1977, *10*, 289–298.

Strain, P., & Timm, M. An experimental analysis of social interaction between a behaviorally disordered preschool child and her classroom peers. *Journal of Applied Behavior Analysis*, 1974, *7*, 583–590.

Sullivan, H. S. *The interpersonal theory of psychiatry*. New York: Norton, 1953.

Tschirgi, H. D. What do recruiters really look for in candidates? *Journal of College Placement*, 1973, *33*, 75–79.

Turner, S., & Adams, H. Effects of assertive training in three dimensions of assertiveness. *Behaviour Research and Therapy*, 1977, *15*, 475–483.

Twentyman, C. R., & McFall, R. M. Behavioral training of social skills in shy males. *Journal of Consulting and Clinical Psychology*, 1975, *43*, 384–395.

Twentyman, C. R., & Zimering, R. T. Behavioral training of social skills: A critical review. In M. Hersen, R. M. Eisler, & P. M. Miller (Eds.), *Progress in behavior modification* (Vol. 7). New York: Academic Press, 1979.

Ullman, C. A. Teachers, peers, and tests as predictors of adjustment. *Journal of Educational Psychology*, 1957, *48*, 257–267.

Urey, J. R., Laughlin, C. S., & Kelly, J. A. Teaching heterosocial conversational skills to male psychiatric patients. *Journal of Behavior Therapy and Experimental Psychiatry*, 1979, *10*, 323–328.

Warren, S. F., Baer, D. M., & Rogers-Warren, A. Teaching children to praise: A problem in stimulus and response generalization. *Child Behavior Therapy*, 1979, *1*, 123–137.

Watson, D., & Friend, R. Measurement of social-evaluative anxiety. *Journal of Consulting and Clinical Psychology*, 1969, *33*, 448–457.

Weinrott, M. R., Corson, J. A., & Wilchesky, M. Teacher-mediated treatment of social withdrawal. *Behavior Therapy*, 1979, *10*, 281–294.

Wessberg, H. W., Mariotto, M. J., Conger, A. J., Farrell, A. D., & Conger, J. C. Ecological validity of role plays for assessing heterosocial anxiety and skill of male college students. *Journal of Consulting and Clinical Psychology*, 1979, *47*, 525–535.

Williams, C. L., & Ciminero, A. R. Development and validation of a heterosocial inventory: The survey of heterosocial interactions for females. *Journal of Consulting and Clinical Psychology*, 1978, *46*, 1547–1548.

Wolf, M. M. Social validity: The case for subjective measurement, or how applied behavior analysis is finding its heart. *Journal of Applied Behavior Analysis*, 1978, *11*, 203–214.

Wolf, M. M., & Risley, T. R. Reinforcement: Applied research. In R. Glaser (Ed.), *The nature of reinforcement*. New York: Academic Press, 1971.

Wolpe, J. *The practice of behavior therapy*. Oxford: Pergamon, 1969.

Wolpe, J., & Lazarus, A. *Behavior therapy techniques*. New York: Pergamon Press, 1966.

Woolfolk, R. L., & Dever, S. Perceptions of assertion: An empirical analysis. *Behavior Therapy*, 1979, *10*, 404–411.

Zahavi, S., & Asher, S. R. The effect of verbal instructions on preschool children's aggressive behavior. *Journal of School Psychology*, 1978, *16*, 146–153.

Zeichner, A., Wright, J. C., & Herman, S. Effects of situation on dating and assertive behavior. *Psychological Reports*, 1977, *40*, 375–381.

Zielinski, J. J., & Williams, L. J. Covert modeling vs. behavior rehearsal in the training and generalization of assertive behaviors: A crossover design. *Journal of Clinical Psychology*, 1979, *35*, 855–863.

Zigler, E., & Phillips, L. Social competence and the process-reactive distinction in psychopathology. *Journal of Abnormal and Social Psychology*, 1962, *65*, 215–222.

INDEX